PELICAN BOOKS

A552

DIAGNOSIS OF MAN

KENNETH WALKER

Kenneth Walker was formerly a consultant surgeon on the honorary staff of several London hospitals. He was also a Hunterian Professor to the Royal College of Surgeons. But he has always interested himself in many other things than surgery – such as philosophy, and the sacred literature of the East. He now devotes most of his time to these studies. His best known works are *Meaning and Purpose, The Physiology of Sex, Human Physiology, Sex and Society, Patients and Doctors, The Circle of Life, The Log of the Ark* (for children), *Diagnosis of Man, I Talk of Dreams, Only the Silent Hear, The Story of Medicine, So Great a Mystery, Life's Long Journey, The Unconscious Mind, The Conscious Mind, The Making of Man,* and *Love, Marriage, and the Family.*

KENNETH WALKER

— * —

DIAGNOSIS
OF MAN

PENGUIN BOOKS

Penguin Books Ltd, Harmondsworth, Middlesex
u.s.a. : Penguin Books Inc., 3300 Clipper Mill Road, Baltimore 11, Md
australia : Penguin Books Pty Ltd, 762 Whitehorse Road,
Mitcham, Victoria

—

First published by Jonathan Cape 1942
This revised edition published in Pelican Books 1962
Reprinted 1964

—

—

Made and printed in Great Britain
by C Nicholls & Company Ltd
Set in Linotype Pilgrim

TO
MY TEACHERS

CONTENTS

PREFACE TO THE PENGUIN EDITION

NEARLY twenty years have passed since this book first appeared and quite naturally Penguin Books have asked me to bring it up to date. I have been surprised how few alterations have been required. Progress has been made in some of the sciences related to the subject of this book, and notably in the science of neurology, but progress with regard to details only. No new general principles have been discovered and the body-mind relationship remains as great an enigma as it has always been. To quote Professor Adrian, the greatest living authority on this subject: 'The whole problem of the connexion between the brain and the mind is as puzzling to the physiologist as it is to the philosopher. Perhaps some day a drastic revision of our systems of knowledge will explain how a pattern of nervous impulses can cause a thought, or will show that the two events are really the same thing, looked at from a different point of view. If such a revision is made I can only hope that I may be able to understand it.'

But new names have appeared in the list of writers who are influencing contemporary thought, and it is here chiefly that additions have had to be made. An entirely new chapter on Existentialism has been added in which I have tried to summarize not only the views of Existentialists but those of their critics as well. The names of those who are regarded as leading authorities on psychotherapy have changed, although psychology itself remains much the same. The study of the human mind is as far from becoming a science as it was when William James declared that psychology showed no promise of ever becoming a science.

One difference between this edition and its predecessors is that it contains additional evidence of the existence of higher levels of consciousness. I should like to express here my thanks to Professor Raynor C. Johnson for permission to reproduce two examples of higher levels of consciousness taken from his book

Watcher on the Hill. Finally I should like to express my thanks to Penguin Books for putting into circulation again a book which was very well received when it first appeared, but which has now long been out of print.

Harley Street, W1
1961

CHAPTER I

THE DARK HOUSE

I N that book of Sufi wisdom, *The Mathnawi* of Jalalu'ddin Rumi, there is a story called 'The Disagreement as to the Description and Shape of the Elephant'. It runs as follows:

The elephant was in a dark house: some Hindus had brought it for exhibition.

In order to see it, many people were going, every one, into that darkness.

As seeing it with the eye was impossible, each one was feeling it in the dark with the palm of his hand.

The hand of one fell on its trunk: he said, 'This creature is like a water-pipe'.

The hand of another touched its ear: to him it appeared to be like a fan.

Since another handled its leg, he said, 'I found the elephant shape to be like a pillar'.

Another laid his hand on the back: he said, 'Truly this elephant was like a throne'.

Similarly, when anyone heard a description of the elephant, he understood it only in respect of the part that he had touched.

On account of the diverse place of view their statements differed: one man entitled it 'dal', another, 'alif'.

If there had been a candle in each one's hand, the difference would have gone out of their words.

The eye of sense-perception is only like the palm of the hand, the palm hath not power to reach the whole of the elephant.

The eye of the Sea is one thing, and the foam another; leave the foam and look with the eye of the Sea.

Day and night there is the movement of foam-flecks from the Sea: thou beholdest the foam, but not the Sea. Marvellous!

The genius of the poet has gone straight to the centre of the problem of knowledge. Our hands fumble over the surface of the elephant, each of us proclaiming what we have found, and

none of us being able to relate the part to the whole. The fact
that we have invented scientific instruments which render our
special senses a thousand times more acute does not reduce our
difficulties. If anything, it increases them, because we become so
engrossed in our minute examinations that we are unable to
listen to what our colleagues at the other end of the elephant are
saying. We have all become specialists, learning more and more
about the part, and less and less about the whole. Even if we
could spare the time to study different specialities, the search for
knowledge has become so intense and so many observations
have been recorded, that no man can ever hope to know all that
others have discovered. The task of synthesizing so many observations is beyond the wit of man. It would seem, indeed, that
the very existence of the elephant has been forgotten, so pressing is the work we have on hand. As a result, we are now engaged solely in compiling vast catalogues of observations on
legs, trunks, or tails, as the case may be. No longer attempting
to synthesize, or obtain, real knowledge, we endlessly subdivide
our subject and accumulate more and more facts about it. It is
analysis driven to extreme, a dispersion of energy along a multiplicity of channels.

This is the unsatisfactory state in which medical science now
finds itself, and what is true of medical science is equally true
of the whole body of scientific knowledge. Medicine studies
man, and man is an indivisible whole which cannot be understood by studying one aspect of him. Man is an object of such
complexity that we doctors have taken him to pieces in order to
examine each piece separately. Now we are finding the greatest
difficulty in putting the pieces together again.

The physician who is called upon to deal with a sick man is
confronted with a truly formidable task. What renders the task
so difficult is the fact that he does not even know what a normal
man is, still less a sick one. He has a nodding acquaintance with
some of man's organs and has a shrewd idea how they work, but
of the nature of man himself, he is woefully and confessedly
ignorant. The physician is, indeed, in the position of a mechanic,
who has been summoned to put right an engine that works in
accordance with principles that are quite unknown to him. He

is like a mechanic, say, who understands the structure of steam-engines, but, because he is ignorant of the existence of electricity, is quite incapable of dealing with an automobile. If all that is wrong with it happens to be some mechanical defect in a pipe, he may be able to put things right, but if the dynamo is wrong, he is completely at a loss what to do. Small wonder that the physician in the privacy of his heart is appalled by his own ignorance, and puts all his trust in the one advantage that he possesses over the motor-mechanic, the help that he derives from the curative forces of nature, the *vis medicatrix naturae*. Indeed, as every doctor knows, all that he does is to act in the capacity of nature's humble and admiring assistant.

In his interesting book, *Man the Unknown*, Alexis Carrel points to a strange disparity that exists between the progress achieved in the sciences of inert and of living matters. During the course of the last century, physics and chemistry have made such stupendous advances that they have outdistanced all other branches of science, and particularly those sciences which concern themselves with the phenomenon of life. It is as though the examiner of the trunk of the elephant had been so industrious and had made such progress in his handling of it that his reports were no longer intelligible to those palpating other portions of its body. The mathematical formulae and the hypotheses of the physicists are truly magnificent, but they are utterly beyond the comprehension of the biologists. The latter are still in the preliminary stages of their task, that is to say, in the descriptive stage. They are still making observations, painfully sorting out and classifying phenomena, but so far they have been unable to produce order in the material they have collected, let alone infer from their observations the laws that govern life. Not that they are to be blamed for this. Progress in science is dependent on the discovery of a suitable technique, and the techniques for examining living matter are greatly inferior to those which are available for the examination of inert matter. Life cannot be handled in a test-tube, or weighed and measured. Life is a phenomenon which disappears when we submit it to analysis. If we are unable to explain even a simple organism, how much less can we understand a living man. How indeed are we to approach the subject which of all others is of greatest importance to us? All that we have been able to do so far is to make certain abstractions from him and study them to the best of our ability. This has entailed the calling in of various specialists, each of whom, when he has completed his work, has presented us with a different description of what man is. The anatomist, the physiologist, the bio-chemist, the geneticist, and the psychologist have all contributed their quota of knowledge, but when we come to add up what we have been given, the sum of it still fails to represent man. The man described by each of the specialists and the man described by all the specialists, is still not a man. There is a residue that remains, a residue that is more important than all that has been abstracted. Indeed, when we come to look at the answers given by the experts more carefully we find that all that they have done has been to hand us a collection of schemata formed around the particular technique which each of them has employed. We have been given a corpse dissected by the anatomists, a collection of organs and extracts by the physiologists, and a pattern of behaviour by the psychologists. In spite of much research on the subject man still remains an enigma.

But it is not only because the subject is so difficult that man's knowledge of himself has lagged behind his knowledge of the outside world. Man has been so occupied with this outside world that he has had no time to study the world that is within. In primitive ages this was inevitable, for the struggle to survive was so fierce that it absorbed all his energy. Tools had to be made, food procured, dwellings erected, homes defended, and children reared. There was little time left over for the study of the phenomena that he carried about in his own person. Later on, when his life was better organized, the study of his nature was left to the priests and the medicine men. Since these possessed no more knowledge than their fellows they resorted to the use of cut-and-dried formulae, and thus hid their ignorance from the world. In this way it happened that long before his attention was turned on himself, man had gained quite a considerable knowledge of the movements of the sun, moon, and stars, of the rise and fall of the tides, of metallurgy, and of the cultivation of crops. But on the whole, man's body and mind worked satisfactorily, so that it seemed that they could be left to their own devices, and attention directed to those objects which by study could be shaped to man's ends. In any case, the external world was a much more satisfactory subject for observation, for the study of it promptly yielded tangible results, results that the mind delighted in contemplating. Our minds have a strong partiality for clear and definite solutions, and instinctively dislike all efforts that lead to a feeling of insecurity. Some sort of order can be discovered in the world outside us, whereas in the world that is within, there is nothing that can be caught hold of, submitted to scrutiny, and fitted into a general scheme of knowledge. There was every inducement therefore to leave man's body and mind alone, and to get on with the study of objects that yielded such profitable results as those which accrued from chemistry and physics.

At a later period necessity, in the shape of injury and disease, drove man, in spite of his distaste for the task, to study his own body. It was clear that the medicine men and priests could not be relied upon to do all that they had promised. They were deprived, therefore, of jurisdiction over the body, but still left in charge of the soul. Physicians appeared, and because, before prescribing a cure, it is necessary to know something about the body, they began to study anatomy and physiology. That this move on the part of the early doctors to gain some knowledge of the mystery of life met with considerable opposition is shown by the obstacles that were frequently put in the way of their studies. Human anatomy had to be studied in secret, and sometimes the help of criminals had to be enlisted in order to obtain material for dissection.

Although the army of physiologists, anatomists, pathologists, bio-chemists, and other experts that medicine eventually pressed into her service has revealed much that was previously unknown about man's body it revealed nothing of his mind and spirit. Knowledge of these did not seem to be necessary to those who only treated disease. It was felt that mind and spirit could be left to themselves or that if help were needed a patient could apply to the priests. But later, when it was found that many of the diseases that the physician had to treat had their origin in the mind, there arose the necessity for studying the mind as well as the body. A new branch of medical science was founded, the science of medical psychology. At first this was looked upon as a sort of Cinderella of the medical family, at whom the older members of the profession laughed, and of whom they were a little bit ashamed. But medical psychology, after a struggle, succeeded in establishing itself as a reputable department of medicine, and great hopes were even entertained for its future. Medical men, it was now felt, were equipped to treat not only the body, but also the mind. There were even those who looked upon Freudian analysis as a new religion that would eventually save the world; and certainly some of its exponents quickly developed qualities that are often attached to the priesthood. Yet, when examined closely, all these new schools of medical psychology told us very little about the real nature of man. What they actually succeeded in doing was to describe and to explain some of the mechanisms that are found in a mind that is sick. They were in no sense of the word complete systems of psychology, and left out of their account the whole of the spiritual side of man. Medical psychologists admitted that they were not interested in the subject of religion, and if pressed to account for the religious urge in man, they generally attempted to explain it as a survival in the adult of the fantasies of childhood.

The foregoing is a brief résumé of the state of medical knowledge of man at the present day. Few doctors have time for any other than a medical approach to this subject, for their profession is an exacting one and it is all that they can do to keep pace with its advances. And what is true of medicine is also true of other professions. We are so engrossed in our various occupations, so preoccupied with our professions, so caught up in our studies and affairs that we have no leisure for pausing and wondering where our work is leading us. The pace of life has quickened, change follows change, theory replaces theory and, swept along by this movement, we have no time to think. What is remarkable is that this ceaseless movement and change have now become prized for their own sakes and not for any goal towards which they may be carrying us. The existence of such a goal has, indeed, been generally forgotten, and only the existence of ceaseless movement is borne in mind. Change has been taken to be synonymous with progress and the fabrication of new theories with truth. The tide of life has proved too powerful for us and, swept along by it, we cease to struggle towards the greater truths or even to believe that it is possible to do so.

This book is an attempt on the part of one who, however ill-equipped he may feel himself to be for such a task, is re-examining certain fundamental questions, and more particularly the question of man's nature. Only if one knows what man is, can one hope to find out what he may become. The task that the writer has set himself is an immense one, since it entails a survey not only of science, but also of religion. A detailed survey is manifestly impossible, and all that can be attempted is to provide a bird's-eye view of the subject which may encourage the ordinary man to think about matters that hitherto he has been content to leave to the experts.

First it will be necessary to examine what the various experts have to tell us about the different aspects of man which they have studied. We shall learn what they have to say concerning the part into which they have divided him, his body and his mind, and then study the means by which the activities of these separate entities are coordinated so that they work in harmony. Then, having discovered that science has really told us but little about the nature of the whole man, we shall seek other sources of knowledge and discover what philosophy and religion have to tell us on this subject. But before attempting to examine such a difficult object as a man, it will be helpful to make a preliminary study of the simpler element out of which he is formed, the living cell.

CHAPTER 2

THE CELL

THE discovery of Copernicus that the earth moved round the sun evoked a storm of indignation, for it displaced the earth from the important position it was thought to occupy at the centre of the universe. Instead, it was proved to be only one of several planets that obeyed the dictates of the sun. Such an idea was thought to be an insult to the earth's chief inhabitant, man. The invention of the microscope and the discovery of cell life provoked another upheaval. Buffon, the naturalist, was shocked by the news when it was brought to him. That a drop of water should reveal the presence of thousands of minute individual lives cheapened the idea of life, and thereby lessened the prestige of man himself. It was true that creation gained in grandeur through the discovery, but this was at the expense of man, and it was some time before he overcame his sense of affront.

Man may be looked upon as being an organized family made up of myriads of cells, a family so cleverly integrated that it appears to have a unity. Nevertheless, in Sir Charles Sherrington's words:

Each of its constituent cells is a life centred in itself, managing itself, feeding and breathing for itself, separately born and destined separately to die. Further, it is a life helped by, and in its turn helping, the whole assembly, which latter is the corporate individual.

But before dealing with the corporate individual, let us return to the consideration of the cell. Each cell can be pictured as being a well-organized and self-contained factory, so constituted that it can carry on numerous chemical processes. It is an entirely self-sufficient factory which takes from the outside world the raw materials that it requires for its work, and gets rid of the by-products that it can no longer use. This factory can hydrolyse, oxydize, pull to pieces, and build up, according to its needs; it can even manufacture its own special proteins from the proteins that it has absorbed from without.

An examination of a cell under the microscope shows that it is a mass of jelly surrounded by a containing membrane. By appropriate staining further details of its structure may be revealed, of which the most important is a small complicated area somewhere near its centre, which takes up the dye more strongly, and is known as the nucleus. This is the organizer of the cell's industry, the most vital structure in its mass. It is the heart and brain of the cell's existence, and the very centre of its being. By means of a special technique that has excited universal admiration, Robert Chambers has succeeded in extracting the nucleus from a cell, and has found that when it is bereft of this little organ the cell promptly dies. Staining also reveals the fact that the jelly that makes up the bulk of the cell is not a homogeneous fluid, but itself has a structure. The most obvious feature of this structure is the presence of a number of minute particles of living matter, like smaller cells within a cell. These aggregates of protein are suspended in the more fluid substance of the cell, so that its internal surface is enormously increased by their presence. Now, it is on surfaces that the chemical reactions of life take place most readily, and part of the cell's secret of life is the immensity of its inner surface. In the interstices of its sponge-work, a hundred different chemical processes may go forward simultaneously, so that the cell is a veritable hive of industry.

Staining a cell kills it, and instead of examining a living cell we find ourselves examining only a brightly coloured corpse. A far better method of examination is to view the cell in its living state, under what is known as the 'dark ground illumination microscope'. This allows us to see the cell's ceaseless activity, so that it appears not as a static, but as a dynamic system. Cells can now be filmed and magnified to such an extent that when thrown on to the cinematograph screen they appear as large as a man, and all their organs are rendered visible. In the middle floats the nucleus, an ovoid elastic-walled balloon containing two smaller bodies, the nucleoli, which slowly and unceasingly change their shapes. And in the whole of the cell there is a ceaseless streaming hither and thither of granules, which zigzag through its substance and penetrate the transitory arms, or pseudopodia, that the cell may project from its surface.

Cells, like animals, belong to various species, which differ from each other both in structure and in function. Those that make up the human body may be subdivided into two main groups, the fixed cells out of which the tissues and organs are built, and the wandering cells that may travel throughout the body's whole length. Each of these groups contain a great many varieties of cell ; for example, amongst the fixed cells, epithelial and connective tissue cells, and amongst the wandering cells, red and white blood corpuscles. Of all the cells in the body, the epithelial are the noblest, since it is out of them that are formed such organs as the brain and the endocrine glands.

By the use of a suitable technique, fragments of living tissue can be grown in flasks. This allows of the cell characteristics being studied, just as the characteristics of microbes in culture can be studied. Each type of cell is found to have its inherent qualities, which remain the same even after several years have elapsed since their separation from the organism from which they were originally obtained. Cells taken from a chick embryo have now lived for nearly a quarter of a century, although the life of a fowl has a span of only two or three years. After three or four days a culture ceases to thrive, and if left would die, poisoned by its own excretions into the serum that nourishes it. To avoid this the culture must be transferred periodically into fresh serum and, provided this be done and no accidents befall it, there appears to be no reason why it should not continue growing for ever. The cell that is most easy to grow is the primitive cell of the connective tissue, but it has also been found possible to cultivate more specialized cells from muscles and nerves, and even from such organs as the kidney. In such cases the cells lose their highly specialized character. No longer dedicated to the performance of special duties, they become free individuals, and revert to a humbler and more generalized type.

The characteristics which are used to distinguish one cell from another are their mode of locomotion, their manner of associating with each other, their rate of growth, their response to different chemicals, the food they require, the substances they secrete, and their shape and internal structure. It must also be remembered that the medium in which a cell lives is of the greatest importance to it. This applies equally to cells living within the body, and to cells grown outside it in flasks. The organic medium that surrounds the cell in the living body must indeed be regarded as forming an integral part of the tissues. It is composed of blood flowing in the interior of the smallest blood vessels, or capillaries, and of plasma, or lymph, that has filtered through their walls. Upon the physico-chemical state of this organic medium in which the cells live depends not only our health, but even the manifestations of our psychic life, our very thoughts and emotions. It was not without some justification that the ancients spoke of the different 'humours' of the body, the 'humours' on which everything depended. Although much of their theory has been discarded, it still survives in a modified form in the theories of the part played by the secretions of the endocrine glands in the physical and psychic life of the organism. This subject will be dealt with more fully in the following chapter, but in the meantime it may be pointed out that it is by their presence in the medium surrounding the cells that the internal secretions exert their influence. When a person's temperament has been changed by the absence of thyroid, or he suffers from undue fatigue through a deficiency of suprarenal secretion, these changes are due to a lack of the necessary secretions in the fluids nourishing the brain.

The cell is said to be bounded by a limiting membrane, but it is a membrane which does not shut it off from the outer world. It is best to picture it as a kind of sieve through the meshes of which a ceaseless exchange and barter is being carried on with the outer world. Nutritive material is absorbed through these meshes, in the form of sugar, fats, and proteins, and through them oxygen is taken in. Respiration is not only a function of the total organisms, but it is the function also of the individual cell. Equally important to the taking in of nutriment is the elimination of waste products. A cell kept in a medium filled with waste products dies like a fish in a bowl of stagnant water, so that freedom to eliminate is in the end as important as freedom to take in.

We may regard the cell as being a self-contained, self-running chemical factory in which the nucleus plays the part of the board of management. Within it a hundred different processes are being carried out; processes of hydrolysis, oxidization, breaking down, building up, taking in, and giving out. Never for one moment are its activities allowed to cease, for life must always be kept going and the cell can never be at rest.

What then is life? To ask for a definition of life is to ask for something that scientists have never been able to supply — unless Bichat's description of life as that which results from the action of forces counteracting death, can be accepted as a definition. Yet this definition was not given in any spirit of cynicism, for it is impossible to describe life by means of any simple formula. Needham has supplied the somewhat technical definition that life is 'a dynamic equilibrium in a polyphasic system, consisting of proteins, fats, carbohydrates, sterols, lipoids, cycloses, and water'. But it were better to avoid seeking a definition, and consider instead some of the characteristics of life.

In round terms, life is an energy-system, the energy of which is directed to maintaining itself. We have seen that the cell fulfils these conditions; it feeds itself, grows, excretes waste products, moves, and reproduces itself. This in turn entails dependence on its surroundings, for it is from these that the cell takes up its energy, and into these that it returns energy. Life is, therefore, an energy-system that can maintain itself as a self-centred balanced unity by giving to and taking from its surroundings. And now comes in a very important feature. Life acts as though it *desired* to maintain itself. It is, above all, this element of purposive intention that distinguishes the animate from the inanimate. A cell sets out to maintain itself as though acting in accordance with some design to which it subscribes. A stone that falls to the ground, a magnet that attracts iron filings, an iron that expands on heating cannot be regarded as desiring to fall, to attract, or to expand, but a cell works as though it desired so to work. It is purposive and resourceful. But to describe life as being purposeful does not give us much aid in defining it, and in practice we find that it is impossible to draw a sharp line between the living and the non-living. As Sir Charles Sherrington has put it:

There is in living nothing fundamentally other than is going forward in all the various grades of energy-systems which we know, though in some less rapidly and less balancedly than in others. Whether atom, molecule, colloidal complex, or what-not, whether virus or cell, or plant or animal compounded of cells, each is a system of motion in commerce with its surround. The behaviour of the living body is an example of this, and we call it living. The behaviour of those newly discovered so-called viruses is an example of this, and there is hesitation whether or not to call it living. There is between them all no essential difference.

Life therefore to the scientists is really a question of complexity of organization. The adjective 'living' would never be applied to a simplified organization, but only to a highly heterogeneous, complex organization that had been integrated into an individual. Some scientists now regard the division of physico-chemical systems into living and non-living as being merely a convenient convention, but a convention that rests on no scientific basis. The old idea of an occult life-principle which, added to matter, brought it to life, is now abandoned. The word 'life' is retained as a useful term to describe all those faculties that are characteristic of living matter. Life is a train of fire that finds fuel for itself and produces ashes, a train that will continue until its force is spent, and then it will go out.

This is the point of view of the modern scientist, but at the same time, he hurries to point out that, although the re-lighting of the fire of life is continually taking place, its starting-point must always be a spark from the living. Life always comes from life, and every search for another starting-point has proved fruitless. Ancient scientists did not always hold that life only comes from life, although William Harvey, the discoverer of the circulation of the blood, believed this to be the case. 'The living thing', he wrote, 'is always from an egg, which is again from a living thing.' Pasteur confirmed Harvey's view by his classical investigation of the processes involved in the fermentation of wine. In his experiments he could find no evidence that germs were ever spontaneously generated.

The examination of a complex organism resolves itself into two parts, first the study of the life of the constituent cell, and second the investigation of the life of the total organism. Although each cell has a separate self-centred life, together the cells form a corporate unity. Each cell helps, and is in turn helped by, its neighbour, the whole agglomeration of cells forming an ideal socialist community, such as politicians may have dreamt of, but have never seen realized. Sometimes the cells are so intimately joined one with another (for example, the nerve-cells) that the microscope is unable to discover any separation between them. Nevertheless, experiment has shown that they still remain individuals, so that the death of one does not necessarily entail the death of the other. Each is a self-sufficient living unit.

One of the factors that integrates the component cells into one whole is the dependence of each individual on its surroundings. Forming part of a cell's surroundings is its neighbour, so that every cell is modified by, and responsive to, its neighbour. There is a balance maintained between them, a balance that determines activity, and particularly the activity of reproduction. In tissue-cultures, where the cells are all of one kind, reproduction goes on indefinitely, untrammelled by the presence and restraining force exerted by neighbours of a different nature. What happens when a cell is entirely egocentric and uninfluenced by the activities of the cells surrounding it is shown when an organism is attacked by cancer. A malignant growth may be regarded as a set of bandits let loose in a peaceful socialist community. Originating, say, amongst the cells of the breast, the cancer cells assume a fierce and completely inconsiderate activity. Watched on a cinematograph film cancer cells are seen to be possessed of a fanatical frenzy, pushing on one side the quiet, well-disposed cells of the body and thrusting themselves into their place. With mad impetuosity they have set out to conquer the body, and since it is by sheer brute force that they will accomplish this, they multiply prodigiously. They are invaders who have no idea other than that of conquest by force.

It is the absence of conformity to a general plan that distinguishes a cancer cell from the ordinary cell of the body. In the healthy body everything is done deliberately and in conformity with design. Although each cell is a self-contained, self-supporting unit, it still remains a unit that works for the common good. It is as though somewhere in the body there was a master-mind at work, a mind that coordinated the work of the parts with the whole, integrating the activity of a million million cells. The number of cells out of which the human body is built is said to be about a thousand billion, all of which obey the law, and all of which are able to trace back their ancestry to one original progenitor. Nobody knows how the beehive and the antheap are coordinated and ruled. Nobody knows the nature of the mind which rules and regulates the activities of the thousand billion cells that constitute the body.

The modern scientist, as we have seen, refuses to admit that there is any essential difference between life and no life. What has he to say on the subject of mind and no mind? In order to find an answer to this question we must follow the hierarchy of living systems downwards, and note the point, if such exists, at which mind quits living matter. We and the animals have minds, and since the Psalmist has referred us to the ant for a moral lesson, we must assume that the insects have minds also. What about the lowest forms of life, the unicellular organisms? Some wit has said that if an amoeba were as large as a dog, we would never hesitate to accord it a mind. An amoeba works according to a plan; its movements are purposive, and from its behaviour it would appear to have primitive desires. It is less adaptable than a dog and would seem to be less capable of being educated. But who has ever attempted to educate an amoeba? The psychology of an amoeba has yet to be written, but if by mind is meant purposive action, the amoeba has a mind.

Teleological explanations are generally taboo in science, but it is quite impossible to approach any biological problem without thinking in terms of purpose and design. Who can watch a battle between the white corpuscles of the blood and invading bacteria without saying that the whole behaviour of the corpuscles is designed to overcome and devour the organisms that threaten not only their own lives, but also that of the whole organism? If the warrior ants who defend the antheap from invaders are accredited with mind, the leucocytes in the blood-stream have just as much right to be accredited with it. What we see when we peer through the microscope is a battle worked out according to the principles of strategy and tactics. First advance those white cells whose role it is to absorb and to neutralize the poisons that have been let loose by the invading bacilli. Next appear the warriors, who, in turn, must paralyse the activity of the invaders by a discharge of poisons, and finally the phagocytes, or scavengers, whose business it is to engulf the dead bodies of the enemy. So pregnant with purpose are all these activities that the adjective 'defensive' is inevitably attached to these cells.

The application of cinematography to cell culture has given us an extraordinary insight into the nature of cell life. There can be few things more impressive than watching a film of young connective tissue cells (known as fibroblasts), and wan-dering cells (similar to the white corpuscles of the blood). The scene is one of intense activity embodying the dramas of birth, the struggle for existence, and death. First of all we see the young cell growing to maturity, and then suddenly dividing into two. This division is an extremely complicated process, the twisted skein that makes up the nucleus splitting down the middle and then rearranging itself into two nuclei, which retire to opposite ends of the cell. A membrane then forms between the two halves, and in a convulsion of activity, the cell breaks into two separate individuals. Transferring our attention to one of them we watch it in turn gradually becoming more mature. Sometimes it repeats the process, but sometimes we watch it growing old, its nucleus shrinking, its substance becoming trans-lucent and its movements feebler. Life for an enfeebled cell is as ruthless as it is for an aged animal in the jungle. The wandering cells of the body approach and attack it, instinctively knowing that it cannot defend itself. Finally it is engulfed, thus providing sustenance for its fellows. To us, watching the whole of the drama, the scheme behind it is all apparent. Birth and death must play their part in the greater life of the tissues. But how would the cell itself, knowing only what was happening in its immediate neighbourhood, interpret its existence? It would know only that it was alive, and that life was difficult, and it would probably come to the conclusion that in living it had served no ulterior purpose. That it was an essential part of a greater life would be beyond its powers of comprehension, and who shall say whether its ignorance in this matter is greater than our own?

The same purposive action of the wandering cells of the body is seen also in free unicellular organisms. According to some patient observers of the paramoecium, this minute creature not only acts purposively, but is even capable of learning from experience, and experience entails the existence of memory. It may well be that the observations of the paramoecium observer are capable of some other interpretation, but until that is forthcoming we must accredit the paramoecium with memory and mind. Mind, indeed, would seem to be coincident with life, not only the Mind of the Great Thinker, but also the mind existing in living beings. His incarnated thoughts. Hobbes once said: 'I know that there have been certain philosophers, and they learned men, who have held that all bodies are endowed with sense; nor do I see, if the nature of sense be set along reaction solely, how they can be refuted.'

CHAPTER 3

THE ENDOCRINE GLANDS

ONE of the questions raised in the last chapter was how the activities of the numerous cells that go to make up the body are coordinated so as to supply the needs of a single integrated individual. Each cell, as we have seen, is a self-sufficient, self-contained chemical factory, and yet they all combine together for the welfare of the whole, of which each forms so tiny a part. This is a problem to which the biologist has not been able to find an entirely satisfactory answer. Some of the coordinating factors in the body are known, but not all.

We have seen that a cell is influenced by the environment in which it lives. If the fluid surrounding it is deficient in the materials it requires for its activity, it ceases to work, and if the same fluid becomes clogged with the waste products of the cell, it dies. Also, it was shown that cells of one kind grown in a flask continue to multiply indefinitely, but that cells in the body that are surrounded by neighbours of a different type maintain a balance in growth, no one type of cell attempting to overcome another by sheer weight of numbers. It is mainly by means of these two mechanisms, the composition of the surrounding fluid and the balanced action of one cell against another, that coordination is secured in simple multi-cellular organisms devoid of any nervous system.

When we come to more complex creatures, two new, and very important, mechanisms come into action : the endocrine glands and the central nervous system. It is these mechanisms that we must now study, so that we may be in a position later on to discuss the nature of man's body and mind. Fortunately it will only be necessary to furnish very simple descriptions of them, for both are highly technical subjects, to the study of which experts have devoted the whole of their lives.

It is an interesting fact that the two systems that play such an important role in coordinating the activities of body and mind are developed from the same structure, namely, the skin. Embryologists have shown that both the endocrine glands and the central nervous system are formed from an infolding of the outer layers of the developing embryo, so that they may be said to be embryologically closely related to the skin. At first sight, this kinship of the brain and the endocrine glands with such a humble structure as the skin would seem to be surprising. But this surprise is due to our regarding the skin as an unimportant structure. The skin is far more than a waterproof covering; it is a highly complex structure, the importance of which is only now being realized. If this were not so, how could we explain the fact that the skin so often reflects the activities and errors of the brain? Skin eruptions often follow a nervous shock, and we are told that some of the saints developed stigmata as the result of their dwelling upon the Crucifixion of Christ.

The story of the discovery of the endocrine glands is one of the most interesting in the history of medicine. As is the case in so many other discoveries, it is difficult to fix any date for it, for long before the existence of internal secretions was proved, their presence in the body was suspected. Perhaps the credit for being the first to formulate a theory of internal secretions should be given to Bordeu. Bordeu was a physician at the court of Louis XV, and he must have been a remarkable man, not only because court physicians are usually too much occupied with their duties to further medical advances, but because he formulated so clearly the role of the ductless glands. This formulation appears in his statement that he personally believed that each organ of the body was the workshop of a specific substance which passed into the blood and regulated the chemistry of the body. Should any of these substances be absent, he added, the harmony and poise of the body suffered. Could any guess have gone nearer the mark than this?

Yet it was only late in the nineteenth century that the accuracy of Bordeu's theory was confirmed. The confirmation came as the result of an accident. The Swiss surgeons Kocker and Reverdin, emboldened by the progress made in aseptic surgery, decided to undertake the removal of goitres. It had been taught that, like the appendix, the thyroid was a gland devoid of any function. But a few months after these two pioneers had removed it independently from their patients, these patients passed into a curious condition that was similar to cretinism. The loss of the thyroid had caused a slowing down of all bodily processes, so that the patient became apathetic, sluggish in body and mind alike. The rate of the heart beat had dropped, the skin became dry and wrinkled, the temperature subnormal, the speech guttural, and the features broadened and coarsened. Although the removal of their enlarged thyroids had relieved the patients from the symptoms from which they had previously suffered, the operation had converted them into cretins. A serious error had been made, and it was now obvious that the thyroid, far from being useless, performed some very important function. A halt was immediately called to its surgical removal.

The experiment that had unwittingly been made on human beings was now repeated on animals, and although the results were less striking they were sufficiently so to confirm the view that the thyroid was essential to the health of the body. Soon afterwards the next great advance was made in the form of what is known as 'replacement therapy', that is to say, the making good from an outside source of what the body has lost. Extracts were made from animals' thyroids and administered to other animals that had been deprived of their glands. The result was a dramatic recovery from all the symptoms that had previously been brought about by removal. The new method of treatment was applied to human beings suffering from signs of thyroid insufficiency, and with gratifying results.

It was soon found that if very large doses of thyroid extract were given, the patients suffered from a number of new symptoms which were exactly the reverse of those caused by a deficiency. There was a speeding-up of all the bodily processes, a quickening of the heart-beat and a deepening of respiration. Patients also became very nervous and emotional, and unable to sleep, and they looked at the world through prominent, frightened eyes.

The secretion formed by the thyroid was handed over to the bio-chemists for analysis, and it was found to consist mainly of an organic compound of iodine. To this product the name of thyroxin was given. Clinical medicine worked in close collaboration with bio-chemistry, each adding its quotum to the growing sum of knowledge. Physicians observed that in certain cases of goitre, the symptoms resembled those caused by excess, rather than by a deficiency, of thyroid. To these cases they gave the name of exophthalmic goitre, a name that is descriptive of the prominent eyes which are a feature of this disease. These patients formed a striking contrast to the cretins, those unfortunate beings with a prematurely senile appearance, thick and lumpy bodies, short squat limbs and fingers, and mental development so low that they might almost be regarded as idiots. And between these two extremes lay a number of cases that exhibited a minor degree of deficiency or excess: in other words, of hypo-thyroidism, or hyper-thyroidism. The hypo-thyroid group had dry thick wrinkled skins and scurfy hair, the hyper-thyroid group, moist transparent skins and glossy hair. The hypo-thyroid cases were lethargic and tired with any effort; the hyper-thyroid, alert, emotional, energetic, and restless.

It will be noted that both temperament and physique are affected by the quantity of thyroid secretion that finds its way into the circulation. The thyroid may, indeed, be looked upon as a sort of governor that controls the speed at which the body and mind work. It also controls the speed of growth, so that a small quantity of thyroid extract placed daily in an aquarium materially shortens the time required for a tadpole to turn into a frog. It is for this reason that stunted and backward children are sometimes given small doses of thyroid.

If he had been alive at this time there was one old man who would have welcomed the news of the discovery of the internal secretion of the thyroid. Many years previously Brown-Séquard had delivered a lecture before the Société de Biologie in Paris on the internal secretion of the testicle. He had been ailing in health and was on the point of giving up his work when he decided to make certain experiments on himself. Believing that the testicle contained an internal invigorating secretion, he prepared extracts from a dog and injected them into himself. He

claimed that he had markedly benefited from the treatment, and
that thanks to it he was enabled to continue his work. It was for
the purpose of reporting these experiments and their results
that he gave his lecture. But the lecture utterly failed to con-
vince his audience and the scientific journals which published
an account of it were frankly satirical. 'Professor Brown-
Séquard's audience', said one of them, 'appears to have received an impression of the intellectual capacity of the aged
scientist very different from that which he, in his elevated
frame of mind, evidently expected to produce. The lecture must
be regarded as further proof of the necessity for retiring pro-
fessors who have attained their threescore and ten.'

No lecture could have had a more crushing reception, and yet
it contained nothing that need have surprised the audience or
the reporters. Since the remotest antiquity men have deprived
their domestic animals of their sex-glands for the express purpose of altering their growth and their disposition. The results
of castration were well known to the world, and certainly to
Brown-Séquard's audience. By castration a bull is changed into
a patient ox, a fighting cock into a fat capon, an unmanageable
stallion into a gelding. By the same means the papal choir-
masters, in former times, prevented the breaking of the voice of
their choristers at puberty, and thus retained their services in
the cathedral. So likewise did the Eastern pashas provide themselves with eunuchs who could be trusted to guard the seraglios.

With these proofs of the effect of castration so long before
them, it is surprising that scientists took so little interest in the
subject. This is probably explained by the fact that they believed that the changes brought about by castration were nervous in origin, that is to say, that the removal of the testicle cut
the path of nervous impulses travelling from them to the brain,
and so altered the animal's sexual behaviour. Having accepted
this theory, they did not bother to find out whether it was true
or not. But curiosity is endemic amongst scientists, and eventually experiments were made. Bertholdt showed that if a capon
was grafted with fragments of testicle the changes that usually
follow castration were avoided. Since the grafts were unconnected with the brain their efficacy could not be through

nervous impulses, but through the action of an internal secretion. Steinach of Vienna continued this work and proved that both the testicles and the ovaries contained specific secretions, one that pushed the body in the direction of maleness, and the other that pushed it in the direction of femaleness. By grafting testicles and ovaries into young castrated animals of the opposite sex, he was even able to change their outward appearance, the males taking on the characteristics of females, and the females those of males.

The final stage in the elucidation of the secrets of an endocrine gland is usually the isolation in pure form of its internal secretion. This has now been accomplished in the case of both the testicle and the ovary. It has been found that the ovary forms two secretions, oestrin and progesterone, and that these secretions are responsible for all the changes that take place in the lining membrane of the uterus, both during pregnancy and during menstruation. Another interesting fact that has emerged from experimental work on the internal secretion of the sex-glands is that maleness and femininity are not sharply differentiated entities standing widely apart. In between the masculine type of man and the feminine type of woman are a number of individuals in whom the characteristics of their sex are less strongly marked. As well as the masculine type of man and the feminine type of woman, there is the womanly type of man and the masculine type of woman. Indeed, it might be said that, in most men lurks something of the woman, and in most women something of the man. This is not surprising when we realize that in the body of a man we find certain secretions that are feminine by nature and in the body of a woman those that are male.

The important discoveries made in connexion with the thyroid and the sex-glands directed attention to other structures in the body that might possibly form internal secretions. There were two small glands that had already aroused interest, the suprarenals. These structures, the size of plumstones, lie at the upper poles of the two kidneys; and Addison, a nineteenth-century Guy's Hospital physician, had already made some observations in connexion with them. In 1855 he described a group of symptoms that were associated with tuberculosis of the suprarenals. These symptoms consisted of a progressive loss of weight in a patient with increasing muscular weakness. The patient also developed a bronze mottling of the skin. Because he had been the first to draw attention to these symptoms and to correlate them with the destruction of the suprarenals, Addison's name has been attached to this disease.

The other methods of investigation that had proved so fruitful in unravelling the function of the thyroid and the sex-glands were now applied to the suprarenals. The second method of investigation, namely, extirpation of the suprarenal glands from animals, proved of little service since the animals died almost immediately of prostration and convulsions. All that could be said as the result of these experiments was that the suprarenals were essential to life. The third line of research, the making of extracts, turned out to be more fruitful. From the glands was obtained a substance, now known as adrenalin, that when injected into an animal caused the contraction of its blood vessels. It was also shown to have the same effect when dabbed on to an open wound, so that it could be used as a means of reducing bleeding from cuts. When given as an injection it acted on the heart, increasing the rate of its beat, and on the breathing, making the respiratory movements deeper. It was next proved that the blood leaving a suprarenal body by its veins contained more adrenalin than the blood flowing in its arteries ; in other words, the suprarenals obviously poured their internal secretion into the blood-stream.

The histologists and the comparative anatomists then made their contributions to our knowledge of the suprarenals. Microscopic examination showed that the suprarenal glands consisted of two parts : an outer part called the cortex, and an inner called the medulla. The comparative anatomists now supplied the information that the two parts developed quite separately, and that in fishes the cortex remained an independent organ, completely isolated from the medulla. This allowed of the removal of one part without damaging the other, and eventually led to the discovery that it was the cortex that was the vital portion of the gland and not the medulla.

This does not mean that the medulla is unimportant to an animal; on the contrary, it is this part of the adrenals that forms adrenalin, the only hormone that up till recently has been isolated from the suprarenal. Both portions of the gland play important, although different, roles in maintaining the health of the body, although it is the cortex that is more essential to life. By some authorities the suprarenal glands have been called 'the glands of emergency', and the name is a good one. They supply one of the means by which an animal suddenly mobilizes its resources in a crisis, preparing it for either flight or resistance. Under the stress of anger or fear the suprarenals suddenly begin pouring their secretions into the blood-stream, thus stimulating the activity of the heart, raising the blood-pressure, deepening the respiration, increasing the blood-sugar that has to supply fuel for the muscles, and generally preparing the animal for the flight, or fight, upon which its life may depend. Moreover, the suprarenals not only prepare the animal for the emergency, but they make certain that the existence of an emergency is sensed by the animal. In order that the danger may be rightly apprehended, the warning signals of palpitation, sweating, and gooseflesh, must be flashed through the animal's body. All these signals, as well as the reactions that they automatically provoke in preparation for fight or escape, are conveyed by the suprarenals to every part of the body through their hormones, or chemical messengers in the blood.

Professor C. B. Cannon has written a great deal about the energizing action of the suprarenals when they have been stimulated by fear or anger. Nor is it necessary to rely solely on animal experiment to understand this. We all know how the sudden realization that a car is about to run over us galvanizes us into activities that we could never emulate in quieter moments. None of these astounding exertions could have been made without the energizing help of the suprarenals. Nor is fear the only emotion that can galvanize us into activity. Cannon in his book, *Bodily Changes in Pain, Hunger, Fear and Rage*, quotes interesting examples of frenzied feats of endurance performed by people acting under the influence of religious mania. He recalls that in 1374 a widespread outbreak of religious fervour occurred in Germany, in which men and women danced in the streets for hours on end without resting. A similar event happened in Wales in 1740. These feats of endurance were made possible by two mechanisms coming into action, first the switching off of energy from other bodily activities, like digestion, so that it could be used entirely by the muscles, and second, the pouring of adrenalin into the blood-stream.

But the suprarenals have other functions than that of mobilizing the muscular responses of the body. The suprarenals are found to be closely linked up with two other structures, the skin and the sex-glands. The former connexion has already been mentioned, for it was seen that the skin became pigmented in Addison's disease. The connexion between the suprarenals and the sex-glands is proved by the fact that children with enlarged adrenals are sexually precocious, possessing the sexual development of an adult. It would also appear that the role played by the suprarenals in the sexual development of a woman is somewhat different from that played by them in the sexual development of a man. An overgrowth of the suprarenal cortex produces masculine changes in a woman but not feminine changes in men. A girl with a tumour of the adrenals slowly becomes more and more like a man, first growing hair on the face and body, and then developing the voice, mentality, and temperament of a male. In great distress of mind she sees herself slowly moving in the direction of the opposite sex, and only if the tumour can be removed will she have any chance of returning to her former condition. The suprarenals may therefore be regarded as glands that play a particularly prominent part in the male. It is for this reason that they have sometimes been called male glands, just as the thyroid which is particularly active in women, is sometimes called a female gland.

One more function of the suprarenals is known. They mobilize the body's resistance to foes that attack it from within, as well as from without. Experiments have shown that an animal with a damaged adrenal cortex is much less resistant to bacterial infection than is another with intact glands. The suprarenals have been well named the glands of emergency, for they take their full share in the body's fight against disease. It need not seem surprising therefore, that after a severe attack of influenza, a patient often shows signs of suprarenal exhaustion in the way of disinclination for any muscular or mental exertion, fatigue, loss of appetite, and depression. The taking of tonics may sometimes help, but no tonic can act as a deputy for an exhausted suprarenal gland. Since chemists are now succeeding in extracting the active principle of the cortex, as well as of the medulla, it is possible that in the future such patients will be spared these distressing symptoms by being provided with the hormone of which they have been temporarily depleted.

Interesting as these glands may be, they are far less interesting than a tiny structure tucked under the fore part of the brain, and neglected by the older anatomists, the pituitary. The understanding of this gland is the key to the understanding of the whole endocrine system. Although it is not greater than the size of a pea, it is the master gland controlling the development and the activity of all the others. If the pituitary is removed from a young animal, the animal ceases to grow. If it becomes overactive in an individual, he may grow into a giant. Without its help the thyroid and the sex-glands fail to develop, and but for its activity, the whole of the chemistry of the body would take a wrong direction. It is not without reason therefore that it is termed by endocrinologists, the leader of the endocrine orchestra.

Quite apart from the importance of the role played by the pituitary amongst the endocrines, it is remarkable on account of its position alone. It is attached by a long stalk to the base of the brain, and if this stalk is examined microscopically, it is found to contain nerve fibres, which run eventually to the thalamus, an important structure, which (as we shall see in a later chapter) is regarded nowadays as the seat of the emotional life. The pituitary, therefore, is the meeting-ground of secretions and nervous impulses. It is affected by what happens in the thalamus, and in turn it has an effect on that structure. It would scarcely be an exaggeration to say that this tiny gland is the centre of our being. Indeed, the difficulty that now faces physiologists is to understand how so small a structure can perform so many functions, and there has been a disposition lately to suggest that it does not act so much by forming a vast number of secretions, as by activating those of its servants.

A careful examination of the pituitary shows that it is divided into two lobes, an anterior and a posterior, of which the former is the more important. From the anterior lobe have been extracted so many secretions that it is difficult to understand how they can all be formed by such a small gland, secretions controlling growth and exercising a powerful influence over the body's chemistry. The posterior lobe produces a definite secretion which, when extracted and injected into an animal, causes a marked rise in its blood-pressure, and contractions in the bowel, and in the womb. It also produces an increase in the amount of urine excreted. Certain endocrinologists also believe that as well as affecting the body, the posterior lobe of the pituitary also affects the character, and people with a well-developed posterior pituitary are supposed to have artistic ability. It is now believed that the pituitary controls certain rhythmic activities of the body, such as the rhythm of sleeping and waking. It is also believed to be the lever responsible for the rhythm of hibernation, slowing down, during the winter months, all the bodily activities, until they are at such a low ebb that the animal seems scarcely alive.

Many of the descriptions that have been given of the action of the secretions of the internal glands on the body are not so simple as has been described. The action, instead of being direct, is indirect, the pituitary playing a part in them, so that three factors are concerned – the body, the appropriate gland, and the pituitary. The full significance of this triparite action will be shown in the later part of this book in which an ancient philosophy is referred to. This philosophy states that *all* phenomena are due to the action of three qualities or forces called *gunas*.

Three other endocrine glands of less importance remain to be described, the parathyroid, the thymus, and the pineal. Very little is known about any of them and as they are not believed to have a marked influence on character they are only of secondary importance to us. The parathyroids are small glands which, as their name implies, lie in close proximity to the thyroid. If they are removed, the patient suffers from tremors, and the calcium chemistry of his body is upset. The thymus lies inside the chest, just beneath the breast-bone. It is well developed in a child, but generally shrinks in adult life. It is therefore regarded as a gland that is only important in the earlier stages of life, and its chief medical interest lies in the fact that, when it is enlarged, it is sometimes responsible for deaths under anaesthesia. The pineal gland, which lies at the posterior end of the brain, was formerly regarded as the seat of the soul. Modern science has, however, deprived it of its exalted position, and looks upon it as a relic of a structure that exists in certain lizards, a third eye. It will be remembered that the Cyclops possessed a single eye in the centre of their skulls. This eye was more or less in the position of the pineal gland, although the Greek authors placed it a little too far forward. The pineal of an ordinary man is, so far as one knows, of very little importance to him, and the injection of pineal extracts has given variable results.

Brief and incomplete though this description of the endocrine glands may be, it is sufficient to furnish an idea of the manner in which the body is acted upon by its internal secretions. It must be remembered that a close relationship is maintained between the different members of the endocrine circle, the thyroid and suprarenals affecting the gonads,* and in turn being influenced by them, the thyroid being called into action by the pituitary, and the weakening of one gland being compensated for by the overaction of another, and the harmony of the whole orchestra being maintained by the leadership of the pituitary. Should this harmony be disturbed, should the balance of the secretions be tilted in one direction or another, the health of the whole body suffers. Sometimes this upset in balance reveals itself primarily in a disturbance of body function, and sometimes it is the personality and psychic life of the patient that is more affected. But because body and mind are so closely bound up together, so inextricably interwoven that it is impossible to unravel them, more usually both suffer equally, so that the patient becomes the victim of what may be called a psycho-somatic disturbance.

The capacity of an individual to survive depends to a great

*The sex-glands.

extent on his ability to adjust himself to changes in his environment. In times of war, a man who has hitherto been engaged in a sedentary occupation finds himself suddenly pitchforked into an entirely new life. His diet, his manner of living, and his emotional environment all undergo a sudden change. Either he must adapt himself to his new circumstances, or failing to do so, he must suffer a mental and physical breakdown. His success or failure in reacting to the novel conditions in which he finds himself will depend to a great extent on the adaptability shown by his endocrine system. If he is successful certain glands will respond by an increase in function, and a new equilibrium will be reached which often may seem to him preferable to the old. Such a man, at the conclusion of the war, will find it difficult to return to his office, and will make every effort to exchange his former sedentary occupation for some more active and open-air existence. If, on the other hand, his endocrine system fails to accommodate itself to the new mode of existence created by active service, he will suffer in bodily and mental health, and finally be discharged as a case of nervous breakdown, or neurasthenia.

The thought that the welfare of body and mind is so dependent on the fine chemistry of the internal secretions may come as a shock to many. It is distressing to think that our dignity as human beings may be balanced on the fine point of our thyroids. Should some accident befall it in the early days of its development, the result may be a cretin, a creature misshapen and hopeless, dwelling in a twilight of consciousness; should, on the other hand, it be stimulated into overaction, a nervous, emotionally unstable, tremulous, and restless person is produced. It is a gruesome thought that about three and a half grains of iodine stand between us and idiocy, that we are to such a large extent not what we want to be, but what this subtle chemistry of our glands makes us.

Should a medieval alchemist return to earth and learn what modern science has to say on this subject, he would show no surprise. For the alchemist there existed no hard and fast division between the realm of the material and the spiritual. Instead he pictured an intermediate state between matter and mind, a psychic realm of subtle bodies to which a mental, as well as a material manifestation was appropriate. To him the soul was something material, but of a materiality infinitely finer and more subtle than the substance of which the body was made. 'All these secretions which you chemists have discovered', he would say, 'we knew about in principle. They are the subtle substances that permeate all the grosser matters. Even the earth which you moderns consider dead is not actually dead but is permeated by subtle matter. This is the earth's life and spirit which are nourished by the stars and in turn give nourishment to all living things, as a mother gives life to the child that she shelters in her womb.'

So the finer chemistry of the body would cause no difficulty to the alchemist, who made no hard and fast distinction between the outer manifestation of his art, the transmutation of the baser metals into gold, and the esoteric side of his calling, the transmutation of the grosser side of his nature into the finer matters of the spirit. He would rather find in the discovery of the endocrine secretions and of the vitamins a confirmation of his own teaching that subtle bodies permeated all grosser matters of nature.

And in linking up the endocrine secretions with the vitamins he would have been right, for these two categories of substances have much in common. Not only do they share the characteristic that a very small quantity of each can bring about immense and far-reaching consequences, but they sometimes exert a similar action. It has been proved for example that a similar body to that found in the ovary, oestrin, can be extracted from plants, and that daffodils can be made to flower all the year round by the use of human secretions. The old distinction drawn between active principles obtained from the body and those obtained from plants has therefore broken down. This justifies us in our use of plant extracts in medicine.

So far we have considered mainly the action of the internal secretions on the body. In the following chapter an attempt will be made to indicate how they may influence the mind.

CHAPTER 4

HUMAN TYPES

THE study of human types is no new one. From the most ancient times efforts have been made to divide men into different categories, not according to race, but to temperament. When the theory of the 'humours' of the body dominated physiology, it was natural that the classification attempted should be based on the predominance of one of the four humours and that men should be divided into the sanguine, the bilious, the lymphatic, and the nervous. But long before the time of Galen, who sponsored this division by means of humours, the Hindus had described three kinds of women, whom they likened to the deer, the mare, and the elephant, and three kinds of men, pictured as the hare, the bull, and the horse. These animal analogues summarized in picture form certain peculiarities of the skin, hair, voice, genital organs, general physique, and temperament of men and women, and it will be noted that all of these characteristics are those that are capable of being produced by differences in endocrine constitution.

The search for a basis for classification continues at the present day. Kretschmer has attempted a division into types, in accordance with certain physical and psychic characteristics, and Jung in accordance with psychic qualities alone. Jung's two main groups are the extraverts and introverts, the former being individuals whose main preoccupation is with the world around them, the latter, those whose attention is chiefly focused on the world within, upon their own feelings, reactions, fantasies, and thoughts. Jung subdivides these two main catagories according to the psychic activity that plays a predominant part in the individual's decisions and mode of living.

This provides four classes, men whose lives are ruled by thinking, feeling, sensation, and intuition respectively. In all, eight categories of men are thus described. But although Jung's method of classification shows ingenuity, few of his psychological colleagues regard it with favour. Professor William Brown denies the validity of even his primary division into extravert and introvert. In his opinion, the person who is turned in on himself is the victim of unsolved complexes and fixations, and must be regarded as pathological. Such a person is so entangled by inner difficulties that he is not only incapable of seeing the world outside, but himself as he is. The division into extravert and introvert, according to Professor Brown, is, therefore, only a separation of the normal from the abnormal. Whilst it is true that one person is more concerned with external, and others with internal, events, this should be regarded as being a classification of interests, and not of individuals.

The homoeopathic school of medicine founded by Hahnemann, has also interested itself in the question of human types. This interest was aroused by the observation that certain men and women when they were ill showed a tendency to develop one set of symptoms, whilst others tended to develop another. It was also noted that patients reacted to the same drugs in a very different manner. To the homoeopathic doctor, therefore, it became of paramount importance to discover the type of patient with whom he had to deal. He considered it far more necessary to know what sort of man was ill, than what sort of illness he suffered from. Only after the patient's type had been discovered would it be possible to prescribe the appropriate remedy.

An allopathic doctor can, if he retains an open mind, learn much from a homoeopathist. Founded originally as a protest against the materialism of nineteenth-century medicine, homoeopathy has avoided some of the errors into which the allopathic school of medicine has fallen. It has never made the mistake of losing sight of the patient in the treatment of his disease, of looking at the part without any reference to the whole. But the homoeopathic practitioner's attempts to divide humanity according to its susceptibility to different derangements, and its response to different drugs, does not provide a broad enough basis for a science of types. It is a practical device that has been found serviceable in homoeopathic medicine, rather than a method for general application.

As so often happens, medical science has been forced to retrace its steps in order to discover a sounder foundation for the classification of humanity. Having discarded psychological divisions, medical men are now searching for new methods of classifying men. Galen's chemistry of 'humours' has been resuscitated in the form of endocrine secretions. It is with this modern version of 'the chemistry of the soul' that we shall now deal.

More and more it is being realized that the general contours of the body, the length of the arms and legs, consistency of the skin, the sound of the voice, and, what is of special interest, the pattern of the emotional life are, to a great extent, conditioned by the endocrine glands. An attempt has therefore been made to classify individual men and women according to the particular gland that appears to be dominant in their endocrine constitution, and, in certain cases, according to the gland that appears to be in abeyance. In this way, men and women are labelled adrenal-centred, thyroid-centred, pituitary-centred, gonad-centred, or thymus-centred, indicating that in their particular make-up this or that gland, or this or that combination of glands, plays a particularly important part. This method of classification is as yet crude and unskilful, for much has yet to be learnt about the secretions and their action on the pyscho-physical complex that constitutes man. Moreover, it is only in certain individuals that one gland, or combination of glands, is sufficiently in the ascendancy to serve as a basis for classification. In many people they would appear to be so well balanced that it is difficult to attach to individuals clearly marked labels. Despite this, the new attempt at classification rests on securer foundations than did its predecessors, and some day it may result in a real science of types.

Even although that day has not yet arrived, and even although many of our present-day theories will have to be revised in the light of new knowledge, it will be advisable to take a general view of the present situation. The best method of doing so will be to discuss the criteria by means of which the various endocrine types are distinguished, and then provide illustrative examples taken from amongst historical personages. Although the data for arriving at any conclusion concerning the endocrine types of such personages is very limited, they are sometimes sufficient to allow of him or her being placed, with a fair degree of assurance, in one or other category. Much of the material used in this chapter has been obtained from two books, *The Glands regulating Personality* by Dr Berman, and *The Glands of Destiny* by Dr Geikie Cobb, and to these authors I acknowledge my indebtedness.

The Pituitary Type. The presence of two apparently antagonistic principles in the pituitary makes the portrayal of the pituitary-centred man or woman particularly difficult. Although this theory rests on very slender evidence, it is generally believed that the anterior lobe determines the more masculine qualities of an individual, and the posterior the more feminine. Perhaps a little unfairly, Berman summarizes the masculine qualities as 'superlative brain tone and action, good all-round growth, and harmonious general function', and the feminine as 'susceptibility to tender emotions, sentimentalism, and emotionalism'. Those who may regard this discrimination as prejudiced may take comfort in the fact that the predominance of the anterior over the posterior lobe is not the prerogative of a man, or the predominance of the posterior over the anterior the inevitable fate of a woman. Many instances could be given of women whose lives, according to this theory, were controlled by the anterior, and of men who were very much under the influence of the posterior lobe of the pituitary.

Correlated with these psychic qualities, and more easily recognized, are the changes in structure brought about by the pituitary. An active anterior pituitary is generally, but not always, associated with tallness, a long skull, a resolute jaw, and well-marked supra-orbital ridges. The teeth are well developed, the arms and legs hairy, and the feet and hands large. Posterior pituitary predominance is more likely to be associated with a short and thick-set body, a head that seems too large for the trunk, and hair scanty on the body, but plentiful on the head. Men of this type are reputed to develop a paunch early in life, and to be temperamentally less stable than their anterior-pituitary controlled colleagues. In view of this description it is not surprising that Berman concludes that many musical geniuses and writers have belonged to this type : for example, Sir James Barrie. Men of this type should be contrasted with forceful virile individuals, like Abraham Lincoln, who, through predominance of their anterior pituitaries, have the power to dominate their fellows and to hold to a predetermined course whatever the difficulties that may have to be encountered.

The pituitary gland lies in a special hollow in the base of the skull, and is surrounded on three sides by unyielding bony walls. Should it become enlarged it may prove too big for its casing, with resulting damage and disturbance. The pituitary is indeed particularly liable to undergo changes at various periods in its possessor's life. Some of the ills that may result from pituitary errors have already been described, on the one hand, giantism, and on the other, dwarfism. Disfunction of the pituitary may, however, manifest itself in changes outside the skeletal system, and endocrinologists are fond of pointing to historical personages, whose careers started brilliantly, but ended disastrously, on account of a failing pituitary. Whether all the examples that have been given are authentic or not is highly doubtful, but it is quite likely that a gland that has played a large part in shaping an individual's early life may, either through exhaustion or accident, begin to fail after he has passed his prime. Should this happen, a man or woman who in earlier years has been an example of hyper-pituitarism, may, within a comparatively short time, display symptoms of the opposite state of hypo-pituitarism.

Of all the examples that have been given of a person whose pituitary failed him at a critical period of his life, the most famous is that of Napoleon Bonaparte. Berman has carefully scrutinized the emperor's career, temperament, and physical features, and has come to the conclusion that this view of Napoleon is correct. Fortunately we know many details of his private, as well as of his public life. From the diary of his physician, Antommarchi, we glean also many facts concerning his imperial master's health, and finally we possess a report of the post-mortem made in St Helena.

Many portraits of Napoleon, painted at various periods of his life, survive, and all of them portray the same general physical characteristics, both the sharply-cut features and the determined-looking jaw. His height was only five feet, his hands small and plump, his hair dark, silky, and straight, and his complexion swarthy. Although Napoleon's small stature does not favour this view, Berman is of the opinion that his early portraits are those of a pituitary-driven man, with strong adrenal development. Adreno-centred men are usually swarthy, but since Napoleon was a Corsican it would be unjustifiable to put much weight on his possession of a dark complexion.

We know that, although he gave way to storms of temper, Napoleon was controlled by his intellect, rather than by his feelings. He had little love for poetry, music, or painting, and possessed not a glimmering of religious feeling. The thyroid, and the posterior pituitary, were, therefore, not very active in him, a fact that can be correlated with his abnormally slow pulse. Nor, in spite of the scandal whispered behind his back, is there reason to believe that sexuality was an important ingredient in his make-up. Indeed, when we remember how many women were prepared to 'fall for' the greatest personage in Europe, it is surprising that his infidelities to Josephine were not even more numerous than they were.

But although Napoleon must be regarded as a pituitary-centred man, all was not well with that superlatively important gland. Quite early in his career, symptoms arose that suggest a certain instability in its functioning. Whilst, in the interval between his brain-storms, his intellect remained dominant, and he showed great mathematical and logical ability, there were days when he suffered from mental discomfiture, followed by severe headaches. It should be noted also that Antommarchi records that his master was bothered by micturition troubles, so that he could not sleep for more than a few hours at a stretch, or remain in the saddle long without dismounting. Whilst some other explanation may have been at the back of this bladder trouble, it is well known that the pituitary is connected with the secretion of urine, and that there is a disease of the posterior lobe, known as diabetes insipidus, which is characterized by the passage of excessive amounts of urine. One other possible sign that the pituitary was not healthy is the fact that his marriage with Josephine was barren, and that only two illegitimate children are known to have resulted from his liaisons. Modern research has shown that a common cause of infertility in men is a fault in pituitary function.

So we see Napoleon as a man dependent on a pituitary that was showing signs of unstable action in the earlier part of his career. As we trace this career towards its close, we find an increase in these signs of pituitary instability, and finally we witness a breakdown in its functioning. Even before he was crowned emperor it was noted that in spite of his activity he was beginning to put on flesh. Soon afterwards he developed a paunch, with fatty deposits round the hips and the thighs. And with the deterioration in the fitness of the body came a weakening of the intellectual faculties. The keen calculating judgement shown at Austerlitz gave place to the vacillating indecision that kept him lingering in Moscow until winter had begun. No longer was he capable of making those lightning decisions that had made him the finest strategist in Europe. For short periods the masterful mind might reassert itself, but the end of the career of the 'intolerable egoist of Europe' was in sight. There is no need even to postulate that Waterloo was lost to France because on the eve of it the Emperor suffered from a fit. The battle was lost long previously when a tiny gland, the size of a pea, began to show ominous signs of disrepair.

Those who accompanied their exiled Emperor to St Helena suffered more than the loss of their homes; they witnessed the rapid decline of the man who had been their god. His physical and mental powers deteriorated so rapidly that they soon discovered that they were living with an utterly different man. He became fat and flabby, sulky, indolent, and indifferent. At times he gave way to storms of abuse, then sank back into gloomy silence.

After his death the findings at the post-mortem were published by an English physician. 'The whole surface of the body was deeply covered with fat. Over the sternum, where generally the bone is very superficial, the fat was upwards of an inch deep, and an inch and a half to two inches on the abdomen. There was scarcely a hair on the body, and that on the head was fine and silky. The whole genital system (very small) seemed to exhibit a physical cause for the absence of sexual desire and the chastity which had been stated to characterize the deceased during his stay at St Helena. The skin was noticed to be very white and delicate, as were the hands and arms. Indeed the whole body was slender and effeminate.' No better picture could have been given of the changes that take place in the body after a pituitary has failed. The bright star in which the Emperor had so fervently believed had set before its time.

The Thyroid Type. Since the thyroid is believed to be intimately connected with the expression of the emotions, and since woman is commonly regarded as being more emotional than man, examples of thyroid-centred individuals are more usually selected from the feminine sex. This is, however, quite arbitrary and it would be possible to discover just as good instances of predominance of the thyroid amongst males as amongst females, for although severe degrees of hyper-thyroidism are commoner amongst women, lesser degrees are frequently found in men. This is particularly likely to be the case in men of strongly artistic temperament, such as poets, and Keats has been given by some writers as an example of a thyroid-centred person.

The activity of the thyroid, like that of the pituitary, is liable to vary at different epochs in life. Many children are definitely sub-thyroid until puberty, and then suddenly their whole temperament appears to undergo a change. Previously they have been listless, easily tired, backward, and difficult children, and then suddenly with the onset of puberty (in their case often late), all these defects disappear. On the mental side the improvement is shown by increased intelligence, quicker powers of observation, better attention, and a brighter outlook on life, and on the physical, by the shaping of the body into the slender delicate outlines of the young adult. Even the face changes, lengthening, becoming more alive, with brightening of the eyes and clearing of the complexion. The whole tempo of life is changing under the stimulating action of adequate thyroid secretion.

The thyroid, as we have seen, is the accelerator of the body chemistry and of the emotional life. It intervenes not only at the crucial time of passage from childhood to adolescence, but at the other critical periods in its owner's life. This is one of the reasons why the thyroid has been regarded as being an essentially feminine gland. The female organism makes a more adventurous voyage through life than does the male, being called upon to undertake the stupendous adventures of pregnancy and childbirth. And even if the fulfilment of this central function of her being is denied her, every month a woman must prepare herself for the possibility of it happening. During the whole of her reproductive life the generative organs of a woman are never static, but every moon go through a complete cycle of changes in anticipation of what may never happen. Keeping step with these changes there is an ebb and flow in the activity of that accelerator of her body's chemistry, the thyroid gland. During pregnancy the extra work thrown on the thyroid is sometimes made manifest by the appearance of a swelling of the neck, by a speeding up of the pulse rate, and by a tendency to perspire at the least exertion. Menstruation may be associated with the same symptoms of hyper-thyroidism.

It has been said that excessive action of the thyroid is likely to lead to emotional outbursts, nervousness, insomnia, and psychic instability. The converse is also true; a severe psychological crisis may be followed by an enlargement of the gland. On questioning a patient suffering from exophthalmic goitre one will frequently be told that the symptoms and swelling of the neck were first noticed after some distressing experience, such as the death of a husband or child. In this association of an enlarged thyroid with an emotional shock, we have one more instance of the interdependence of mind and body, mind acting on body and body on mind.

Just as the pituitary may become exhausted by the wear and tear imposed on it by life, so may the thyroid, after playing a prominent part in its owner's affairs, later show signs of failure.

Geikie Cobb in his analysis of Henry VIII gives it as his opinion that the chief levers that controlled the royal machinery were, on the psychological side, a sense of inferiority, and on the endocrinological, an active thyroid-pituitary combination. Towards the end of Henry's life his thyroid began to give out; he put on flesh, became lazy, puffy under the eyes, and, as revealed by Holbein's portrait, lost the outer halves of his eyebrows. This thinning of the outer parts of the eyebrows is regarded as being characteristic of hypo-thyroidism. There was one compensation attached to the diminution of the activity of the royal thyroid; His Majesty became distinctly more manageable by his wives.

The Adreno-centred Personalities. Berman has termed the adrenal-controlled man or woman 'the Atlas of the twentieth-century World'. Perhaps the term would be more complete if he had added the word Western to his definition, since it is the Westerner who is generally energetic. The adrenals are organs for the mobilization of physical and mental energy, for the combating of shocks, and for the meeting of emergencies. They work overtime in war, and since even in the intervals between wars Western man still remains at loggerheads with his environment the adrenals are rarely at rest. The skin furnishes one of the chief clues to the adrenal personality. It is darkly pigmented and the hair on it is thick, coarse, and dry. The scalp usually descends low on to the forehead and the body is well covered. Psychologically, adrenal people are characterized by a capacity for dogged persistence and super-effort. They are the Shackletons of the world, the great explorers, and the holders of Marathon records. Their adrenals have made them what they are by fitting them for great physical and mental efforts.

In a woman, an active adrenal tends to swing her in the direction of masculinity. The advance of emancipated womanhood into the realms that once were inhabited only by men has made a call on the activity of her adrenals and the glands have generally responded. The modern world is full of vigorous, persistent, manly women, furnishing yet another example of the influence of activity on structure.

The Gonad-centred Type. The action of the internal secretion of the sex-glands upon the body and mind is well known. The stronger the sex-glands the more emphatically is a man stamped a man and a woman a woman. A man even more than a woman is dependent on an adequate complement of the sex secretion, for the body itself has a distinct bias in the direction of femininity. It is for this reason that, when the supply of internal secretion is deficient, the man is more likely to become womanly, than the woman to become manly. Only if the woman's adrenals become more active than before is the latter metamorphosis likely to take place.

Male eunuchoids are distinguished by their lack of initiative and push. They are usually gentle, unassuming weaklings, who even when grown up retain many of the attributes of childhood. Such men lack the drive of the male, and are unambitious and retiring. Because the onset of puberty slows down the growth of the long bones, and because puberty is late when the sex hormones are deficient, the eunuchoid is often taller than his fellows. In later life he puts on flesh and shows a tendency to become gross and flabby.

The gonad-centred man is the reverse of all this. He is thick-set and muscular, like his adreno-centred brother, inclined to hairiness, exhibiting in superabundance all the characteristic traits of the male. Usually, although not always, this make-up is associated with strong sexual desire and capacity.

As the gonado-centric male exhibits strongly the distinguishing marks of his sex, so does the gonado-centric woman exhibit the characteristics of hers. Geikie Cobb draws a comparison between two well-known sovereigns, Queen Elizabeth I of England and Queen Catherine of Russia. Both of the queens are known in history to have been successful and graceful personalities, who managed the affairs of State with efficiency and skill. Yet the methods they used in controlling their ministers were entirely different. Elizabeth, in spite of her liaison with Leicester and her vain display of dancing before the Spanish ambassador, deliberately discarded her womanhood in order to rule as a man. She was a pituitary-centred female who gradually developed into a sharp-featured and skilled politician. Catherine, on the other hand, remained throughout her life a woman who employed for her own ends the efficient instruments of her own sex. Empress although she was, she was still in essence a woman and a mother. It is true that she heartily disliked her offspring, the unpleasant Paul, but her feeling for her lovers, in the latter part of her life, was that of a mother for her sons. Her essentially feminine nature revealed itself, not only in her innate dislike of cruelty and war, but in her gentleness and consideration for all the men who served her. If she was guilty of sexual excess – as she undoubtedly was – it must be remembered that she lived in a court where moral ethics were never discussed.

Thymo-centric Personalities. As has already been said, but little is known of the internal secretion of the thymus gland, other than that it functions mainly in childhood. Some endocrinologists are of the opinion that if the thymus does not become less active at puberty, the work of the other endocrine glands is deranged. When this happens something of the child is perpetuated at the expense of the mature man or woman. To quote Berman : 'In women the external manifestation of the thymocentric personality may be limited to thinness, delicacy of the skin, narrow waist, rather poorly developed breasts, arched thighs, and scanty hair, with scarcity and delayed menstruation'. Or there may be obesity associated with juvenility, if, for one reason or another, the pituitary functions poorly.

Berman regards Oscar Wilde as an example of the thymocentric male, and in support of his view quotes Henri de Regnier's description of that unfortunate poet. At the time of his meeting with him in Paris 'this foreigner was tall and of great corpulence. A high complexion seemed to give still greater width to his clean-shaven face. It was the unbearded (glabrous) face that one sees on coins. The hands ... were fleshy and plump.' Another sign of thymus dominance was Oscar Wilde's voice, a beautiful tenor when under control, but high-pitched and strident when he was irritated. Such a quality of voice would be produced by a larynx that had failed to develop after puberty. There was something of the child that persisted in both the body and the mind of Wilde.

From a strictly scientific standpoint this attempt to portray different personalities in terms of endocrine endowment is unjustifiable. As yet we know so little about the influence of the endocrine glands on character that the preceding sketches of individual men and women whose lives have been regarded as being controlled by this or that gland are speculative, rather than scientific, studies. Until we are able to identify and measure the small quantities of secretion circulating in the blood and express our findings in an endocrine formula, we will only be able to recognize gross disturbances of the endocrine balance, and will be able to say little or nothing concerning the endocrine pattern of the normal man or woman. At the present moment all that we really know is that the endocrine pattern of an individual is a very important factor in determining his character.

CHAPTER 5

THE BRAIN AND CENTRAL
NERVOUS SYSTEM

IN the previous two chapters a description has been given of the endocrine glands, and their bearing on temperament was discussed. Temperament is a word that admits of various interpretations, and many attempts have been made to define it. For our purpose we shall accept McDougall's description of it as 'those personal qualities that are determined by the chemical influences of the body metabolism exerted upon the general working of the brain or nervous system'.

So far we have considered only the chemical influences. It now remains to deal with that upon which these chemical influences work, the brain and the central nervous system. Very primitive organisms are without any central nervous system, all the messages of the body being conveyed by the bloodstream, or, in the case of unicellular organisms, by the movement of the more fluid contents of the cell. But such means of communication are comparatively slow and for quick delivery and response some speedier method is required. This is provided by the development of the central nervous system. Physiologists invariably liken this to a telegraph system, in which the brain represents the General Post Office, the spinal cord the main distributing centres, and the nerves running from the spinal cord to various parts of the body, the telegraph wires. This picture is a good one and can be filled in with still greater detail. Just as in a busy telephone exchange there are special lines reserved, some for incoming, and others for outgoing calls, so also in the central nervous system there are sensory tracks that convey only incoming messages from the body to headquarters, and outgoing tracks that carry messages to the muscles.

Without straining the metaphor between the central nervous system and the post office unduly, it would also be possible to say that in the body the telegraphic and telephonic communications are divided into two more or less distinct systems, the voluntary, which we may liken to the facilities afforded to private individuals and businesses, and the autonomic system, which is mainly concerned with administration. The voluntary system is engaged in carrying to their destination outgoing messages from the brain and the spinal cord, and also in conveying incoming messages (sensations) from various parts of the body. The autonomics sympathetic, or vegetative, system, as it has variously been called, is relieved of this work and acts as a kind of accessory nervous organization that deals entirely with involuntary messages. Its function is to regulate those parts of the body that are not under the control of the will : that is to say, that are purely automatic in action. This accessory autonomic system is of special importance in connexion with the endocrine glands, for it is through it that the work of the glands is regulated ; for example, stimulation of the sympathetic nerve fibre running to the suprarenal glands results in an increased output in secretion. The action is reciprocal, for an increase in adrenalin in the blood reacts in turn upon the sympathetic system, heightening its response to stimulation.

The sympathetic system regulates not only the action of the endocrine glands, but also that of all other organs not under the control of the will, such as the heart, the blood-vessels, and the digestive system. In describing the suprarenals it was said that the sympathetic system was the physical basis for the appreciation and expression of the emotions. Long before the function of the sympathetic system was known, the solar plexus was reputed to be the seat of the emotions. The solar plexus is one of the largest networks or plexuses formed by the sympathetic system. It lies just below the diaphragm in the 'pit of the stomach'. This linking of the solar plexus with the emotions is fully justified by modern discoveries.

Although it has been described as a separate concern, the sympathetic system is closely connected with the brain and spinal cord. Anatomically, it is intimately linked up with the voluntary system of nerves. If we trace the path of the fine nerve fibres of the sympathetic system and follow them as they travel in the direction of the brain, we find that they lose themselves finally in the thalamus, a great mass of grey matter that lies at the base of the brain. This structure is of particular interest to us. Modern physiologists believe that it is the thalamus, rather than the solar plexus, that should be regarded as the seat of the emotions. But as the sympathetic nerves (including the solar plexus) and the thalamus are all parts of one system the localizing of emotions in the thalamus is merely the shifting of the centre of gravity from one part of the system to another.

In its work of controlling the mechanism of the body the sympathetic system makes use of two sorts of fibres, one set of which stimulates and the other diminishes the activity of an organ. The sympathetic nerves running to most of the organs in the body contain both varieties of fibres, known to physiologists as pressor and depressor fibres. An excellent example of their mode of action is provided by the nerves that regulate the tone of the blood-vessels. Experiment has shown that if the pressor fibres running to an artery are stimulated electrically, the blood-vessel becomes constricted, and that if the depressor fibres are stimulated, it dilates. Normally the tone of the blood-vessels is maintained by a balanced action of the two sets of fibres, the one opposing the other. Should more blood be required for the efficient working of an organ, the depressor fibres immediately come into action, overpowering the influence of the opposing fibres and flooding the organ with blood.

Because the sympathetic system is affected by the emotions, the action of the pressor and depressor fibres may be called into being by psychological states. The pallor of the face associated with fear and blushing caused by shyness are examples of pressor and depressor action respectively resulting from a psychic stimulus. In a precisely similar manner, the frequency of the heart-beat is regulated by the opposing action of two sets of fibres, one of which tends to increase it, and the other to diminish it. It is scarcely necessary to point out that the heart-beat is readily affected by emotional states. The body is full of these balanced actions, ready at an instant's notice to meet the requirements of life by either diminishing or heightening activity. Normally they are self-regulating mechanisms influenced by the emotions, but not subject to voluntary control. Only in exceptional individuals, and as a result of special training, can the sympathetic system be brought under the influence of the will. These cases of voluntary control over the sympathetic system will be mentioned later (see Chapter 11).

So far we have discussed only the gross structure of the central nervous system, but, before proceeding further, it will be necessary to say a few words about its finer structure, revealed by the microscope. The unit out of which the whole of the central nervous system is built up is the branched nerve-cell, or 'neurone'. There are many branched cells in the body, but the nerve-cell or neurone is distinguished by the fact that one of its branches is enormously elongated into the nerve-fibre. The central cores of these elongated branches, known as axis cylinders, are the conductors along which the nervous impulse travels, the shorter branches of the neurones serve to make connexions with neighbouring nerve-cells. Usually a message from the brain has to pass through several relays of cells and axis cylinders before it reaches its destination in the muscles. In this process we again find a close parallel with the telephone system, in which the necessity for laying down innumerable wires is obviated by the employment of an operator, whose work it is to connect a subscriber with any branch he requires by 'plugging in' on a switchboard. It may indeed happen that in order to speak from, say, York to Torquay, connexions will have to be made at several different switchboards, so that neither in the telephone system nor in the body does a message travel along a single continuous wire. And as telephone wires are carefully insulated by means of a rubber and silk covering, to prevent leakage of current, so in the body are the nerve-fibres insulated by special sheaths, where fat and connective tissue play the part of rubber and silk.

For the sake of mutual protection many different neurones are packed together into a single nerve, and they travel together during the major part of their course, only parting company when they near their destination. From the brain and the spinal cord (its prolongation down the backbone), a vast number of these complicated cables of nerve-fibres are given off, in the form of the cranial and spinal nerves.

When examined under the microscope, the brain and the spinal cord are also found to be composed of innumerable nerve-cells and fibres held together by a minimum of packing, and covered by their own special membranes, or meninges. The whole of the central nervous system is, therefore, nothing but a vast network of paths for nerve impulses, a network that is so complicated that in comparison with it even London's telephone system appears to be a simple affair. In spite of the enormous difficulties the work entailed, scientists have, by painstaking research, succeeded in tracing many of the paths taken by nerve impulses in the body. It has even been possible to state how many relays occur in the passage of a sensation, say, from the hand to the brain, and how many in the return journey from the brain to the hand muscles.

When we come to discuss the parts played by the brain and the spinal cord in the control of the voluntary movements of the body, it may be said that in general the spinal cord deals with movements that are more or less automatic in character (e.g walking), and the brain with those that are deliberate or intentional. If the sole of the foot is lightly tickled, the toes bend downwards and the foot is rapidly withdrawn. This is an automatic movement and no effort of will enters into it. An automatic movement of this nature is termed a reflex action. Another reflex action is the spasm that is provoked in the eye-lid when a speck of dust enters the eye. What really happened when the sole of the foot was tickled was that the stimulus sent an impulse along the sensory nerve-fibres to the cord. The stimulus then passed by means of their interlocking branches from the sensory to the motor-cells of the cord, so that it was transmitted back to the muscles of the foot. As a result of this, certain muscles contracted and caused the foot to be with-drawn. A stimulus that started to the cord as a sensation re-turned therefore to the foot as a command to withdraw. That the whole action was mechanical is shown by the fact that it could equally well have been provoked had the subject been asleep. It would, of course, have been possible for him to have contracted the same muscles by an act of will. In this case the action would have been a voluntary one in which the brain had played a part. This, indeed, is the history of many actions that are automatic, such as walking, which must be learnt before it becomes automatic. In other words, a young child, by deliberate effort and directed attention, must learn to move his legs, and then, often quite suddenly, the spinal cord takes over the work from the brain, and he has learnt to walk. If it were not for this power to delegate to the spinal cord what it had mastered, the brain would be so fully occupied with other functions that it would have no time left over for the work for which it alone is fitted.

As will be seen later, there is a school of psychology that puts so much emphasis on automatic action that it seeks to interpret the whole of life as a series of reflexes. According to the views of the Behaviourist school, not only movements, but feeling and thought are nothing but a succession of reflexes occurring in the network of fibres that make up the substance of the brain. This subject will be dealt with later, but in the meantime it may be pointed out that this view of the Behaviourist school of psychology, extreme though it be, is not without some justification from the point of view of brain structure. Indeed, it may be conceded that the physiology as well as the anatomy of the brain, so far as they go, support the Behaviourists' thesis. The brain's activity, like that of the cord, depends to a very large extent on the stream of impulses that reach it from the outside world. If the brain could be entirely deprived of the stimuli that reach it along the various sensory paths of the body, it is doubtful whether it would continue to work, for its function seems to be that of responding to, rather than of initiating activity. Michael Foster records the case of a boy who suffered from cutaneous anaesthesia, who was blind in one eye and deaf. His sole tie with the outside world, apart from the weak links of taste and smell, was through his remaining eye. When this was covered, he immediately went to sleep. The stream of impulses that reach the brain along the sensory track of the central nervous system may therefore be looked upon as a sort of driving belt to the brain. Speed up the impressions reaching it, and the brain becomes more active, slow them down and it becomes more sluggish, remove the belt altogether, and consciousness disappears. But this statement must be qualified. An uninterrupted flow of stimuli from the outside world is not an essential to thought. The memory of past stimulation may act as an incentive to mental activity, as well as external impressions received at that actual moment. A man sitting in a dark and silent room may still remain mentally active, the flow of vivid memories stored in the records office of his brain taking the place of fresh visual and auditory impressions.

In a non-technical work it would obviously be impossible to give more than an elementary description of the great coordinating and regulating centre of the central nervous system, the brain. All that can be attempted is to give sufficient information concerning its structure to allow of later discussions being understood. As an introduction to the subject, it will be useful to look at the early stages of the brain's development. At a very primitive stage in the embryo's life, the head end of the streak that later is to form the brain and spinal cord swells out into three so-called primary vesicles. These three swellings are the forerunners of the fore-, middle-, and hind-brain respectively. Like the spinal cord, of which they are really an expansion, these three swellings surround a central canal, which later becomes the brain's cavities or ventricles. All the complex structures of the brain are eventually formed by the thickening of the walls surrounding these central cavities.

From the thickened walls of the lowermost swelling are developed the hind-brain, that is, the medulla oblongata (mainly concerned with such bodily functions as the regulation of the blood-vessels and of the body's temperature), and the cerebellum (controlling complicated movements such as maintaining balance in walking). From the thickened walls of the middle swelling are formed the mid-brain, in which run the great bundles of nerve-fibres connecting the fore-brain with the rest of the body, as well as with the cerebellum. From the foremost swelling is developed the fore-brain or that part of the brain in which we are more especially interested. This, in turn, may be subdivided into two parts, one of which is chiefly concerned with the life of thought, and the other with the life of feeling. Thought is one of the functions of the two cerebral hemispheres, which start as two separate outgrowing buds from the fore-brain. These outgrowths finally become so large in the case of man, that they overwhelm, and bury beneath them, the whole of the fore-brain from which they have arisen. It is indeed this enormous development of the two cerebral hemispheres that distinguishes the human brain from that of members of the animal world. Only amongst the apes can there be found anything that is comparable to that which has occurred in man.

The degree of development of the cerebral outgrowths may indeed be regarded as a measure of an animal's intelligence, for as we progress in our survey from such lowly creatures as birds and reptiles, whose cerebral development is insignificant, to the lower mammals, and thence to the apes and man, we find that with each stage there is an increase in the bulk and complexity of the cerebral hemispheres. To be more precise, it is the surface of these structures that is of importance from the point of view of intelligence, for it is here that we find the coating of grey matter which may be regarded as the physical basis of thought. And because there must be a limit to the surface area of the brain that a man is able to carry, Nature has overcome the difficulty by throwing this surface into a number of folds, or convolutions, thereby increasing the amount of grey matter available. By this means the thinking area of the brain is doubled without any addition having been made to its size. As a result, men of great intellect are not necessarily men with big heads, but if their brains are examined, they are generally found to be more deeply furrowed than are the brains of their less highly endowed fellows.

Even if the fore-brain had not given origin to the thinking apparatus of man, it would still be of importance, because in it are situated the great nuclei that are the centre of the emotional life. If we cut horizontally across the central cavity, known as the third ventricle, we find lying in the mass of white substance, two grey ovoid masses, nearly two inches long, known as the thalami. These constitute the largest collections of grey matter in the brain, and, as greyness indicates richness in nerve-cells, the two most important masses of nerve-cells. In addition to the thalami, other great nuclei are found in the fore-brain, nuclei that are associated with the life of movement and sensation. But it is the thalamus that interests us most, for it is this structure that is concerned with the origin and expression of the emotions. By means of the nerve-fibres travelling from this nucleus to the central cortex, emotional tone is imparted to thoughts that would otherwise be colourless. It will be remembered also that in dealing with the pituitary and the sympathetic system generally, attention was called to the close connexion that existed between these structures and the thalamus, so that in this area of the fore-brain we have the meeting-ground of affective stimuli and the chemistry of the pituitary. The thalamus in the lower animals is considerably larger in relation to the cerebral hemispheres than it is in man, since the higher brain in man has taken on many of its functions. Another difference between the brains of animals and men is that in men many more fibres travel from the thalamus to the cortex of the cerebral hemispheres, so that man is more conscious of affective stimuli than are the lower animals.

For a description of the finer structure of the brain it would be impossible to improve on the picture drawn of it by Sir Walter Langdon Brown in his book, *Thus We Are Men*. In this description the fore-, mid-, and hind-brain are regarded as piled one on top of the other, so that the cerebral hemisphere becomes the top floor, the fore and middle the first floor, and the hind-brain the ground floor. Sir Walter Langdon Brown likens the brain

to an office consisting of several storeys. The lowest part is concerned with vital functions; above this is the cerebellum, which is chiefly concerned with maintaining the balance of the body and regulating muscular movements. The storey above this is concerned with the expression of the emotions. The floor above is the sorting department where all the messages received from below are dealt with and sent on to the appropriate departments above, where the directors sit, each in his allotted room. These are on the surface, or cortex, of the brain. Starting from behind and working forwards (that is to say, travelling over the surface of the cerebral hemispheres from back to front), we find first the departments concerned with vision, in the front portion of which visual memories are carefully and systematically stored for ready reference, like a card index. In front, and slightly below this, is the central hearing department, with similar stores of memories of sounds, including spoken words. Coming further forward, neatly arranged on one side of a deep fold in the surface, are the rows of offices for receiving the ordinary sensations sorted out from all parts of the body, and facing them on the other side, a corresponding row whence messages ordering or checking movements are sent out. At one end of this row is a special office, on the left side only, for speech, but this cannot work without drawing on the word memories stored up behind. And then, in front of all in a spacious office sits the Head of the Firm – the thinking You, with all this complicated and elaborate machinery at your command, as you imagine, although you are really entirely dependent on it.

This picture of the brain as a vast and complicated building, full of offices given over to different businesses and each fitted with its own telephone for the reception and dispatch of messages, and with its own card-index system for the storing of its memories, is an excellent one. The only point at which the analogy drawn between a successful business concern and the brain becomes doubtful, is when we tap at the door of the head of the firm whom we presume to be sitting in his spacious office, in the front part of the cerebral hemisphere. Will we actually find the director of all these manifold activities there? Does he indeed exist at all, this integrated 'You', that exercises full control over all the complicated machinery of the body and mind? Sir Walter himself appears to harbour some doubts about this, for he is careful to point out that the 'You' that imagines it has all this complicated and elaborate machinery at its command, may find in the end the situation is quite different. Perhaps the machinery controls this 'You', and the 'You' does not control the machinery. Here is a mighty question. Who is the 'You' that directs this machinery? Does he indeed exist at all? It is to this enigma that we shall attempt to find some sort of answer in the later chapters of this book. In the meantime we are only studying the machine, not the person, if such person exists, who controls the machine. The time for searching for the 'self' has not yet arrived.

The story of the discovery of the functions of the different areas of the cerebral cortex is one of the most interesting in physiology. Three methods are available for the mapping out of the brain in terms of function : the first, the careful investigation of structure; the second, animal experiments; and the third, the noting of the disabilities that result from damage or disease of different areas of the cerebral hemispheres. Of these, the last two are by far the most instructive. In the case of animal experiments, two courses may be adopted. The first is to damage a certain area of the brain and then to note what activity has been destroyed ; the second is to stimulate various parts of the surface of the brain electrically, and to observe the results. What has been done deliberately to an animal may happen as the result of a disease or accident to a man. The brain, like other organs of the body, may become the site of a growth. When this happens, the symptoms produced by the pressure of the growth on the brain are carefully catalogued, and subsequently, either during an operation, or after the death of the patient, the exact situation of the growth is noted. By such means, and after many years of patient research, the centres controlling many of our activities have been mapped out ; such as the centre for voluntary movements of various parts of the body, the areas of the brain recording sensations, the region of the brain concerned with sight, smell, and hearing, the control centres for speech and writing, and of many other functions in addition.

While these investigations were being made, one important area of the brain remained without a label, the foremost part of the cerebral hemispheres. Neither animal experiment nor observation of human beings gave any clue to its activity. Why did this region refuse to give up its secret? Certainly it must have some function, but all the available methods of investigation had failed to reveal it long after other activities of the brain had been located. Help in revealing the role of this frontal area was derived from an interesting case, recorded as far back as 1848. The patient was a workman named Phineas P. Gage, who was seriously injured by a crowbar. This penetrated his left orbit and completely destroyed the left frontal lobe of his brain.

The patient survived his injury for many years, and presented no disability other than a change in character and mentality. His judgement and reason had obviously been impaired by the accident and his temperament altered. After the accident his temper became fitful, so that he gave way to unprovoked outbursts of rage. So erratic did his moods become that he gave up a job as soon as he had started upon it, and finally, unable to settle anywhere, he spent his time wandering from place to place. Previously of good character, he was now obviously a dishonest man and a liar. Formerly careful in his speech, he now indulged in gross profanities. In a word, from being a decent, honest, steady, and efficient workman, he had been converted into a thoroughly disreputable character. He died in 1860, twelve and half years after his accident.

Since this case was recorded, several other reports of patients suffering from disease confined to this area have been carefully studied. All of them have strengthened the conviction that the foremost part of the cerebral hemisphere is concerned with those psychic activities that may be said to distinguish a man from an animal. One observer has formulated this difference in one way, and another in another. We can accept Penfield's summary that the frontal lobes are concerned with 'apperception, memory, spatial orientation, the ability to carry on abstractions, such as mental arithmetic, the manifestation of initiative, and the preservation of mental alertness with the capacity for planned administration'.

An examination of the minute structure of this part of the brain explains the ability of a patient to correlate thought and emotion. Thought must be activated by feeling before any bodily reaction occurs, for a thought uncoloured by emotion provokes no response. In order that this blending may take place, impulses from the cognitive sense areas of the brain are connected up with the frontal lobes by special fibres. To the same region run fibres from the thalamus, the structure that we have learnt to regard as the centre of the emotions. It is therefore in the frontal lobes that these two streams of consciousness, the cognitive and the emotional, blend and reach adjustment. In this area thoughts become coloured with feelings, and feeling in turn provokes action. A number of synthetic processes of this kind determine behaviour. Reason, judgement, imagination, fears, hopes, and many other emotions all contribute their quota and from this conglomeration of impulses a pattern of action eventually emerges.

If the endocrine glands help to colour man's behaviour, it is in the fore-brain that the colours are utilized and the pattern is finally formed and fixed. Here all the different forces meet, and from here emerges the resultant behaviour pattern, a pattern determined not because some supreme director has planned it, but because an equilibrium in forces has been reached. The means by which this is achieved is vastly complicated. To blend the cognitive forces of vision, hearing, body, sensibility, and smell with the primitive emotions of hunger and anger, and of sexual and parental feeling, would not be a very difficult business, and it can take place quite satisfactorily in the small frontal lobes of an animal. When, however, these cognitive and emotional elements have become a hundred times more complex, when thoughts have been expanded to the nth power, and when from the primitive emotions have been derived such abstruse sentiments as scorn, wonder, admiration, and a number of equally fine feelings, the blending becomes an infinitely more complicated matter. Small wonder, therefore, that the well-developed fore-brain and the imposing brow are the distinguishing marks of a man.

Having examined the gross structure of the brain we can now turn our attention to the elements of which the brain is composed, the nerve-cells. The cell population of the brain is enormous, and according to Judson Herrick, the number of cells living in the cerebral cortex of a man is somewhere in the neighbourhood of ten thousand million. This profusion of nerve-cells is the reason for the greater size of the higher types of brain, but even in the brain of a dog the cerebral hemispheres contain a greater number of cells than the whole of the rest of its central nervous system. In man the preponderance of nerve-cells situated in the brain is even greater and that is believed by physiologists to account for the pre-eminence of the human mind. Others would formulate this differently and would say that it is the pre-eminence of the human mind which accounts for the largeness of the human fore-brain.

We have seen that the cell is characterized by its purposive activity, and that purpose may be taken as being synonymous with mind. Has the brain-cell more mind than a cell in a lowlier position, for example a leucocyte in the blood-stream? No answer can be given to this question for our only means of judging purpose in a cell is to watch its movements, and a brain-cell has no movements that can be observed. The brain-cell would appear to have given up its personal freedom for the sake of its higher calling and is securely anchored by all its branches. At one time it was supposed that one brain-cell had the power of disconnecting itself from another by withdrawing its tendrils. This withdrawal was regarded as being the means of producing a temporary block in the path of a nerve current, and was supposed to take place automatically in sleep. But the withdrawal of the branches of brain-cells has never been observed and this theory has been abandoned.

Except for this immobility, which the brain-cell shares with many others in the body, there is no special characteristic that distinguishes it from its fellows. It is markedly granular in appearance, but then so are many other cells in the body. One feature of the brain-cell is that it is specially sensitive to changes in its environment. Loss of consciousness may follow a slight reduction in the pressure of its oxygen supply. Shortage of oxygen has long been known to impair mental activity. Professor Barcroft reports that in the high Andes he had a marked disaptitude for arithmetic. Sugar is also an urgent requirement of the brain, since, unlike many other organs, it has no facilities for storing it. Sugar is indeed a vital food to the brain-cell and prolonged shortage first impairs mental activity and then produces unconsciousness. Many narcotics act by diminishing the power of the brain to oxydize sugar, thus causing sleep.

The insistent demands made by the brain-cells for oxygen and sugar are a sign of the high pressure at which they live. The activity of the chemical changes in a cell may be regarded as a measure of their intensity of living. Judged by this standard the brain-cell is far more alive than a cell forming a part of connective tissue.

It is, however, by electrical means that the activity of brain-cells can best be measured. A nerve impulse, in other words the process by means of which nerve-cells communicate with each other, is in its essence an electrical phenomenon. By suitable means nerve impulses of less than a thousandth of a thousandth of a volt can be recorded as they pass over any spot in the central nervous system. But in addition to conducting an impulse, the brain-cell initiates it. It is also continually engaged in maintaining the efficiency and repair of the axis-cylinder along which the impulse travels, so that it is not only the operator in the telephone exchange, but also the engineer who maintains the efficiency of the wires. When therefore the brain-cell is said to be at rest, in the sense that nerve impulses are not being initiated, or are not travelling along it, the expression 'at rest' is only relative. At rest or not, the brain-cell is continually on duty. It is no wonder that it requires so much nourishment.

The electrical disturbances passing over the surface of the brain can be recorded and two kinds of changes in potential are made manifest, a fall followed by a rise. Since in this situation the neural processes can only be of two kinds, activation and arrest of activation, these changes of opposed electrical signs fit into the physiological picture. We are also able to pick up rhythmical electrical waves from the brain of a human being by placing two pad electrodes over the skull. The chief seat of this rhythm is the occipital or visual area of the brain, and it is found that the electrical waves coming from this area can be altered by mental activity. If a light be flashed in the eye of the subject of the experiment, a whole series of waves is picked up by the recording instrument from the visual area of the brain.

Although brain-cells are extremely sensitive to stimuli, they are not sensitive to all stimuli. The writer of this book had his forefinger two inches deep in a fellow-creature's brain without his patient being aware of the liberty he had taken. Yet the patient was fully conscious of everything else that was happening. Aristotle was probably aware of the fact that the exposed human brain is insensitive to touch when he made the heart rather than the brain the organ of the mind. But because the brain does not respond to touch, it does not mean that it is insensitive to appropriate stimuli. A wireless set answers to its switch but it is not likely to respond to a blow.

There is nothing, therefore, that is essentially distinctive in the brain-cell. It is even possible that a cell from elsewhere in the body might be trained for such a high destiny. In an embryo frog, the cells that are eventually to form the brain can be replaced by those from the skin of the back. So far as we can judge from the adult frog's behaviour, the cells that have been diverted from their natural destiny fulfil their new function faithfully. It should also be noted that many of the cells in the spinal cord that transmit the involuntary impulses of locomotion are indistinguishable from their more highly placed fellows in the grey matter of the brain cortex.

Physiology has therefore advanced so far as to be able, by means of its electrical instruments, to watch the brain at work and to take the brain to pieces and examine it under the microscope. We have been admitted into the telephone exchange and allowed to examine its switches. But this examination has not given us the answer for which we have been searching. What we really want to meet is the subscriber who makes use of the telephone. It is the mind and not the brain that we are after, and here our collaborators, the physiologist, the chemist, and the electrical experts, fail us. They are like the engineering staff of the post office that is only concerned with the switches, wires, and other paraphernalia of the telephone system. They have nothing to do with the subscribers; for that we must go to another department.

Thoughts, feelings, aspirations, despairs, and all the varied manifestations of the psyche, lie outside the realm of natural science. Whilst science is prepared to study, and at one time was even prepared to explain away, life on physico-chemical principles, she refuses to advance into the realm of the soul. Thus far and no farther, is her reply when we press her to go forward.

Mind presents itself as thoughts and feelings [said Sir Charles Sherrington in his Gifford lectures], and they are the outcome of the brain. The brain is matter and energy. Matter and energy can only be matter and energy. Therefore thoughts, feelings, and so on are matter and energy. Therefore the mind is matter and energy? ... The reply by the followers of Natural Science today, as I surmise it, would be: Thoughts, feelings and so on are not amenable to the energy (matter) concept. They lie outside it. Therefore they lie outside Natural Science. If, as you say, thoughts are an outcome of the brain, we, as students, using the energy-concept, know nothing of it; and as followers of Natural Science, we know nothing of any relation between thoughts and the brain, except as a gross correlation in time and space.

With this answer from the lips of a leader in the world of science we must for the time being rest content.

CHAPTER 6

MEDICAL PSYCHOLOGY

THE last three chapters have been devoted to the study of the physical basis of thought and feeling. Physiology has left us in doubt as to whether there exists in the fore-part of the brain a general manager or as to whether our life consists only of a series of predetermined actions set in motion by the impact of sensory impressions on the central nervous system. Such a result was inevitable. The engineer who sets out to investigate the body will interpret it in terms of mechanism as certainly as the chemist will interpret it in terms of chemistry, and in this preliminary examination of the physical basis of behaviour and personality we have taken the body to pieces and viewed the pieces with the eye of an engineer.

There is another reason why scientists show a natural tendency to interpret human behaviour in terms of mechanism. This is because physics has advanced so rapidly that it has come to be regarded as the standard and basic science. We tend, therefore, to assess degrees of 'reality' in our thinking, according to its conformity or not with the laws derived from our study of physics. 'Make me a model of it, and then I will be prepared to accept it' is not only the demand of the Kelvins of this world but also of ordinary men and women. But, in using the laws of physics as a measuring rod of 'reality', we are attempting the impossible task of explaining the higher in terms of the lower, the animate in terms of the inanimate. This dilemma in which we find ourselves would have been avoided had biology, rather than physics, been accepted as the basic science, and the laws that we had derived from the study of the living been taken as the criteria by means of which we gauge the 'reality' of our thinking.

But it is natural that the study of physics should have gained this pre-eminent position in the intellectual life of man. Man has established his ascendancy in the world through his success as a maker of tools. From the earliest ages he has been preoccupied with the nature of the material world outside him, and for an entirely practical reason. He has chiefly been concerned how best he could convert to his use the various substances and natural forces that lay around him. In the process of answering this question he has stumbled upon the laws of physics and chemistry, and having tested their validity by the practical results that he derived from them, he has accepted them as proven and real. It is not surprising therefore that during the nineteenth century, when science was piling up its conquests over the material world, physics should have established itself as the basic science, and that the laws which the physicist enunciated should have appeared to have a special validity.

Medicine is a handmaiden of science, and as this book is written by a medical man it approaches its subject from a scientific angle. Nineteenth-century medicine was entirely materialistic and viewed disease in terms only of broken mechanisms. The doctor looked upon his patient as a collection of organs, one of which had gone wrong. The idea that disease might be psychic in origin and that, in addition to possessing organs, a patient also possessed a soul, had not yet found any place in medical thinking, and even those practitioners who recognized the existence of such troubles as hysteria sought an explanation for them in terms of diseased organs. A woman was hysterical not on account of some mental conflict but because her womb was misplaced !

Fortunately the modern doctor is becoming far less mechanistic in his interpretation of disease than were his predecessors. A new and fuller meaning has been given to the old dictum 'Mens sana in corpore sano'. Not only is a healthy body necessary for the possession of a sane mind, but a sane mind for the possession of a healthy body. The 'psyche' of his patient can no longer be neglected by the physician. However materialistic he himself may happen to be in his outlook on life he is driven to take a broader view of his patient's condition, and to consider his psychological as well as his physical state. The old distinction between the hysterical and the real in disease has broken down and the physician, willy-nilly, is being forced into a new role, that of being his patient's father confessor, as well as the prescriber of physical remedies. Hence the increasing importance of psychology in the medical curriculum, and the necessity for the doctor himself to find some philosophy of living that may furnish a basis for the advice that he gives to his patient.

It is to Freud that the medical profession is chiefly indebted for pointing out the importance of the mind and for the establishment of psycho-therapy as a branch of medical treatment. Born in 1856 of poor Moravian Jewish parents, he qualified at the Medical School of Vienna. Before starting practice he spent a year in Paris, where he met Charcot and his, by then, still more renowned pupil, Janet. Freud was deeply impressed by their methods of treating nervous disorders by means of hypnotism, and on returning to Vienna he made up his mind to devote his life to the study of nervous diseases. At this juncture he fell in with Breuer, another nerve specialist, who described to him the interesting case of a woman who suffered from paralytic symptoms and a speech difficulty of a functional nature. When encouraged to talk about her trouble under hypnosis she traced it back to a time of emotional stress with her father, to whom she had been deeply devoted. What was of particular interest was that after having recalled to memory the origin of her trouble her symptoms had disappeared. Freud and Breuer, profiting by this experience, decided to treat patients by means of questioning under hypnosis.

But Freud did not long remain satisfied with the method that he and Breuer had devised, the cures often proving only temporary. He therefore began experimenting with a new method of reaching the 'unconscious' of his patients. By getting them to lie relaxed on a couch he encouraged a dreamy state in which they gave free utterance to every passing thought. Each idea was allowed to call up of itself the next associated idea until slowly the patient had retraced his past life back to the beginning of his trouble. By recalling to consciousness the circumstances, and the conflicts associated with the origin of his difficulties, a complete cure of the patient's symptoms was often effected.

From these beginnings was evolved the technique of the analysis that forms so important a part of modern psychotherapy, the technique of free association. The patient is told to let his thoughts and feelings go as they will, without attempting to direct them and without selecting or repressing them. When consciousness abandons the helm, the unconscious takes it over, and the thoughts and feelings that present themselves are those connected with its own special preoccupations, sometimes partly known to the person undergoing analysis, and sometimes completely unknown, or in any case, not recognized as being the real motive behind his apparently random ideas. Nor is the task of getting at these submerged stresses so hopeless as it might seem, for the repressed impulses are on the analyst's side and are continually trying to push through into consciousness. At last, the patient makes contact with this vital part of his unconscious, and what he is trying to hide, or to express, by his illness emerges. The explanation of his illness destroys its utility, and sometimes removes it. But this is not always the case because an intellectual recognition is not necessarily synonymous with a full emotional realization. Such in broad outline is the technique of psycho-analysis.

As the result of his empirical work on patients, Freud eventually arrived at several generalizations. The chief of these concerned the unconscious mind, repression, and transference. Freud asserted that in our ordinary waking life, ideas and impulses originate in the unconscious where they are experienced as emotions and not formulated in words. Many of these unconscious ideas are repressed, that is to say, prevented from becoming conscious. In order to explain the repression he postulated the existence of a restraining force, which he termed the 'endopsychic censor'. This censor only allowed to pass over the threshold of the pre-conscious into the daylight of consciousness those ideas of which it approved, driving back into the dark anything that was in conflict with the patient's view of what was desirable or fitting. These ideas when repressed into the unconscious carried with them their own quota of energy or life force, and this, having no natural outlet, expressed itself in the form of neurotic or hysterical symptoms.

Freud soon came to the conclusion that the energy, or life force, that he had postulated was sexual in origin, and gave to it the name 'libido'. Later on, and possibly influenced by the storm of protest that his views aroused, he widened his definition so as to include within it all enthusiasm and likings, as well as sexuality. But to his way of thinking the sexual impulse still remained the most potent of all the basic energies of which the libido was composed.

Freud's investigations led him to believe that a patient's failure to remember some past incident in his life, and the difficulty that he often encountered in narrating events associated with it, were due to the action of this defence mechanism. Such thoughts were too painful to the patient and were therefore ejected from his consciousness. Only when this mechanism was overcome and the painful incident revived and reviewed in the light of later experience could the stresses and strains in the unconscious be removed.

The analytical idea of transference has frequently been misunderstood and has often been regarded as synonymous with the patient's falling in love with the analyst. Actually, as often as not, transference is expressed in terms of anger, hatred, or resentment, the patient transferring to his doctor some of the old forgotten emotional feelings he entertained for the parents, nurse, brothers, and sisters that surrounded him in his youth. Transference may be described as being the power of attaching to the analyst the unsatisfied emotion left over from some previous, and perhaps very early, experience.

It must be remembered that Freud was essentially an empiricist. He was working on sick human beings and his first concern was to cure them. Analysis was a form of treatment, and his theories were working hypotheses that he and his followers found to be useful. But as time went on, what was merely a method of treatment grew into something like a system of psychology. The old enigma concerning the nature of the 'self' obtruded itself, and Freud felt constrained to furnish an answer to it. He elaborated therefore the cumbersome doctrine of the Ego, Super-ego, and the Id. It will be unnecessary to give a full description of what he meant by these terms, for it is not by any of these theories that Freud will be remembered. It is for having stressed the importance of conflicts in producing neurotic symptoms and for having initiated a method of relieving them that he will be regarded as a pioneer in medical psychology. Freud himself defined the Ego as 'a coherent organization of mental processes' and the Id as an unknown and unconscious basis on whose surface the Ego rests. The Super-ego was a kind of moral standard to which the patient subscribed. According to Freud the problem before the 'Ego' was to win freedom from both the 'Id' and the 'Super-ego'. This could be done by the Ego (the reasonable, conscious, and discriminating self) extending further and further into the unconscious fields of the Id and the Super-ego. But Freud himself recognized the weakness of this part of his work for he referred to it as follows:

these ideas are not the basis of the science upon which everything rests; that, on the contrary, is observation alone. They [the Id and the Super-ego] are not the foundation stone, but the coping of the whole structure and they can be replaced and discarded without damaging it.

Amongst Freud's earliest pupils was Alfred Adler, like him a Jew, but unlike him a keen socialist, a man who saw man always as a member of a community. Adler was a student of Nietzsche and Schopenhauer and he held that it was not sexuality but the 'will to power' that was the main driving force in man. It was not surprising therefore that as Freud continued to give exclusive importance to sexuality, and Adler to the desire for power, a widening rift should have opened up between master and pupil.

Adler maintained that every human being suffers from some sense of inferiority, and that in order to overcome this he consciously, or unconsciously, devises some scheme of action, which Adler termed his 'style of life'. Any inferiority, or faulty bodily development, acts as a spur to persistent effort to overcome this defect and its consequence, and to emulate those whom the child regards as superiors, or all-powerful. When the attainment of this goal is frustrated by the actualities of life, or because the goal is impossible, a neurosis is produced, the disabilities of which are made use of as a means 'for continuing the struggle for power'. The man or woman who has become ill, in this way finds a justification for withdrawal from life, and may even use the illness itself as an instrument for domination and aggression in the household. Hence the tyranny that is often exerted over a home by a querulous invalid.

The aim of analysis, according to Adler, was to discover the patient's particular 'style of living', and having found it to induce him to establish another that was of greater service to the community. After working with Freud for several years Adler found that the differences of opinion between them were too great. He therefore left his master and founded a new school of his own which he called the School of Individual Psychology.

Adler's place at Vienna was filled by a young Swiss doctor from Zürich, Carl Jung, a different type of man to both Freud and Adler. Primarily Jung was a teacher, and a teacher with a strong religious bias, not so much in the direction of orthodox Christianity as of Eastern religious writings. He felt that it was not enough to liberate a patient from the compulsions from which he was suffering and then leave him; it was also necessary to give him some help for his future guidance. In this he came into conflict with Freud, who considered that advice to a patient was an unwarrantable interference with his freedom. Moreover, Jung had as little liking for Freud's preoccupation with sexuality as had Adler, and regarded the 'libido' merely as a term for general vital energy. He even took a different view of the unconscious by asserting that it was a repository for racial memories, such as the memory that made a duckling take to the water as soon as it was hatched. According to Jung this racial memory played an important part in man's unconscious and was frequently reproduced in his dreams and fantasies in the guise of symbols.

Nor did Jung lay stress like Freud on the necessity of looking always for the cause of a neurosis in the past. He sought rather to find it in the present. The question he asked was: 'What is the essential task in the patient's life that he will not fulfil, and from which he recoils?' His treatment was directed towards enabling the patient to recover the submerged function of feeling and thought in order that some natural adaption could be made. In the words of Dr Karin Stephen in *Psycho-Analysis and Medicine:*

> Freud's outlook may be compared to that of Adam before the Fall – the pursuit of pleasure in a paradise of desire, marred only by the interdict placed upon the fruit of the forbidden tree. Jung's outlook is that of Adam after the expulsion from the garden, confronted with the task of adaptation, if he would live.

For all of these pioneers of psycho-therapy the activities of life were linked up with purpose ; for Freud, with an attainment of pleasure and the avoidance of pain ; for Adler, with the acquisition of power and superiority over one's fellows ; and for Jung, with adaptation to life. It was not surprising that they parted company on the subject of the chief motive power behind action. What could be more natural than that the young Adler, filled with ideas of an ideal socialist state and finding himself an obscure Jew in the aristocratic capital of the Austrian monarchy, should reach the conclusions that are the basis of Adlerian psychology? It was equally natural that Jung, well-read in sacred Eastern literature, should react against the materialistic views of his master. Each brought to Vienna his own personal luggage and each left it with that luggage intact but wrapped in the analytical language of Freud.

Side by side with these new medical schools of psychology there arose another which had its origin in the physiology departments of medicine, rather than in its consulting rooms. This was known as the Behaviourist school led by Dr J. B. Watson. Its protagonists were frankly sceptical of the speculations of the clinicians, and disliked their terminology even more than their methods. They felt that it would be more scientific if the psychologist were to make his observations in a laboratory, and under conditions that could be defined and repeated, or varied, at will. This new school of experimental psychology approached the problem of human nature from the standpoint of the physiologist. Its exponents assumed that the psychic life was entirely dependent on the central nervous system, all mental events being but an emanation from chemico-physical processes in the brain. Since in their opinion mental life only existed as a function of the brain and had no casual efficacy, the fittest place for its investigation was in the laboratory of the physiologist.

Pledged to be strictly scientific (the model science being physics) the members of this school set two principal aims before them : the first to find mental units comparable to the atoms of the physicists, and the second to explain life in terms of mechanics. A most serviceable unit was available in the form of the reflex action. It was not surprising therefore that this was selected as a starting point. Physiologists had fully established the importance of reflex action in the working of the body, and since nervous tissue everywhere consisted of a tangled network of protoplasmic filaments it was safe to assume that the structure underlying a reflex movement was a path of low resistance through this tangle. When the sole of the foot is tickled the excitation process spreads along the path of lowest resistance until it reaches the leg muscles and brings them into action.

What made the reflex arc a still more profitable unit for a really scientific system of psychology was the fact that Pavlov, the great Russian physiologist, had shown that new reflexes could be created or conditioned. Pavlov utilized for his investigations the reflex regulating the flow of saliva into a dog's mouth. The natural stimulus to this flow is the taking of food. Later on, because the sight of food had always been followed by the taking of it into the mouth, the mere sight of it was found to be sufficient. The secretion of saliva produced by the stimulus of sight was called a conditioned reflex, and that caused by its actual presence in the mouth a natural one. Pavlov found that he could condition a new reflex secretion by the repetition of some artificial stimulus such as the ticking of a metronome at a certain rate. If the food were presented to the dog immediately after the beating of the metronome, in time the sound of the metronome alone was sufficient to start the secretion of saliva. Pavlov's next step was to show that a negative as well as a positive reflex could be created. In his first experiment he had set the metronome beating at the rate of 100 per minute immediately before the meal was presented and also while the dog was

eating it, and after a series of such experiments (usually about
125) the positive reflex had been established. He now arranged
that the metronome should beat at the rate of 50 per minute
and that the meal should be taken away. This new experiment
was repeated a large number of times. At first the dog did not
appear to distinguish between the metronome beating at 50
and at 100 per minute, but gradually with the repeated withdrawal of food at the lower rate, the secretion of saliva began
to fall when it was set at 50. In the end two conditioned reflexes
were established, a positive produced by the metronome set at
100 beats, and a negative produced by the metronome set at 50.
Finally Pavlov set the metronome between the two speeds at 75
per minute. This produced confusion, the nervous system of the
dog partly exciting and partly suppressing the secretion of
saliva. The dog was kept oscillating between the two tendencies,
went off his food and sleep, and finally became neurasthenic.
He is said to have been relieved by taking bromide.

Another experiment of the Russian physiologist suggested
that acquired reflexes could be transmitted from one generation
to another. By ringing a bell shortly before mice were fed, the
mice could be conditioned to secrete gastric juice at the sound
of the bell. This new reflex was only obtained after the experiment had been repeated a great number of times. The mice
were then allowed to breed and the new generation treated in
the same way. They learnt to respond to the bell much sooner
than had their parents. The experiment was repeated on the
next generation with a still greater shortening of the period
before the bell reflex was established.

Pavlov did not confine his experiment to animals but repeated them with suitable modifications on children. A young
child was laid on its back with a rubber bulb under his chin so
arranged that every time he opened his mouth the movement
was communicated to a manometer. By a suitable contrivance
chocolates could be liberated so that they fell into the child's
mouth. Pavlov found that the child could be taught to open his
mouth to a neutral stimulus provided that the stimulus had
previously been associated with the dropping of a chocolate.
What was felt to be of greater importance was the fact that

the child could be conditioned far more rapidly than an animal.

With this work as a background, the new 'scientific' school of behaviour psychologists carried out their own strictly controlled experiments. As an example may be quoted Dr J. B. Watson's fear-conditioning experiments on an eleven months baby known as Albert B. Watson found that fear response to white rats could be produced in Albert by means of loud noises. Previously he had enjoyed playing with them and had never shown any nervousness. There was no doubt, however, about his natural fear response when a heavy steel bar was struck in his immediate neighbourhood. In Dr Watson's words, on the first occasion,

there was an intake of the breath and an upward fling of the arms. On the second stimulation the lips began to pucker and tremble, on the third he broke into a crying fit, turned to one side and began to crawl away as rapidly as possible with head averted.

The stage having been set for a scientific experiment, the friendly white rat was introduced in the usual manner into Albert's room, and just as he was reaching out to touch it 'the bar was struck immediately behind his head. The infant jumped violently and fell forward, burying his face in the mattress. He did not cry, however'.

After Albert had recovered, the experiment was repeated. This time the infant 'began to whimper. In order not to disturb him too seriously no further tests were made for one week'. To cut a long story short, by means of a steel bar, a new fear reflex to white rats was soon established in Albert. To quote Dr Watson again : 'The instant the rat was shown the baby began to cry. Almost instantly he turned sharply to the left, fell over, raised himself on all fours and began to crawl away so rapidly that he was caught with difficulty before he reached the edge of the table'.

Not only was Albert now terrified of white rats but of rabbits, dogs, and anything of a furry nature, of a sealskin coat, cotton-wool, and even of Dr Watson's head. The conditioned fear for the rats was therefore transferred to many other objects.

With the reflex as its fundamental unit, the Behaviourists

have built up a school of psychology in which everything is explained by such means. Reflexes of a lower order are conceived to have been shaped mainly by heredity, and those of a higher order by environment. An instinct, according to this view, is a 'hereditary pattern reaction, the separate elements of which are movements principally of unstriped muscle'. This conception of instinct was formerly held by William James, who wrote:

The actions we call instinctive all conform to the general reflex type; they are called forth by determinate sensory stimuli in contact with the animate body or at a distance in his environment.

Not only are the more obviously automatic reactions explainable by such means, but also all forms of psychic activity. According to the Behaviourists all mental growth and all education is accompanied by the linking together of more and more reflex arcs, and by a greater and greater elaboration of an already vastly complicated network of neurones.

Although it is true that the linking together of numerous reflex arcs would furnish a reasonable physical basis for some types of thinking, it is impossible to regard it as an explanation of all forms of psychic activity. In the thinking known as 'associative', one idea or even one word automatically calls up another, and it can easily be assumed that the sequence of these ideas is determined by the links existing between contiguous reflex arcs in the brain, the excitation travelling from one to another. But associative thought is not the only psychic activity of which man is capable. Thought may be on different levels; it may be purely automatic, as in the initial excitation stage of an anaesthetic, it may be associative and determined only by similarity of words or phrases, or it may demand all the attention and the concentration of which a man is capable. All of these types of thinking are within a man's power. But even although most of his mental activity is of a kind that can easily be accepted as automatic and therefore explicable along behaviourist lines, all cannot be so explained. Occasionally, in the creative work of the artist, in the greatest efforts of the mathematicians, philosophers, and scientists, and in the flashes of direct perception of the mystic and the saint, we have clear instances of psychic activity on a higher level that are beyond the capacity of the Behaviourist to explain.

The idea of different levels of thought is far more prominent in Eastern than in Western systems of psychology. It is stated clearly by Patanjali, who divides mental activities and states of consciousness into five categories: clear thinking, confused thinking, fancies, sleep, and memory. Because the mind, the instrument of thought, is usually caught up and controlled by the external world (*prakriti*) it is rarely capable of clear thinking. Only when it is detached from this and controlled by the spirit (*purusha*) can it reveal truth. This idea is formulated in the 24th Sutra of Patanjali's fourth book: 'Though the mind has its automatic reactions, directed thinking is the result of its association with purusha.' It again appears in the 10th and 12th Sutras: 'The law of cause and effect is inherent in mind and is co-existent with mind. The yogi who has gained liberation (*Kaivalya*) is no longer in bondage to mental limitations and is able to transcend the law.'

What explanation would the Behaviourist offer of these higher levels of thought? He would offer none, for the simple reason that he denies their existence. The Behaviourist entirely ignores the subject of consciousness and holds the view that because states of consciousness 'are not objectively verifiable, for that reason they can never become data for science'.

The mistakes made by Pavlov and by the Behaviourists lie in what they deny, rather than in what they affirm. No one can fail to appreciate their work on conditioned reflexes. Reflexes may occur at different levels in the central nervous system, at the levels of the spinal cord, the sub-cortical regions of the brain, and the cerebral cortex itself. The cortex of the brain would appear to be the level at which positive and negative conditioned reflexes manifest themselves, and the study of these is of the utmost importance to psychologists as well as to physiologists. Although the former are chiefly concerned with the psychic manifestations of man, they are keenly interested in the physical changes associated with these manifestations. Where the psychologist must part company with the Behaviourist is when the latter denies that the psychological aspect of his subject is of any importance to science. Psychology must be based on the study of man's psyche as well as on the study of the physical basis of his thought and behaviour, and it is ridiculous to ignore the existence of consciousness merely because it provides no data which can be weighed or measured. It has to be ignored in Dr Watson's particular technique of investigating human behaviour, and because this is the case he can tell us little about the real nature of man. Watson, like Freud, has made valuable discoveries in a very limited field of psychological research. It is unfortunate that both of these researchers have been tempted to make philosophical pronouncements beyond the scope of their inquiries.

When we examine these four medical schools of psychology we find that although they are marked by many differences, they possess two features in common, the emphasis they put on mechanism, and their disregard of what may be called the spiritual side of man's nature. If we accept the validity of the technique of analysis we at the same time tacitly accept a large measure of psychological determinism. We assume that the apparently disconnected and rambling thoughts of our patients are not really disconnected and rambling at all, but obey some general law, even although we may not have discovered that law. However disjointed these thoughts and feelings appear on the surface, they are the results of definite happenings in the unconscious part of the brain. If we knew the causes acting in the depths of the mind, we could foretell exactly how the patient would react: in other words he has no choice in what he says or what he does.

The form taken by our minds is invisible and intangible to us, so that any structure we may assign to the mind in our description of it is a metaphorical description only. So also when we speak of the mind in terms of psychic or mental energies, instead of in terms of structure, we are speaking again metaphorically. Nevertheless descriptions of this kind are of great use. It is quite true that we have no means of measuring the amount of mental energy possessed by any individual but it is still possible for us to think of psychic energy quantitatively. Some individuals seem to possess more of it than others do and we have all experienced the feeling of being entirely depleted of psychic energy. So likewise it is of the utmost importance for us to learn how to use economically what is undoubtedly the most valuable of all our possessions – our daily allowance of nervous force. In the ordinary way we are utterly spendthrift with it, pouring out our nervous energy in completely useless expenditures, such as when we fly into a rage, or when we spend our time deploring some foolish action which we committed long ago. Some psychologists take the view that the energies expended in our various psychological functions are specific ; emotional energy, they maintain, differs from intellectual energy so that the one form of energy is not convertible into another form. I myself think that, broadly speaking, there exists only one variety of psychic energy, the way in which it finds its outlet differing. Only when we have to deal with what may be called the higher functions of man in other words, the functions of man's spirit or higher mind, does it become necessary for us to consider the possibility, to which I personally subscribe, that there exist also higher and finer varieties of energy. In this book man's higher and finer forms of energy will not be discussed.

Freud chose a mechanical and a dynamic model for his description of the human mind, and his choice was an excellent one. A great deal has been learnt from studying the mind in this way. It represents the scientific method of investigating things, but we should remember whilst using it that in another field the physicists are now finding it impossible to explain all of the properties of the atom and of the 'quanta' of energy entirely in terms of machinery. The mind often behaves as a machine behaves, but this does not necessarily mean that it is a machine and nothing but a machine. It is a machine but a machine plus something else.

CHAPTER 7

DIFFERENT PATHS TO TRUTH

I T will be noted that the medical schools of psychology of the twentieth century have deliberately severed the study of mind from the study of philosophy and religion. J. B. Watson in his book, *Psychology from the Standpoint of the Behaviourist*, complains that in the past psycology has been too much under the dominance of traditional religion and philosophy, and that, as a result, its development has been retarded. He is of the opinion that as astronomy had to free itself from astrology, chemistry from alchemy, and neurology from phrenology before they could progress, so psychology must now disentangle itself from philosophy and religion. He states that psychology must become an exact science, employing only those methods which scientists have found to be reliable, namely, experimentation and the study of objective phenomena.

Whatever scientific value there is in the colossal number of volumes written in terms of consciousness, it can be better defined and expressed when the psychological problems which give rise to them are solved by genuine objective methods. States of consciousness provide no objective data that admit of scientific examination, nor can the Behaviourists find any evidence for 'mental existence', or mental processes of any kind.

It will be helpful to examine the scientific method in which Dr Watson has so much confidence that he believes it to be the only one by means of which the mind should be investigated. The instrument used by science is the intellect and the five special senses, and more particularly the special sense of sight. Through our sense organs messages reach us from the outside world and are conveyed thence to various parts of the brain. There certain physico-chemical disturbances are produced and we experience certain sensations. With the help of memory the intellect interprets these sensations and makes inferences. By this means it discovers the existence of an ordered pattern in the world outside it. But when we analyse critically the method by which the senses and the intellect work, we find that they are capable of telling us very little about the objects which surround us. Generally it is assumed that they tell us a great deal, but further reflection tells us that the information relates to what is happening *inside* us, and not to what is happening 'out there'. What actually happens when we see a red pillar-box is that certain vibrations towards the lower end of the spectrum impinge on the corneas of our eyes, are refracted on to the retinas, and from there send impulses along the optic nerves which finally set up a commotion in the occipital area of the brain. As a result of this inner agitation, and of relating it to certain similar agitations that we have previously experienced and still remember, we state that we have seen a red pillar-box. If, however, we had happened to be colour-blind, we would have been equally justified in calling the pillar-box green, for the colour that we have seen is projected by us on to it. Of the real nature of the box, or indeed of its real existence, we can never be sure.

How large a part of what we know of the external world is inferred by our minds instead of being directly perceived is admirably expressed by Sir Arthur Eddington in his book, *Science and the Unseen World*:

Consider how our supposed acquaintance with a lump of matter is obtained. Some influence emanating from it plays on the extremity of a nerve, starting a series of physical and chemical changes, which are propagated along the nerve to a brain cell; there a mystery happens, and an image of sensation arises in the mind, which cannot purport to resemble the stimulus which excites it. Everything known about the material world must in one way or another have been inferred from these stimuli transmitted along the nerves ... The mind as a central receiving station reads the dots and dashes of the incoming nerve signals. By frequent repetition of their call signals, the various transmitting stations of the outside world become familiar. We begin to feel quite a homely acquaintance with 2LO and 5XX. But a broadcasting station is not *like* its call signal; there is no commensurability in their natures. So, too, the chairs and tables around us which broadcast to us incessantly those signals which affect our sight and touch cannot in their nature be like unto the signals, or to the sensations which the signals awake at the end of their journey ... It is an astonishing feat of deciphering that we should have been able to infer an orderly scheme of natural knowledge from such indirect communication.

Clearly there is one kind of knowledge which cannot pass through such channels, namely, knowledge of the intrinsic nature of that which lies at the far end of the line of communication.

Mind is the first and most direct thing in our experience; all else is remote inference ... We have an acquaintance with the mental and spiritual nature of ourselves known in our minds by an intimate contact transcending the methods of physics.

Having stressed the roundabout and inferential character of our knowledge of the outside world, Eddington contrasts this with the directness and immediacy of our knowledge of the inside world of thoughts, feelings, and sensations. Here we are not attempting to interpret the nature of the objects which surround us by means of messages reaching us along a long line of communications, but we are viewing *directly* what is occurring in ourselves. Our knowledge is not an inferred knowledge, but a knowledge of something as it is in itself. Mind is therefore the most direct thing in our experience and something which can be studied very closely. The only point on which I would differ from Eddington is that, in my opinion, none of us avail ourselves to this capacity to see our thoughts and feelings. Although in theory we can have self knowledge, we do not actually possess it. Instead of seeing ourselves as we really are, we create in our imagination self portraits that have but little relation to reality. Hence the ancient injunction, 'Know thyself'.

But are the special senses and the intellect the only instruments of cognition in our possession? Man has long believed that this is not the case, and that the heart has its knowledge as well as the brain. He has even come to the conclusion that in certain fields of experience this other faculty may prove to be a more sensitive instrument than the intellect. A variety of names has been given to this non-intellectual cognitive faculty, such as emotional perception, intuition, inspiration, and spiritual insight. None of these names is satisfactory. Not only have these terms been used loosely and without discrimination, but they are often employed in quite different senses by different writers. This is not surprising when we realize that the word emotion itself has been employed to describe a great number of psychic phenomena ranging from such a purely instinctive reaction as fear to the religious ecstasy of the mystic. It must be remembered also that even non-instinctive emotions are generally automatic and sensuous reactions, which, far from extending our power of cognition, usually reduce it. It is for this reason that Bertrand Russell is of the opinion that all emotional reactions are an obstacle to understanding.

They generate material opinion, since emotional associations seldom correspond with collocations in the external world ... With the sole exception of curiosity, the emotions are, on the whole, a hindrance to the intellectual life, though the degree of vigour required for successful thinking is likely to be correlated with a considerable susceptibility to emotion. (*An Outline of Philosophy*)

The word 'intuition' is also unsatisfactory as a description of this non-intellectual method of cognition. It is a word which has recently been brought into prominence by Bergson, who uses it to describe a form of sensuous perception which is closely allied to what in animals is called instinct. According to this philosopher this faculty alone is capable of apprehending the flux of change which is reality. He contrasts it with the intellect, which, in his opinion, focuses the attention on a limited and static field in order that appropriate action may be taken. Because Bergson uses the word intuition for a sensuous and sub-rational faculty allied to instinct, Guénon has called our capacity to apprehend directly, and not through the intermediate link of the special senses, 'intellectual intuition'. He points out that although modern scholars know nothing higher than reason in the order of intelligence, scholars of the Middle Ages regarded intellectual intuition as being the highest of all man's faculties. As used by this writer, intellectual intuition would appear to have much in common with McDougall's 'implicit reason'. In Sanscrit there is a word which describes more accurately this method of obtaining knowledge. It is the word *buddhi*, which comes from the root, *buddh*, meaning 'to awaken'. This implies that the faculty to apprehend directly exists more particularly in the man who is spiritually awake, and that although it is of an emotional character, it is far removed from the passions, prejudices, and imaginings that form such a large part of our emotional life. By means of it the whole is directly apprehended without dividing it into parts, the truth grasped without seeing the steps by which it has been reached. And it is this capacity to grasp the meaning of the whole without first subjecting it to analysis which characterizes the method of cognition which we are describing. Another feature which distinguishes it from thinking is that this capacity is not achieved by a mere accumulation of information, but is always dependent on the attainment of a certain degree of spiritual development. Only by means of it can the deepest things in life be understood, and in its absence religion becomes either a meaningless ritual or a system of ethics, and philosophy degenerates into dialectics.

To many scientists the idea that there exists a method of attaining knowledge other than the intellect may appear illusory and dangerous. Yet even in the realm of science it is often some form of emotional insight which reveals the true meaning of the information which the intellect has amassed in the course of some painstaking research. In a flash Kekulé saw the fourfold valency of the carbon atom, and Darwin an explanation of the origin of species. There is, indeed, a strong similarity between the creative vision of the scientist and the inspiration of the artist, and but for the intervention of this non-intellectual faculty, it is probable that many a line of scientific research would never have reached its successful conclusion. There is yet another factor in cognition to which modern Western writers pay no attention, the factor of consciousness, and yet it is the degree of consciousness which exists that determines the depth of our knowledge. Western psychologists take no interest in this subject and generally assume that changes in consciousness are limited to sleep and awakening. Only recently have they discovered lower levels of consciousness which are described under the general term of 'the subconscious'. But no interest has been shown in what may be called the supraconscious, probably because it is usually assumed that thought and consciousness are synonymous terms and that consciousness cannot be increased. Even when Western psychologists admit that the existence of higher levels of consciousness is theoretically possible, they do not regard this as being of any practical importance. It is in fact of the greatest importance. This subject will be dealt with more fully in a later chapter. Here we are discussing only scientific methods of investigating man.

Science works on the assumption that every event must have a determining cause, an uncaused event being unthinkable. Acts of will are events, and, being predetermined by some cause or other, cannot possibly be free. The whole of the universe, according to the view of the scientist, work in the mannor of a gigantic machine, and man being part of the universe, he, also, is a mechanism. If he were to be an exception to this rule, we should have two categories of events in the universe, the vast majority predetermined by mechanism, and the remaining few resulting from the operation of man's will. Such an idea is intolerable to the scientist whose whole method of investigation rests on the basis of tracing a relationship between causes and effects. There is no place for 'will' within the frame which he has set up for his investigations.

In order that a scientist may discover the relationship between a cause and its effect, he must take to pieces the object with which he is dealing so as to examine its component parts. Each separate part, the known and the unknown, is scrutinized separately, and from the relationship that is found to exist between the unknown and the known parts new light is thrown on the mechanism. Science cannot but proceed in this way, and the results that it has obtained from this method of investigation have amply justified its use. Nevertheless, two assumptions have been made by the scientist : the first the assumption that effects can always be calculated from causes, and the second that an object is analysable without remainder into its parts and is capable of classification in terms of these. Another way of putting this is to say that the nature of the whole can be discovered from an examination of its parts, an idea that is vigorously denied by a large number of philosophers. According to the 'holism' of Smuts and other philosophers, the whole is more than the sum of its parts ; something new emerges from the whole that is not revealed in the examination of the separate parts.

A striking example of the fallacies that result from the scientific method of examining an object is summed up in B. A. Howard's prescription for a man, quoted and commented on by C. E. M. Joad in his *Guide to the Philosophy of Morals and Politics* :

> To make a man take the following:
>
>> Enough water to fill a ten-gallon barrel;
>> enough fat for seven bars of soap;
>> carbon for 9,000 lead pencils;
>> phosphorus for 2,200 match-heads;
>> iron for one medium-sized nail;
>> lime enough to whitewash a chicken coop; and
>> small quantities of magnesium and sulphur.

Take these ingredients combine them in the right proportions, in the right way, and the result, apparently, is a man. This, at least, is one of the things that a man is. There is in other words, a scientific formula for the production of men, as there is for the production of any other commodity. And, if it be objected that the formula applies only to the body, and that the mind has been left out of the recipe, we have only, as we have seen above, to go to the biologists and geneticists for information as to genus, species, race, initial inheritance, and distribution of chromosomes and genes, and to the psychologists for a statement of inherited disposition, temperament, mental structure, and unconscious complexes, and the mind and character can be brought within the bounds of the formula ... So treated a man inevitably appears to be determined. His constitution is determined by its constituent parts just because, *from this point of view*, it is the sum of its constituent parts, and his present is con-ditioned by his past antecedents just because when *he is so regarded*, it is the outcome of his antecedents.

A jury of scientists therefore is bound to bring in a verdict of 'not responsible' when a man is put into the dock and tried for what he has done. No other verdict is possible to those who have taken their oath on the bible of Science.

And this method of taking a thing to pieces and examining

each part separately is the only one possible to science. To deny the applicability of the method or the validity of its results is to deny the competence of science to deal adequately with the study of man, and this to a great many scientists is anathema. It is anathema, apparently, to Dr J. B. Watson. Hence his desire to free science from the trammels of Philosophy and Religion and to exclude from his consideration such entities as states of consciousness, which disappear when the man is taken to pieces, and thus upset calculations.

But the nature of man can never be discovered by ruling out all methods of investigation that do not conform to scientific standards. The scientific approach has undoubtedly given magnificent results, and, as we have seen, endocrinology, the investigation of the anatomy and physiology of the central nervous system, and the contributions of the various schools of medical and behaviourist psychology have all given us valuable information. Each kind of investigator has examined man within a certain framework, the limitations of which are clearly reflected in his findings. Man is this, and Man is that, but he is something more, and for the discovery of the 'more' the help of other methods of research are necessary. Philosophy and Religion can both make their contributions, and it would be as rational for us to decide that we can examine satisfactorily the contents of a room by looking through a keyhole as to conclude that we can best describe man by excluding all philosophical and religious accounts of him. P. D. Ouspensky in *A New Model of the Universe* writes as follows:

People of our time posses four ways that lead to the Unknown, four forms of conception of the world – religion, philosophy, science, and art. These ways diverged long ago. And the very fact of their divergence shows their remoteness from the source of their origin, that is, from esotericism. In ancient Egypt, in Greece, in India, there were periods when the four ways constituted one whole. If we apply the principle of Avva Dorotheos, which I quoted in *Tertium Organum* (page 286), to the general examination of religion, philosophy, science, and art, we shall see clearly why our forms of conception of the world cannot serve as a way to truth. They are for ever being broken up, for ever being divided, and they for ever contradict both themselves and each other. Obviously, the more they are broken up and separated from one another, the farther they depart from truth. Truth is at the centre, where the four ways converge. Consequently the nearer they are to one another, the nearer they are to truth, the farther they are from one another, the farther from truth. Moreover, the division of each of these ways within itself, that is to say, the sub-division into systems, schools, churches, and doctrines, denotes great remoteness from the truth; and we see in fact that the number of divisions, far from diminishing, increases in every domain and every sphere of human activity. This in its turn may show us, provided we are able to perceive it, that the general trend of human activity leads, not to truth, but in the very opposite direction.

It is noteworthy that it is never the great scientist, but always the second- or third-rate scientist who regards the scientific as being the only path to truth. Great learning inevitably brings great humility. As the circle of light broadens in which the seeker after knowledge stands, so does the encircling darkness appear greater. What is known, compared with that which remains unknown, seems infinitesimal. Why should anyone, who is so conscious of how little he can see, proclaim that he alone is fitted to show the way to his fellows? He does not proclaim it, but on the contrary, welcomes his fellow-pilgrims, those who follow a different path. Max Planck, one of the most eminent of all living scientists, writes:

There can never be any real opposition between religion and science; for the one is the complement of the other. Every serious and reflective person realizes, I think, that the religious element in his nature must be recognized and cultivated if all the powers of the human soul are to act together in perfect balance and harmony. And, indeed, it was not by any accident that the greatest thinkers of all ages were also deeply religious souls, even though they made no public show of their religious feeling. It is from the cooperation of the understanding with the will that the finest fruit of philosophy has arisen, namely, the ethical fruit. Science enhances the moral values of life, because it furthers a love of truth and reverence – love of truth displaying itself in the constant endeavour to arrive at a more exact knowledge of the world of mind and matter around us, and reverence, because every advance in knowledge brings us face to face with the mystery of our own being.

But science, philosophy, and religion have not always seemed divergent paths to truth. Nor did there always exist any feeling of antagonism between them, the scientist maintaining one point of view and the religious man another. Nor was it necessary for the religious man to deny the validity of the scientist's findings, or else, as has been the tendency lately, to act on the defensive and attempt to drag his own experiences into line with those of the scientist. Not only in Ancient Egypt, Greece, and India was science closely linked with religion, but also in Medieval Europe at the time of the Moorish occupation. It was to the Moorish centres of culture, then established in Southern Europe, that we owe the beginnings of the experimental method that has proved so successful in science. Roger Bacon never wearied of declaring that familiarity with Arabic and Arabic science was for his contemporaries the only way to true knowledge, and Arabic culture at that time was closely linked with religion. Buffault, in his *Making of Humanity*, goes so far as to declare that:

Science is the most momentous contribution of Arab civilization to the modern world. Not until long after Moorish culture had sunk back into darkness did the giant it had given birth to rise to its might. It was not science only which brought Europe back to life. Other and manifold influences from the civilization of Islam communicated the first glow to European life.

And the civilization of Islam was a civilization that was founded on religion, a religion that opened the doors of its universities to all who might care to enter.

Christians, Jews, and Mohammedans spoke the same tongue, sang the same songs, participated in the same studies. All the barriers which separated the various people were effaced, all worked with one accord in the work of a common civilization. The mosques of Cordova, where the students could be counted by thousands, became the active centres of philosophical and scientific studies. (RENAN)

What really Dr Watson should demand is that psychology be freed from the restricting bonds imposed on it by formalized and institutionalized religion; the 'religion' that imprisoned

and bullied Galileo in order to force him to deny his discoveries
and which still issues its 'ukases' when scientific findings are
not to its liking. With such a demand all seekers after truth,
religious as well as scientific, will be in agreement. The dead
hand of dead religion has always lain heavy on scientific discovery, and the sooner such encumbrances are removed the
better it will be for humanity. Not only will science gain from
this burial of religious corpses, but religion itself. The ground
is encumbered with dead creeds, the outer shells, rituals, and
observances from which the inner life has long departed. They
make a mockery of true religion and had best be hidden under-
ground.

But religion is something else than the creeds and dogmas
that in the end grow up and choke it.

It is the vision of something which stands beyond, behind and
within the passing flux of immediate things; something which is a
remote possibility, and yet the greatest of present facts; something
that gives meaning to all that passes and yet eludes apprehension;
something whose possession is the final good, and yet is beyond all
reach; something which is the ultimate ideal, and the hopeless
quest. (WHITEHEAD)

Because our task is so exceedingly difficult, let us enlist the
help of all branches of knowledge in our search for an understanding of the nature of man. To the question, 'What is man?'
modern science gives the answer, he is an automaton, every
action of which is predetermined by his mechanism. There is
truth in the answer, yet it does not embody the whole truth. It
will therefore be necessary to turn to the philosophers and the
men of religion and to hear also what they have to say on the
subject.

It may be advisable at this point to forestall a criticism. It
will be felt by some readers that in the chapters that are to follow, I have given undue prominence to Eastern systems of philosophy, at the expense of those of Western origin. I make no
apology for this. At a very early period of history the paths of
the East and the West diverged. Whereas the attention of the
Western thinker was turned mainly to the world outside himself, that of the Eastern thinker looked more at the world

within; whereas the Westerner sought adjustment by altering that which lay without him, the Oriental sought salvation by altering that which was within. The result of this different orientation of attention is obvious. Each thinker has reaped his reward; Western man, all the achievements of science; Eastern man, the greatest system of philosophy and religion that the world has ever known. It is the greatest possible error to suppose that because the Eastern sage's standard of living and system of sanitation is below that of a British or American working man, he must be regarded as backward in every other respect. If the West has brought to the East all the achievements of her science, the East possesses riches from which the Westerner can gain equal profit should he wish to do so. It is not by accident that all great religious geniuses have arisen in the East.

Guénon has drawn attention to an essential difference between Eastern and Western philosophy. Whereas Eastern philosophy has always remained in harmony with what he calls 'traditional knowledge', Western philosophy has no connexion with this. By traditional knowledge, Guénon means ancient knowledge based on knowledge obtained on higher levels of understanding, which has generally been handed down by word of mouth from teacher to disciple. Western philosophy does not recognize the existence of such knowledge, or of any higher principles to which its findings must be related. Each philosopher starts afresh from certain premises, and after refuting the arguments put forward by some opposing school, builds up his own philosophical system. Because of its different attitude to traditional knowledge Eastern philosophy is much more closely allied to religion than is Western philosophy.

Formerly Eastern literature was closed to all Westerners except to the few who had a knowledge of Sanskrit. Now, however, there exist translations of all the more important oriental books so that Westerners have at their disposal the thoughts and discussions of some of the greatest minds in the world's history. What is of particular importance is the fact that these minds have directed their attention to just those problems, such as the nature of man, that Europeans have neglected. Alexis Carrel, in his book *Man the Unknown*, points to the fact that

Western Science has been too much preoccupied with matter, and must now turn its attention to the still more important questions of life and living. He looks to a future in which man will make discoveries about himself that will be as important as those he has made in physics, discoveries that will enable him at the last hour, and just before it is too late, 'to become master of his destiny'. According to Alexis Carrel the key that will unlock the door to man's true progress has yet to be forged in some vast Rockefeller laboratory for the study of mankind. May it not have already been forged and be lying somewhere lost, neglected, and covered with dust? The search that Alexis Carrel would now initiate in the West has been followed in the East for thousands of years. It may not be necessary to build in New York an Institute of Man.

But before dealing with Eastern philosophy it will be advisable to see what light is thrown on man's nature by Western philosophy. The subject is an immense one, and it would be beyond the scope of this book even to provide a summary of the more important systems of Western philosophy. But fortunately this is not necessary. Instead of dealing primarily with philosophy we shall continue as before to discuss man's nature from the point of view of science, breaking off occasionally to note what philosophy has to say on the subject. Science works by drawing inferences directly from observations, but there is a point beyond which it will not venture. It is at this point that we must enlist the aid of philosophy if we are to attempt to overstep the limits that science has set for itself.

CHAPTER 8

EXISTENTIALISM

DURING and since the war the philosophy of Existentialism has made a strong appeal to youth, and more particularly to the youth of France. It has also been the subject of many articles in the popular press and this being so it will be necessary to examine it and see whether it is likely or not to retain its influence on twentieth-century Western thought. In order to discover what message, if any, Existentialism has for us we shall take as our departure point the term 'existentialism' itself. What does it mean? The word has been derived from the noun 'existence' and the adjective 'existential'. Existentialism tends to emphasize the importance of the individual's goal in life and the values he has discovered *for himself*. In other words it affirms the priority and the primacy of his own existence.

But priority over what? Over his Essence. Ontology distinguishes between two different metaphysical principles which the existentialist calls Essence and Existence. The Essence of a man is what he *is*, that is to say, a living organism with certain human characteristics. When we speak of an object's essence we are referring to the characteristic it shares with all objects of a similar kind. These constitute its universal characteristics and when we are talking of the universal characteristics of a man, we are referring to the characteristics which he has in common with all humanity. In addition to these universal characteristics, he possesses also certain individual features by means of which we distinguish him from other human beings. But as Paul Fontguré has pointed out in his small volume on Existentialism, Essence does not necessarily carry with it the assurance that such things are actualized – that they exist. *Existence is, in fact, that which actualizes Essence*. 'Our use of language clearly reveals this distinction of the two metaphysical principles in things. When I say "I am a man", "I *am*" affirms existence; "*man*" designates Essence. Only in God is Existence indistinguishable from Essence. That is why in Exodus III, 14 Jehovah defines himself as "that which is": "I am that I am".'

The problem which the existentialist is attempting to solve, and which he does solve in a certain way, is the following problem: when a man is in question, to which of the two principles should primacy be given, to his Essence or to his Existence? Up till the nineteenth century, philosophers never doubted the primacy of Essence and this being so we can call them Essentialist philosophers. What distinguishes the Existentialist from the Essentialist philosopher is that the former always accords primacy to *existence*.

It will help us to understand Existentialism better if we look first at the characteristics of the opposite philosophical school, the school which gives primacy to Essence. Plato can be taken as an outstanding example of an Essentialist philosopher. He starts by drawing a distinction between two worlds, the world revealed to us by our special senses and the world revealed to us only by our intellects, in the sense in which Plato used the word intellect. The first world can be called the sensible world and the second world the intellectual world or world of Ideas. The uneducated and unthinking recognize the existence only of the first world in which there is revealed to them many individuals of a similar type, that is to say a large number of houses, horses, trees, and men; of the higher world of Ideas they know nothing. Plato called the objects of this higher intellectual world 'Ideas' and he regarded them as the models for everything in the lower world of the senses. But the copies of ideal models to be found in the lower world of the senses are poor ephemeral things which in the process of becoming, die. All that these transient objects are capable of doing is to act as pale reflections of the Ideas in the world of the intellect. For example, although a man may possess some of the attributes of Goodness he can never be a true representation of Goodness itself. In order to illustrate to his readers how illusory and imperfect are the objects in the sensible world, Plato makes use of the allegory of the cave. He asks us to visualize a deep cavern in which a number of prisoners are chained facing a wall of rock, on which the sun is casting the shadows of a procession of people and of things passing the mouth of the cave. Knowing only these shadows the chained prisoners naturally mistake them for reality. But if one of them were to be freed from his chains and were to be conducted into the real world outside of the cave he would be so dazzled by the brightness of the light that he would at first see little or nothing. Only after long training would he be able to realize that out there he was seeing real things, and that what he had previously seen were only the shadows cast by these realities. This is the picture that Plato gives us of the relationship between the sensible and the intellectual worlds. According to Plato it is only in the world of Essense that we have a chance of gaining understanding and this being so Essence must be given primacy over mere Existence. This is the opposite of what the Existentialist believes.

So also St Augustine laid stress on Essence by identifying it with the 'Word' or the Divine Mind. For him the 'Word' was the source of all real knowledge for it was ... 'the true Light which lighteth every man that cometh into the world'. Up till the time of the Renaissance, theology, 'the queen of the sciences', lorded it over both science and philosophy. Consequently all philosophers accorded primacy to Essence and showed little interest in the experimental investigation of Existence.

It was only during the Renaissance that men of science and philosophy managed to rid themselves of theological shackles. Descartes and Francis Bacon assisted them in this act of liberation and also encouraged them to move in a new direction. But this does not imply that their methods of thinking suddenly changed. Scientists showed very little interest in the concrete and the individual; their aim lay rather in establishing certain general scientific laws, and whilst accomplishing this the concrete and the individual remained of very little importance to them. Even in the nineteenth century, observations on the individual and the exceptional were neglected. What the scientist sought, above everything else, was to obtain completely disinterested knowledge. This entailed his taking as objective a view of the whole as it was possible for him to take.

Paul Fontguré regards the Existentialist movement as being a

reaction against a cut-and-dried and intransigent form of intel-
lectualism. He points out that it has now led to a sudden realization of many of the impasses into which the secularization of
all morality has led humanity. At the end of the nineteenth
century the teaching of a morality founded on God was suddenly abandoned in France. This abolished what remained of
theological Essentialism, for the French promoters of secular
morality were strongly convinced that public morals could be
preserved in the complete absence of any belief in God. In this
way they preserved in France an Essential philosophy but one
resting on a new basis. The new Essential philosophy envisaged
a human type which all would regard as being an ideal model
towards which everybody should strive. The Existentialism of
today is supposed to have come into fashion as the result of
the subsequent rejection in France of this ideal type of man.

The great majority of Existentialists prefer to expound their
ideas indirectly in novels and in plays, rather than in philosophical treatises. This preference was shown also by the Dane,
Sören Kierkegaard, who is now usually regarded as being the
real founder of the Existentialist movement. It is also true of
two of the modern exponents of Existentialism, Jean-Paul Sartre
and Simone de Beauvoir, but less true of Martin Heidegger. But
what is Existentialism? Primarily it represents a reversal of the
policy of Essentialism which was deliberately fostered on the
French by the promoters of secular morality. As a result of our
intellectual and scientific training we are disposed to notice in
other people only those features which they have in common,
failing to register their *individual* and *personal* characteristics.
We also approach them armed with a number of different psychological categories hoping to be able to place them in one or
other of these divisions.

We are inclined to treat ourselves in a similar scientific way.
Instead of observing and setting store on our inner life as it
flows uniquely and individually in each one of us, we arrest the
flow by placing what we may have caught sight of under its
appropriate heading.

The Existentialist has reacted from this conceptualized approach to our inner life. He tries instead to watch the flow of

his personal existence and to prevent his intellect from interrupting it by attempting to analyse it. As Kierkegaard has put it in his *Postscript to Philosophical Fragments*: 'Instead of abstract thought having for its task the abstract comprehension of the concrete the Existentialist has, on the contrary, the task of understanding the abstract *concretely*, for example as personified in some novel or play. He is not concerned, as the old Essentialist philosophers were, with speculating about human life in general, for that would be to lose the *individual* and the concrete in a haze of abstract conceptions.

Jean-Paul Sartre gives us a personal example of what the Existentialist is trying to do. He describes one of those vivid moments in which an individual becomes acutely aware of his own *personal* existence and puts his words into the mouth of Roquentin, the hero of one of his novels, *La Nausée*:

So I was sitting in the park. The root of the chestnut tree thrust out of the soil just under my seat. I no longer remembered that it was a root. Words had vanished and with them the significance of things, their uses, the faint land-marks that man has traced on their surface. I was sitting, a little bent, my head bowed, alone face to face with that black knotty mass utterly crude, and it frightened me. And then I had this illumination.

It took my breath away. Never, until these last few days, had I had any conception of what it was to *exist*. I was like everyone else, like the people walking beside the sea in their spring clothes. Like them I said, 'the sea is green, the promontory white, that is a sea-gull up there', but I did not *feel* that any of all that existed, that the sea-gull was an existing sea-gull. As a rule existence hides itself. It is there all about us, and *in* us, it is ourselves, we cannot say two words without speaking of it, and yet ultimately it is beyond our reach. When I imagined I was thinking about it, you must understand that I was not *thinking* at all, my mind was empty, or there was only one word in my mind, the word 'being'. Or rather I was thinking – how shall I put it? . . . I told myself that the sea belonged to the class of green objects or that green was one of the qualities of the sea. Even when I looked at it I was a hundred miles away from thinking that *they existed*; they seemed to me like stage scenery. I took them in my hands and they served me as tools, I avoided them as obstacles. But all that took place on the surface. If anyone previously had asked me what existence was, I should have replied in good faith, that it was not anything, just that one empty form had been added to external things, without in any way altering their nature. And now, all at once, it was present, it was clear as day; existence had suddenly been unveiled. It had lost the inoffensive aspect of an abstract category, it was the very substance of things. That root was saturate with existence.

Occasionally we stir in our sleep, experience the mystery of our existence, look around us, wonder what it all means, and then imperceptibly slide back into sleep again. The rest of the time we are so entangled in our thoughts, our feelings, our movements, and our dreams that we have lost all sense of a personal existence. And usually we are absent from the present moment and are dreaming of something which happened long ago, or else conjuring up, with the help of our imaginations, something which may or may not happen in the future.

A well-known Existentialist, Gabriel Marcel, draws attention to the change which occurs when we 'come to' in the present moment and in the present place. 'Whoever practises the philosophy of *hic et nunca*, one might say, is the real ; he will never become accustomed to the fact of existing ; existence is inseparable from astonishment . . . One cannot speak of existence apart from objects presented in an immediate relationship to a consciousness.' (G. Marcel, *Journal métaphysique*.) Here Marcel draws our attention to the actual cause of the changes occurring in our thoughts and our feelings at these moments – *a raising of the level of our consciousness* from our usual level of waking-sleep to wakefulness.

Like all other psychologies and philosophies Existentialism possesses its own jargon and if we are to understand it we must know something about the meaning it attaches to its terms. What, for example, does the Existentialist mean when he uses the word existence ? Fontguré answers this question by declaring that existence is not a state, but an act, the actual transition from possibility into reality ; as the etymology of the word indicates, to 'exist' is to take leave of what one '*is*' *(ex)* in order to become '*oneself*' (Latin, *sistere*), on the level of that which formerly was only possible. He also tells us that in order to exist one must choose what one wishes to *be*. And the choice must be repeated many times in our lives because existence should be a 'perpetual transcendence', that is to say, a passing beyond that which one is. We only exist in the progress towards a further stage of being, realized by acts of free choice. Since what we *are* is determined by our essence it is our essence which we choose, when we decide what sort of person we wish to be.

The Existentialist accords to man a certain range of choice. He also recognizes that the range of choice is a limited one; what we become will depend very largely on the chromosomes which transmit to us our ancestral heredity; on the surroundings in which we have been reared and, to some extent, on our own choosing. Our way of choosing is to take up some particular attitude rather than another, and by our attempting to 'live' our own thoughts. Admittedly it is difficult to choose, for we lack the kind of indispensable knowledge on which our selection should be based. Unlike the Essentialist, the Existentialist possess no fixed ideal and does not even admit a 'norm' for man. It is for each to make his own norm: what he must be is nowhere written down; it is for himself to invent it. Undoubtedly he can consult, or hand over the direction of his life to someone in whom he has confidence; but the choice of his adviser or director contains implicitly that of certain principles of life and, for a thinking person, is no less difficult.

It is at this point of 'choice' that there may enter the 'anguish' on which Sartre lays such stress in all his writings. Having rejected all notion of an ideal world, such as Plato's world of Ideas, the Existentialist is placed in the very difficult position of having to choose, without possessing any principles on which to base his choice. Nor has he anything by which he can subsequently decide whether the choice he has made is a good one or not: this is the basis of the existential anguish, which is not so much the fear of any precise danger, as the lively sentiment of having been placed here without having wished it, and of being forced to make choices whose consequence we cannot foresee, and which cannot be justified; a sentiment at once painful and noble, for it places us once more in authentic existence.

Choice is notoriously blind, and since it is choice which determines to a large extent the direction in which the Existentialist moves, one would expect that the philosophies chosen by different Existentialists would vary very greatly, and this proves to be the case. There exist a number of different versions of Existentialism; there is the nihilistic and atheistic Existentialism of Jean-Paul Sartre, the Protestant Existentialism of Kierkegaard, the Catholic variety of Gabriel Marcel, and that strange hybrid philosophy, the Essentialist-Existentialism of Louis Lavelle. Existentialism makes only one demand, namely that the choice of the Existentialist should be a sincere one. It is admitted that the act of choice constitutes the chief danger in Existentialism and if there is anything obvious to everybody it is the confusion of thought often to be found in the philosophy chosen by the individual Existentialist. The nihilistic and atheistic philosophy of Sartre is a striking example of this. Developed during the war and the occupation of France, Sartre's variety of Existentialism is clearly the product of crisis. It reminds me of the philosophy of meaninglessness which became so fashionable after the First World War. Many of us gave up a great deal in order to play our part in the first world conflagration and we were romantic enough to regard it as a Crusade. It was a 'war to end all wars', and a war 'to save democracy'. It was in this belief and fortified by the feeling that we were Crusaders in a noble cause that we suffered the horrors, the immense casualties, and the privations and the mud of Flanders and the Somme. Then came the terrible disillusionment of the conference and of the Treaty of Versailles. We had expected the arrival of a new age, but the news brought to us by the paper clearly showed that nothing had changed. At Versailles were displayed all the old political tricks, all the nationalistic schemings which had followed previous wars, but played on a larger scale than before. Our war to end the lunacy of war had dismally failed. Overwhelmed by the mockery of it all, my own and the younger generation became cynics. We adopted the bankrupt philosophy of meaninglessness and tried to laugh it off. There was no meaning in anything and we had been fools even to have thought that there was. It was in a similar spirit of bitterness that Sartre's version of

Existentialism must have been evolved by the young intellectuals and artists, sitting in the cafés of the Faubourg St Germain. 'Laugh, drink, and be merry' may serve as a philosophy for a time but only for a time. There is no nourishment in the bitter fruit of the Dead Sea. Some of the followers of Sartre have defaulted but, I gather, not yet the leader himself.

Sartre and those who follow him have accepted Nietzsche's message that God is dead. Formerly the Deity communicated with men, but now silence reigns. This being so man must forget God and must make use of his freedom and his own creativeness. Sartre also assures his followers that there is no Universe other than a human universe of human subjectivity. This being so, man has to invent his own values.

The Jewish psychologist and philosopher, Martin Buber, counters this pessimistic conclusion by pointing out that the silence of God has been accepted by Sartre without his having considered the possibility that it is man's lack of hearing which is responsible for it. And in Buber's opinion it is the fact that man has substituted an 'I – It' for the former 'I – Thou' relationship which accounts for the cessation of all communication between man and God. Buber places great stress on the difference between these two relationships. The destructive feature of the 'I – It' relationship is that the individual gives only a part of himself to the It, whereas in the 'I – Thou' relationship he surrenders himself to the Thou entirely. Buber writes: 'In our age, the "I – It" relation, gigantically swollen, has usurped the situation practically uncontested, and is the lord of the hour. This selfhood that has become omnipotent, with all the It around it, can naturally acknowledge neither God, nor any genuine Absolute which manifests itself to men as of non-human origin. It steps in between, and shuts off from us the light of heaven.' (*Eclipse of God.*)

There are three relationships which man has to establish before he can be said to have made a satisfactory adjustment to his environment; his relationship to the world; to his fellow human beings; and to the mystery of his own existence. And, as Buber has pointed out, modern man encounters much greater difficulty in establishing these relationships than men formerly encountered. One of the explanations of this great difficulty is that many of the social units which formerly helped man to establish a satisfactory 'I – Thou' relationship with his fellow men have weakened or even disappeared. By the term social units Buber means such things as the family unit, the companionship with fellow-workers which men formerly enjoyed, and the small social groups to be found in towns and in villages.

In the end, the wide attraction of Existentialism may be seen as a specific product of the pessimism which a world war and a cold peace inevitably bring. While giving every credit to the value both of the theoretical distinction between Existence and Essence and of the agony of personal choice on which Existentialism insists, I personally take comfort in the thought that history shows a constant swing between pessimism and optimism and that Buber's 'I – Thou' relationship may be the start of a swing back to idealism and optimism.

CHAPTER 9

CONSCIOUSNESS

PHYSIOLOGISTS generally suppose that consciousness is related to only a very small part of the human organism, the brain. According to the majority of scientists even the brain is not wholly conscious, but only that part of it, the cerebral cortex, in which sensory impressions are registered, and from which voluntary impulses to the muscles depart. Sir Henry Head and other researchers have, however, brought forward evidence in support of the view that the subcortical, as well as the cortical, region of the brain may be conscious. In this area lie the great masses of brain cells and fibres – and more especially cells – that were of so much interest in the study of the emotions, the cells of the thalamus. But it must be remembered that the relationship of consciousness to bodily structures is a subject of immense difficulty (see page 116). What is given here is only the physiologist's view of it.

As will be seen later, the ordinary conception of consciousness presents many difficulties. According to it conscious life is a series of disjointed impressions imprinted on different areas of the cerebral cortex. For example, 'I' become conscious of the light reflected from the box of cigarettes on my desk through the messages conveyed via my eye to the occipital region of my cerebral cortex. 'I' realize that 'I' would like to smoke. 'I' send a message to a series of muscles by means of which I take up a cigarette. 'I' remember that 'I' have already smoked more than 'I' meant to. 'I' replace the cigarette. Here is a series of 'I's, each representing a separate moment of consciousness each provoked by stimulation of my cerebral cortex. And yet, although this description of life as a continual shifting of the focus of consciousness from one object to another is partly true, there appears to exist something that combines these separate impressions into a whole. If this were not so, a symphony played by an orchestra would be a series of disjointed notes, the picture being painted by an artist, separate dabs of colour placed on a canvas. Fortunately, by means of some other faculty, we are able to feel the symphony, and to see the artist's picture, not as an aggregate, but as a whole, that is to say, as something which is brought into existence by the coming together of its parts, so as to form a new and complete entity over and above the sum of its parts. Psychic life, therefore, cannot be entirely explained by a flicker of consciousness travelling over the surface of the brain and lighting up now this area, now that, in the way that some physiologists have supposed. This physiological view of consciousness explains something, but not much.

Logical thought is apt to deal only in extremes. We state that something is either this or that; if it be not this, then it must be that. If the brain only is conscious, then all else is unconscious, as though the phenomenal world were clearly marked out in pure colours without any gradations in between. Although the brain may be distinguished by the intensity of its consciousness, there is no reason to suppose that all other structures are entirely unconscious. Indeed a certain modicum of consciousness may be assigned to every living cell. What distinguishes living from inert matter is its purposefulness, and, as we have seen in considering the cell, it is impossible to study living matter without considering purpose; it is impossible to study biology without using teleological arguments.

Intelligence is innate in all living tissue. Where lies the intelligence that converts the separate notes of a symphony into a beautiful and meaningful whole? Where lies the intelligent force that shapes the body to its own ends? As a surgeon, I am sometimes called upon to cut away the ureter (the narrow channel that connects the bladder with the kidney) and to implant it into another part of the bladder. When my work has been completed, I am ashamed of its crudity. Compared with the job done by a plumber, my joint is a poor and botched concern. Yet when I examine it a year after I am scarcely able to tell which is Nature's joint and which is my own. Some intelligence in the patient's body has made good my failure, paring off redundant tissue here, adding new tissue there, until perfection has been attained. Does that intelligence exist only in the brain ? No, for if I divide all the nerves that reach that spot from the brain, the work is performed just as well. If we concede intelligence to the body, we must also concede to it some degree of consciousness.

P. D. Ouspensky in speaking of Hatha Yoga states that yogis believe that the life of the body consists of thousands of separate lives, and that these lives presuppose the existence of a 'soul', or a consciousness. His own study of dreams confirmed this view. He believes that not only does the head think, but also the limbs and the visceral organs. This thinking of the body does not reach our consciousness in a waking state because the head consciousness dominates everything else.

But when the head consciousness calms down and becomes clouded in the state of sleep, especially in the deeper forms of sleep, immediately other consciousnesses begin to speak, namely those of feet, hands, fingers, stomach, those of other organs, of various groups of muscles. These separate consciousnesses in us possess their own conceptions of many things and phenomena, for which we sometimes have also head-conceptions and sometimes have not. This is precisely what most prevents us understanding our dreams. In sleep the mental images which belong to the legs, arms, nose, tips of the fingers, to the various groups of motor muscles, become mixed with our ordinary verbal visual images.

Many thinkers in the past have gone further and have believed that the whole of Nature, animate and inanimate alike, is alive and intelligent. Fechner is strongly of the same opinion. According to him, original sin in scientific thinking is that which regards the spiritual in nature, not as the rule, but as the exception. Instead of believing our life to be fed at the breasts of a greater Life, our individuality to be sustained by a greater Individuality, which must necessarily possess more consciousness than that of all that it brings forth, we habitually treat what lies outside ourselves as inert and without intelligence. Or, if we do believe in some Divine Spirit, we look upon it as bodiless, and Nature as without a soul. Fechner has therefore returned to the animism of the Greeks. Not only do the trees and the forests have souls, but also the earth on which we live. The earth has a consciousness to which we, as individuals walking on her surface, stand in the relation of sense organs. She absorbs our perceptions into her larger sphere of knowledge, and combines them with the other data that she possesses.

It will be said that Fechner, in his book *Zend-avesta*, speaks as a poet, rather than as a scientist, and that this being so, his view need not be taken too seriously. But a poet is as well entitled as a scientist to tell the story by which he explains the universe. Science possesses no monopoly of truth. In this region she is practically impotent. Science, we have been told, is measurement, and what means of measurement has she in the realm of consciousness? Perhaps the poet, equipped with intuition, is in this region able to see more than the scientist. So before examining scientific and philosophical views on consciousness, it will be of interest to include Fechner's account of how he arrived at his own inspired view of Earth-consciousness.

On a certain morning I went out to walk. The fields were green, the birds sang, the dew glistened, the smoke was rising, here and there a man appeared, a light as of transfiguration lay on all things. It was only a little bit of earth; it was only one moment of her existence; and yet as my look embraced her, more and more it seemed to me not only so beautiful an idea, but so true and clear a fact, that she is an angel – an angel carrying me along with her to Heaven ... I asked myself how the opinion of men could ever have so spun themselves away from life, so far as to deem the earth only a dry clod ... But such an experience as this passes as fantasy. The earth is a globular body, and what more she may be, one finds in mineralogical cabinets.

This idea that nature is animate, which, under the name of Panpsychism, is an element in many philosophies, was clearly recognized by Wordsworth.

> With bliss ineffable
> I felt the sentiment of Being spread
> O'er all that moves and all that seemeth still

But we must turn from the poets to the study of man. We have three entities to consider: consciousness, thought, and the brain.

How is the body related to the mind? This has remained one of the central problems of European philosophy from the days of Plato and Aristotle onwards. Three main theories have been advanced in explanation, each of them capable of many variations. It will be necessary to summarize these three general theories as briefly as possible.

The first is the theory of psycho-physical materialism. According to this view, the physical changes in the brain are themselves the cause of consciousness. Psycho-physical materialism was particularly popular during the last century before matter had crumbled in the scientist's hands and when he could still hope to explain the whole universe in terms of machinery. Hobbes (1588-1679) taught this extreme form of materialism. Impressed by the mechanistic explanations that Galileo and Descartes had applied to physical phenomena he stated that matter and motion were the sole ultimate realities. They accounted for everything and even for human knowledge since all knowledge was derived from sensations, and sensations were produced by the impact of matter on sense organs. Sensations and thoughts alike, according to this view, were only certain kinds of motion.

The mental life according to this idea was a by-product of chemical activity, consciousness being pictured as a sort of glow that travelled over and lit up different areas on the surface of the brain. Being only a result of physico-chemical changes, thought was entirely dependent on the brain and could initiate nothing of itself. The mistake which the materialists made was an elementary one, namely, that of assuming that because consciousness is *associated* with certain physico-chemical disturbances in the brain, it is *caused* by those physico-chemical disturbances. They did not stop to reflect that the movement of matter can only produce movement of matter, or else be converted into potential energy. Even if by means of a technique at present beyond our powers we could express the changes that occur in the brain of a man listening to a musical symphony by means of chemical formulae, these formulae would throw no light on the nature of his thoughts, or tell us why he found beauty and enjoyment in the symphony. Moreover, since according to this theory there can be no such thing as mental activity *per se*, all speculation ceases to be of any value, including speculation on the subject of mind and matter. Materialism, like the theory of Behaviourism, ends in a *reductio ad absudum* ; if thought be merely cerebral chemistry, and the theory of Behaviourism a conditioned reflex, neither materialism nor Behaviourism need be considered seriously. Like the scorpion, who is reputed to sting himself to death when surrounded by a ring of fire, both theories commit *hara-kiri*.

It is obvious, however, that the strongholds of pure materialism are in any case crumbling not through the direct assault of idealists, but because the material out of which they have been built shows signs of disintegration. The science of physics, which, as we have seen, has been taken as a model by all other sciences, has proved untrustworthy. Formerly, matter was matter and force was force, and no one doubted the antithesis between the two principles out of which the universe was constructed. But now that the search into their nature has grown fierce enough, matter and energy are continually changing into each other. Energy in the cosmos turns into precipitate mass, function in living beings materializes into precipitate structure. The old conception, therefore, of matter as an inert mass through which energy manifested itself, and of brain being structure which formed, as a by-product, the emanation of consciousness, is badly in need of modification.

The second theory of the mind-brain relationship is provided by Idealism. Bishop Berkeley (1685-1753) is probably the best known of English Idealist philosophers. He formulated his philosophy in order to combat the materialistic thought of his age, taking Locke's essays as his text. He maintained that our ideas and sensations not only of the primary, but of the secondary, qualities of matter cannot be 'copies' of anything objective, but are our own mental experiences. It is, therefore, superfluous to assume the existence of material bodies at all. Our ideas, and not material things beyond them, are the real objects of knowledge. 'All the choir of Heaven and furniture of Earth ... have not any substance without the mind ; ... their *being* is to be perceived or known.' When not perceived 'they must either have no existence at all or else subsist in the mind of some Eternal Spirit.' The only realities, according to Berkeley are God, other spiritual beings created by Him, and the various ideas and experiences which He has ordained to be apprehended according to a certain sequence. For Berkeley then, consciousness is the reality, and matter the shadow. The processes in the brain, with which consciousness is linked up, are not something additional, but merely the way in which one consciousness appears to another, or perhaps to itself. You can never hope to see into my mind, but if you could invent a special microscope and open my skull, you might conceivably see movements of molecules, atoms, and electrons taking place in my cerebral cortex. This does not mean that two processes are occurring – my consciousness, and the changes in my brain; all that it means is that to *you* the former appears as the latter. But as Professor Wiliam Brown points out, this philosophical conception does not really help us. It is a restatement of the psycho-physical problem rather than a solution of it.

Psycho-physical Interaction is the third and the oldest of the theories that attempt to explain the relationship of brain and mind. It was brought into prominence by Descartes (1596-1650). This philosopher began by doubting all that he could reasonably doubt in order to find a rock on which he could build his philosophy. Discarding all conceptions incapable of proof, he fell back on the famous dictum, 'I think, therefore I am' (*Cogito, ergo sum*). This Descartes regarded as a conclusion that he could accept, all others being axiomatic. It bore, however, the implication that the mind knows its own processes (namely thinking) better than it knows the objects about which it thinks, and this led him to draw a very sharp line between what was 'mind' and what was 'not mind', thus separating mind from body.

According to Descartes' view, there are two entities: the mind and the body. The brain is the organ of the mind and each interacts on the other; in active states the mind acts on the brain, and in passive, the brain on the mind. When a man wills to move his arm, he initiates certain physico-chemical changes in the motor area of his cerebral cortex which travel down the nerves and lead to the contraction of muscles. When light enters the eye, it initiates changes in the retina, changes that are conveyed along the optic nerves to the hind-part of the cerebral hemispheres. As the result of the agitation caused there, the mind becomes conscious of some object in the external world.

Although this explanation of the relationship between body and mind appeals to common sense, it causes great difficulty to the philospher. How can two orders of existence that are so different make contact, so that one may react on the other? Innumerable philosophers have struggled unsuccessfully with this problem. Giving up in despair his attempts to answer this question, Leibnitz fell back on a subterfuge; his mind and brain did not interact, but kept time, like two perfectly synchronized clocks. How did they manage to keep such perfect time, the one with the other? Leibnitz replied that it was because they had been wound up and set going at exactly the same moment with the result that each tick in one synchronized with each tick in the other. Even Descartes was aware of the difficulty he had created and had to fall back on the view that the perfect harmony which existed between mind and body was evidence, not of any casual relationship between the two, but of both having been created by God, and of having been set going together, harmoniously tuned.

There is yet another difficulty in this theory due to the fact that according to the ordinary view of the nature of mind and matter, matter has extension in space, whereas mind has no extension. This difficulty, like the preceding one, is the result of our having so divided up the universe of mind and matter that the two can never meet. In spite of these philosophical difficulties, the common-sense arguments in favour of psychophysical interaction are many. One is that the existence of mind as a separate entity explains the unity of consciousness. It is difficult to see how otherwise a series of separate disturbances widely distributed over the cerebral cortex and in different levels of the brain could ever be realized as a unity unless they meet at some point. This difficulty would be overcome if it were postulated that they met in the unity of the mind.

Aristotle gave a mind-body theory which remained the theory

of traditional philosophy for many centuries. This Aristotelean view, or hylomorphism, holds that mind is the 'form' of the body. Matter receives its whole specification and perfections from its 'form', or soul. Soul and matter do not interact (this would constitute a dynamic union) but are joined by 'substantial information'. Neither the body nor the soul is a complete entity in itself, but from their union results a complete entity, namely, man.

It must be borne in mind, however, that the difficulty of explaining how the separate states of consciousness that make up our lives are unified exists only for Western thinking. For many Oriental philosophers no explanation is necessary, since they believe that life consists only of a series of separate sense impressions, and changing states of consciousness. In order that he may see that this is so the Buddhist disciple is recommended to seat himself in some isolated spot and to contemplate the procession of thoughts and images that pass through his mind, like a long unedited cinematograph film passing through a projector. By so doing he will realize that his life is but a succession of disjointed phenomena, and that he does not possess any co-ordinating and integrating 'I'. When a man says 'I' he is merely employing a useful term to describe an ever-changing combination of physical and psychical phenomena. Nor is the Buddhist alone in believing that there is no integrated and enduring 'I' within us. Hume (1711–76), after careful observations carried out on himself, repudiated Bishop Berkeley's assumption that a man intuitively apprehends his own self. He wrote: 'For my part when I enter most intimately into what I call *myself*, I always stumble on some particular perception or other ... I never catch myself.' Hume was an accurate observer, and he refused to be misled by an assumption merely because it was widely held. All that he could find in himself was a multitude of disconnected sensations and impressions, which, by habit, he had come to regard as casually connected events. As a result of self-observation he was convinced that previously by mistaking similar for identical impressions he had fallen into the error of regarding as enduring what was really transitory. Now all that he could be sure of was the existence of a flux of changing events. Hume was baffled by his inability to find an enduring self. Unwittingly he had joined the company of the Buddhists. To the followers of the Eightfold Path the difficulty of explaining how the disturbances widely distributed over the cerebral cortex are unified would not exist. On the contrary, they would maintain that this is a true picture of reality. Buddha is reported to have said:

There are the petals, the pollen, the corolla, and the stalk, but there is no lotus flower. There is this or that passing idea, this or that transitory emotion, this or that image, but no organized whole behind them which can be called the ego, or the self.

The difficulty of explaining how brain and mind can interact has become so acute that Interactionists have been forced to search for arguments to support their original thesis that somehow or other they *do* interact. They have contested the view of the materialists that consciousness is merely a by-product of the physico-chemical activity of the brain, by means of the biological argument of utility. The fact that consciousness has been evolved at all is, they say, a proof that it must be of some use to the organism, for Nature is an economical housewife and does not produce anything that has no purpose. But if it has a purpose, how can anything be achieved if it is prevented from acting on the organism? This argument may be of some assistance in supporting the view of interaction, but it does not give us any help in understanding how interaction is effected. It must indeed be admitted that all the suggested answers to the problem of how the mind acts on the body are unsatisfactory. This almost certainly means that the formulation of the question itself is unsatisfactory, and that our conception of the two entities, body and mind, is in error.

Henri Bergson has re-examined the problem in a new way, starting with an attempt to find out what we really mean by matter, and what we mean by mind. Our knowledge of matter is based on perception. Instead of accepting the usual philosophical view that *we* endow the material universe with such properties as sound and colour, Bergson holds the view that the material universe actually possesses these qualities. The only difference between matter as we observe it, and matter as it really is, lies in the fact that we see only a part of it, not the whole of it. We make contact with the external world through our central nervous system. This is built up of sensory and motor fibres, which are given to us in order that we may react and adapt to our environment. We see an object, such as an apple, as it is, but only those characteristics of the apple to which we can react. It is green, and if I stretch out my hand and touch it, the apple feels hard. But these messages that pass through the tactile and visual nerves to the brain do not by their action on the brain produce consciousness of the apple. For actual perception of the apple at least a brief duration of time is necessary, for memory must come into play in order to summate a number of rapidly successive views of the object perceived in our consciousness. Memory, according to Bergson, is of the nature of spirit, whilst perception is physical. It is memory that produces the summation of momentary impressions, and gives us a picture of an apple, acting in the capacity of a projector that summates the separate photographs in a film so as to give them meaning. Thus the separate vibrations of light reflected from the apple are combined by memory, so as to give us the appearance of green. If the mind could be so slowed down that it could count the successive vibrations, it would see the apple, not as green, but only as a series of vibrations. Theoretically, pure perception is distinct from memory. 'Pure' memory is, however, unconscious, and what we call 'conscious' memory is memories on the way to perception. Our conscious life is, therefore, a result of the working together of perception and unconscious memories, which insert themselves into the series of motor reactions which serve for our perceptual activity.

Bergson's theory is based on the view that memory is spirit and that all our memories remain in our minds from the earliest times. They are, however, unconscious, but if the mechanism of the brain is excited, they are brought to the mind as conscious memories. According to him there is no such thing as a loss of memory. Even if the brain is damaged this can only result in a loss of the machinery that allows memories to actualize themselves; they are not destroyed, but in abeyance.

It is interesting to note how nearly Bergson approaches the Eastern view of intellect. To the Vedântist and the Buddhist the organ of ordinary thought is placed on the same level as the special sense organs. To the five sense organs of sight, hearing, taste, smell, and touch, the Vedântist adds the sixth organ of the mind (*Manas*). They are all of the same nature and equally limited and liable to error. Whilst the senses are of great practical value in providing us with the means of appreciating and reacting to changes in our environment, they are quite incapable of apprehending reality. Bergson would say that determinism is the sort of view that the intellect is forced to take of the nature of reality. This is so because of the intellect's habit of cutting up everything into little bits. When an individual's personality is divided into bits so that his life appears to be merely a succession of states of consciousness which persist unchanged until they are replaced by other states, and when the intellect proceeds to reason about each of these isolated snapshots, it must come to the conclusion that the one state is conditioned by the other. But the life of an individual is not in reality a sequence of unchanging states and actions. His life is a continuous and indivisible flow, just as all life is a continuous flow of the *élan vital*. It is of the very nature of life to be creative, and the individual (not in a cross-section of time but taken as a whole) is of necessity creative by virtue of the very fact that he is alive. If his life is creative, it is clear that it cannot be completely determined by what has gone before; for this would mean not the creation of anything that is new, but merely the expression of something that is old.

The ingenuity shown by different Western philosophers in trying to solve the riddles of mind and matter, life and death, free-will and determinism, must excite our admiration. These subjects have been approached from every direction, and every trick known to the intellect has been tried, in order to come nearer the solution of the enigma. All the time, the working of the instrument itself, the intellect, has to be carefully scrutinized in order to make sure that it has infringed none of the principles of sound reasoning. Each philosopher has analysed the findings of the opposing school of thought in the hope of discovering there some slip in logic, and has substituted his own theory after having satisfied himself that it was incapable of refutation. The whole game has been played strictly according to the rules of logic. But unfortunately the rules of logic, themselves, are liable to change with time, and the logic employed by Aristotle would not be accepted by all the philosophers of today. Moreover, logical arguments show an unfortunate tendency to degenerate into a series of verbal exercises, ending in a pyrotechnic display of dialectics. Nothing is easier than that a discussion which began as a search for truth should end as an argument about words. Each philosopher attaches to a word a slightly different meaning, and Truth, like an elusive butterfly, slips out between the meshes with which the philosophers are trying to catch her. Which of the words that we use in our discussions represent ideas that are real, and which do not? And when, having defined our position, we have reached the final stage of our argument with that comforting assumption that a thing is either 'this' or 'that', who can say that this is so? Let Chuang Tsu answer that question : 'Suppose I am arguing with you, and you get the better of me. Does the fact that I am not a match for you mean that you are really right and I am really wrong? Or if I get the better of you, does the fact that you are not a match for me mean that I am really right and you are really wrong? Must one of us of necessity be right and the other wrong, or may we not both be right and wrong?' Chuang Tsu had but little faith in dialectics.

The problem of the relationship between mind and body is really the same problem as the relationship between the body and its physico-chemical substratum. Because the Western scientist regards matter as real and physics as the basic science, he has sought to explain biology in terms of physics, and psychology in terms of biology. This attempt to interpret the higher in terms of the lower is inevitably doomed to failure, for the relations of consciousness to living organism and matter is one of an increasing abstraction from reality. By starting from the more fundamental concept of consciousness the Eastern sage has avoided falling into these errors.

As will be seen in the following chapter another difference between the Eastern and Western schools of philosophy is that whereas the latter has complete faith in logical thought, the former has not. It is only in the Oriental school of philosophy that there exists clearly the idea of different levels of thought,

of lower and higher mind. The importance of this idea is repeatedly emphasized in this book, and has been ably dealt with in the preface to the second edition of Ouspensky's *New Model of the Universe.*

The human mind can rise to a level almost inconceivable for us, and we can see the results of the work of higher minds, those most accessible to us, in the Gospels, and then in Eastern Scriptures: in the Upanishads, in the Mahabharata; in works of art, such as the Great Sphinx at Gizeh, and in other memorials, though they are few in literature and art. The true valuation of the meaning of these and similar memorials, and the realization of the difference between them and others which have been created by ordinary man, or even by a genius, needs experience, knowledge, and a special training of the mind and perception and, perhaps, special faculties not possessed by everyone.

The existence or non-existence of higher levels of consciousness and of higher levels of thought cannot be proved. They may be experienced, or some quality in the products of higher thought may strike a man or woman as being of a kind that does not exist in ordinary literature. To those who have faith in the intellect alone as a guide to truth, such an assertion as this will have little meaning. For those who feel otherwise it may have some significance.

Having seen how Western philosophers have attempted to solve the riddle of the interaction of mind and body, we will now turn our attention to the East. The first of the systems of philosophy to be examined will be the Indian *Vedânta.* But at this point our method of procedure must change. Instead of following science as far as it can take us and then attempting to extend our knowledge by means of philosophy, we shall begin our journey again from the starting-point of Eastern philosophy. This change in technique is necessary if for no other reason than that the Vedânta is a complete, self-contained, and self-consistent system of knowledge, which, if it is to be rightly understood, must be studied as a whole. The Vedânta is not only a philosophy; it is also a science, a religion, and a treatise on psychology.

CHAPTER 10

THE VEDÂNTA

THE word *Veda* literally means superior knowledge. It is applied in India to certain extremely ancient books considered to be direct revelations from God, books that embody truths that could not have been reached by any ordinary human mind. Hindu scholars state that humanity owes these works to the *rishis*, men who have attained higher levels of consciousness and have passed on the knowledge so gained to their disciples.

Vedic literature consists of four main divisions: the *Rig-Veda*, the *Yajur-Veda*, the *Sama-Veda*, and the *Atharva-Veda*, each of these being further subdivided into three portions, the first, the original text, the second, texts dealing with ritual, and the third, the *Upanishads*, dealing with philosophy. It is believed by scholars that the *Rig-Vedas* are the most ancient records of the religious sentiment of mankind, and quite apart from their intrinsic merit they are of immense historical interest.

It is with the Upanishads (the basis of Indian philosophy) that we are chiefly concerned. The word *upanishad* is derived from three Sanscrit words meaning 'sitting down near', and denotes the sitting down at the feet of a teacher. The Upanishads are also known collectively as the *Vedânta*, or literally, the 'End of the Vedas', either because they were attached to the end of the Vedas, or because they represent the conclusion arrived at by the Vedas.

The central theme of the Upanishads is 'the search for unity' in the midst of diversity.

What is that, by knowing which, everything in the universe is known? The answer is to be found in the conception of God, or Brahman, as the Ultimate Cause of the universe: Since the effect is not different from the cause, it is possible to know the universe by knowing Brahman, as by knowing one lump of clay, all that is made of clay is also known; for the modification is but an effort of speech, a name, and the only reality is the clay. (SWAMI MADHAVANANDA)

In addition to the original Vedânta we have many commentaries made on it by different philosophers, and in this chapter we shall deal principally with the commentaries made by the sage Shankara. It must be borne in mind that, from time immemorial, Indian thinkers have fully recognized the fact that every man differs in what he has the capacity to think about and perceive, and that the same truths can be given in a variety of ways, suited to different stages in intellectual development, and to different tastes and aptitudes. The Vedânta is an attempt to sum up the whole of human knowledge and it makes use of the whole of human experience; at one time, it is a religion, at another, a philosophy, and at another a science. Its aim is the solution of the mystery of existence. The Upanishads came from many different teachers and did not give an entirely consistent and coherent view of the universe. It was Shankara's aim to reduce the whole of the Upanishads to a single consistent system, free from all contradictions. To him, the principle of non-contradiction (*abadha*) was the test of truth. That which is true does not contradict itself. Dreams are contradicted by waking experience, which in turn is contradicted by the direct apprehension of truth in higher states of consciousness. This is the highest knowledge available to man, and there is nothing that can contradict it. It is beyond logical proof, which applies only to the empirical world, and can be regarded as a working tool of the mind that is serviceable within a limited range of experience. Shankara, like Bergson, regarded the intellect as an instrument that has a limited and an eminently practical utility. It is like the police constable's bull's-eye lantern that concentrates illumination on one particular spot, so that we can take note of a particular object, which at that moment has a particular significance for us. For the practical purposes of living the intellect is an excellent contrivance, but as a means of revealing 'the whole' it is as useless as is the constable's bull's-eye lantern in revealing the world.

In dealing with any contradictions that seemed to exist in the

Upanishads' view of the universe, Shankara generally steered between two extremes; for example, he denied the Sunyavada view that there existed no permanent self, but only a series of impermanent mental states, and stated that the self was both known and unknown. We know that the self exists, but we do not know what it is. Nor can we hope to know the self by means of thought, since thought is but a part of that flux of states belonging to the region of the non-self. The self can never be a creature of the natural world, for there would not be any natural world were not the principle of the self presupposed. Rather can we think of the self as

undifferenced consciousness alone which is unaffected even when the body is reduced to ashes and the mind perishes. (RADHA-KRISHNAN)

This description of the true self in terms of consciousness, and the clear distinction Shankara draws between thought and consciousness, is of great interest. Western psychological systems as a whole fail to differentiate between thought and consciousness, and in identifying the true Self with consciousness, the Vedântist philosophy is in harmony with knowledge gained in higher states. However much Eastern and Western thought may differ on lower levels, such differences entirely disappear on higher levels of consciousness. That this is so is clearly shown by a comparison of the Vedânta philosophy with the writings of Western mystics.

And because the seeker after the highest truth must be able to command perfect concentration, or 'one-pointedness of mind' (*ekagrata*), the aid of *yoga* is enlisted as a means to that end. *Yoga* (mind control) and *vichara* (inquiry) are complementary, each reinforcing and amplifying the other. The Eastern philosopher in his search for truth takes a different path from that followed by his Western colleague. Whilst the intellect is sufficient for ordinary purposes, the higher truths, he would say, can only be apprehended by him who prepares himself carefully for their reception. The philosopher must, therefore, polish the mirror within him, in order that its surface may be able to reflect the truth without distortion.

Philosophy in the East is a quest to which a man dedicates his whole life, for knowledge is not only empirical but also spiritual, and for its apprehension much that a man has already learnt must be unlearnt. Until he has been able to get rid of the *upadhis*, or finite categories in relationships that belong to what is conditioned, he will not be able to pass on to the higher branches of his study. 'Knowledge', says the *Bhagavad Gita*, 'is enveloped in nescience, and thereby mortals are deluded.'

But it is impossible to remove this veil of nescience all at once. The limitations imposed on the seeker after knowledge by the lower part of his nature can only be got rid of by a gradual course of development. Just as in the study of nature it is necessary to proceed step by step, beginning with experience and then rising gradually from sensations to the establishment of principles and the classifying of phenomena, so in the attainment of spiritual knowledge is it necessary to rise by slow degrees from the perception of what seem to be the accidental relationships of the finite to a grasp of the entire universe as a harmonious whole. The final step of all is, as the Advaita (non-dualistic) Vedânta puts it, to rise still higher and reach the stage of complete Self-realization

> Pin your faith to natural knowledge, stumble through the darkness of the blind; pin your faith to supernatural knowledge, stumble through a darkness deeper still. Natural knowledge brings one result, supernatural knowledge another. We have heard it from the wise, who have clearly explained it. They that know and can distinguish between natural knowledge and supernatural knowledge shall, by the first, cross the perishable in safety; shall, by passing beyond the second, attain immortal life. (Upanishads)

This does not mean that the Indian philosopher neglects pure reasoning in his effort to reach higher truth; it means that he believes that the intellect alone can only take him a certain distance, and that in order to go further, other faculties must be developed. He draws a clear distinction between that which is necessarily true for all possible intelligences, and that which is only contingently and relatively true for us and for people like us, but is not true for all possible intelligences. And in order that he himself may be able to attain these higher truths, he employs definite methods, such as those of Raja Yoga.

The life of Shankara, the exponent of the Advaita system of the Vedânta, is an excellent illustration of the attitude of an Eastern philosopher to his vocation. This great thinker lived in the first quarter of the ninth century, when the Vedânta philosophy was already many hundreds of years old. He went to a Vedic school, where Govinda taught him the main principles of the Advaita system. As a young man he became a recluse, or *Sannyasin*, wandering from village to village and discussing philosophy with the teachers of other systems. Later he achieved fame as an exponent of the Advaita philosophy, which he developed by a series of commentaries on the ancient texts. He also became a religious reformer, not preaching a single exclusive method of salvation, but doing his utmost to revive and purify the various forms of Hinduism with which he came in contact. Of the diversity of his gifts there can be no doubt. He was a philosopher and a poet, a savant and a saint, a religious reformer and an adept in yoga practices.

It is possible to present the chief doctrines expounded by the Vedânta under a series of headings. The arrangement of these headings has been taken from V. J. Kirkitar's *Studies in Vedânta*.

1. There is only one Ultimate Reality, the *Brahman*, from which the Universe proceeds. It is self-existent and Alone, and not being originated is Eternal and Real. All else being the effect of causes is unreal. Before it was not, and when its form disappears, it will not be.

2. Brahman is All-Pervading. There is no object without Brahman as its substratum; divorced from Brahman an object has no existence. No object has any independent existence. Its reality is only relative and phenomenal.

3. Whilst Brahman is Immanent, it is also Transcendent, that is to say, only a part of the Brahmic sphere is represented by the visible universe.

4. Brahman is all Intelligence and all Bliss. It is not the thinker but pure thought.

5. Though Brahman is One, it has also become many by its Own will; It is thus many when viewed from the standpoint of the universe.

6. The universe is born from Brahman, that is, brought into being by the Word (Logos, Thought, and Will). It lives in Brahman and in the fullness of time is dissolved again into Brahman. Brahman is therefore that in which 'we live and move and have our being'.

The following principles in Vedânta are enunciated differently by different exponents.

7. Some maintain that the universe is the product of a power called Mâyâ in its association with Brahman. Rigorous Monists, ignoring this intermediate agency, insist that Brahman Itself is the substantial and operative cause of the universe.

8. Monists, such as Shankara, state that individual souls are identical with Brahman; others like Ramanuja admit the individuality of souls.

9. Brahman is not the author of Good and Evil, which are of man's making and enter the world when he violates the higher laws of his being.

10. Every embodied existence with its environment is the result of its own past – *Karma. Karma* cannot be avoided; it must be worked out to its end. The Vedânta, therefore, recognizes freedom of will by asserting that a man's happiness or misery entirely depends on his own actions, past and present. By good deeds he may even destroy evil effects which are to arise in the future, and thus accelerate progress towards the goal of perfection.

There are two verses in the Upanishads that summarize this view of *Karma* and Rebirth:

'When the body grows weak through age or disease, the Self separates itself from the limbs, as a mango, a fig, a banyan fruit separates itself from the stalk; man hastens back to birth, goes as before from birth to birth. Whatever his conduct and character in one life, he has it in his next; if good in one, he is good in another; his good *karma* makes him good, his sinful *karma* makes him sinful. Hence they say that soul is full of desire. He wills according to his desire; he acts according to his will; he reaps what he sows.'

11. Man's difficulties on earth are due to his ignorance, which encourages him to look upon his bodily existence as his real life. Because of this his actions are egoistic.

12. The Vedânta therefore lays down rules for the social, moral, and spiritual development of man. Following these rules he may eventually surrender his lower self and become merged with a higher and spiritual Self. The duties the Vedânta inculcates are not only towards his fellows, but also towards every living creature,

since they are all parts of the whole. These duties must be performed
without attachment or hope of reward, either present or future.

13. The *Karma* that results from this method of living leads eventually to the purification of the heart and to the acquisition of
higher powers that make it possible for a man to realize that the
individual self is not merely related to Brahman, but is identical
with It.

14. True salvation comes with complete realization of this identity
of the higher Self with Brahman.

15. Until this higher state of spiritual perfection is attained, until
the sense of 'I' and 'Thou' and 'Mine' and 'Thine' has completely
disappeared, a man has no right to deny the reality of the universe.
Until then he is bound to recognize the three-fold distinction of God,
Man, and Universe. For ordinary man the world is not illusory, nor
is the relation in which he stands to it an illusion. It is only when
the sense of the individual and personal 'ego' has become completely extinct and when the great truth *Tat-twam-Asi* ('Thou art
the that') has been fully experienced that the true character of the
Supreme Self and the identity of the individual self with that Self
are realized. Then the illusory nature of the world as a self-subsisting entity is evident.

The Vedânta is both a philosophy and a religion, for to the
Eastern there is no real division between the two. The apprehension of divine truth necessitates the living of it to the utmost
of one's ability. That which is known theoretically only still
remains unknown. Theory and practice are mutual adjuvants
to full understanding. The Vedânta prescribes for the student
certain rules of conduct that will eventually lead to his knowing
and living in a larger and larger Self, to the utter extinction
finally of his lower individual self. Brahman, the one Reality, is
consciousness and Being. Associated with his own power *Mâyâ*,
Brahman modifies itself into all the individual existences of
which the world consists; it is broken up, as it were, into a
multiplicity of intellectual and sentient principles (*Jîvas*, or
individual souls). What is real and eternal in each *Jîva* is only
the universal Brahman, but the *Jîva* blindly identifies itself
with the body and the sense organs, and looks for its true self
there. If a man remains in this state, oblivious of his higher
nature, he is bound to a succession of embodied existences. The

round of births and deaths ceases only when the *Jîva* realizes fully its identity with Brahman.

The various philosophers who have made commentaries on the Vedânta have offered slightly different explanations of the derivation of the many in the universe from the One, and all accept these different texts as being necessary for people of different capacity. Shankara states that the explanations that he gives in his commentaries may be either true or only metaphorical. His personal opinion is that they are metaphorical, for only by the use of metaphor can spiritual truths be expressed.

The word *Mâyâ* is often misunderstood by readers of Eastern philosophy. It is generally taken simply to imply that which is illusory – not real. But Shankara himself has described it as

The power of the Lord from which the world springs. The divine power in which names and forms (that is, all finite existences) lie uninvolved, and which we assume to be the antecedent condition of that state of the world in which names and forms are evolved.

For all practical purposes the universe that has come into being through *Mâyâ* is real.

The problem that has exercised the minds of dualistic philosophers, the interaction of body and mind, does not cause any difficulty here. According to the Sankhya philosophy, the concept *Prakriti* covers all that is mental as well as all that is physical. Mental and physical events are both abstractions if they are taken as entirely separate and distinct from each other. They do not constitute two distinct entities but two cooperating wholes within one whole, the *Prakriti*. The relation between body and mind and between the body and its physico-chemical substratum is not one of interaction or parallelism, but of co-operation. Their operations within a single sphere are self-determining and at the same time other-determining. The duality between the physical and the physiological, and the physiological and the mental, and the mental and the conscious is only an apparent duality, for there is a continuity of process between each and the other.

It is interesting to note that the Vedantist philosopher, like Descartes, starts from the existence of the self as being self-

proven. There is no need for any external authority to define
what is even more immediate to a man than is his body. Nor is
any effort required for knowing this so-called self. It is needed
only for removing the error of identifying the true Self with
that which the Vedânta asserts to be the not-self. In the early
stages of his development a man views himself and the object
world as self-subsisting and independent entities, marked off by
sharp and clearly defined outlines. Every event appears to him
to be the effect of some antecedent cause. All objects appear
as occupying space, all events as occurring in time. This is an
illusion due to the limitations of ordinary thinking. In a further
stage of development he finds that these relations of cause and
effect, space and time, are relations which his mind itself has
created for its own purposes and that they are true only for
the mind. They are termed phenomena, or dependent realities,
by Eastern and Western idealists alike.

It has been pointed out that the Vedânta is eminently practical, and does not condemn these views as illusory in the sense
that they have no utility for everyday purposes. A man must
live his life and discharge his obligations to his fellows and for
such purposes these ideas are sufficient. 'All this universe', says
Shankara, 'is for a man's edification and to help him to attain
Self-realization.' But he must go further than these ideas if he
is to reach his goal. There are two paths, *pravritti* and *nivritti*,
the one leading to the external world and the other to Self-
knowledge; the one providing the worldly experience necessary
for a useful life, the other leading to philosophical and spiritual
enlightenment.

Death said: God made the sense turn outward, man therefore
looks outward, not into himself. Now and again a daring soul desiring immortality has looked back and found himself. (*Upanishads*)

Only when in the later stages of development the path of
nivritti is trodden, will the inconsistencies that his mind has
made for him disappear. Then does a man cease to identify
himself with the ever-changing products of Nature (*Prakriti*),
and with the five sense organs (including the organ of ordinary
thinking), which instead of being the true or divine sense are

only its instruments. Only when he finally knows that reality is the Supreme Self, or Brahman, and that the world has no independent existence apart from this, do the differentiations that his mind has made disappear. That is what the Vedântist describes as 'The return into identity from difference'.

According to the Sankhya philosophy, the creative force of Nature is made up of three *gunas*, or qualities.* When this creative force is lying dormant, these three principles or qualities are in equilibrium. When *Purusha* (spirit) acts on them, this equilibrium is disturbed, and from the disturbance arises all the diverse phenomena of Nature (*Prakriti*). The three principles, or *gunas*, are called respectively *Rajas*, *Tamas*, and *Sattva*, and to each is attached a certain distinctive quality. *Rajas* is the restless urgent principle, *Tamas* the heavy, inert, and enveloping, and *Sattva* the light and illuminating. All, subservient to spirit, run like three twisted cords through the whole of Nature. The diversity of Nature is due to one quality predominating over another, but at the same time, the predominant quality is dependent on the other two, and cannot act alone. The Sankhya philosophy explains this contrariety of properties as follows:

If the only operating quality were *Rajas*, the universe would be an increasing round of activity, so nature provides against this by the restraining influence of *Tamas*. Again, if there were no enlightening agency in the shape of *Sattva*, nature would be nothing better than a mass of blind forces acting at haphazard.

In the chapter on the endocrine glands, attention was called to this idea of three principles entering into every phenomenon. Physiology provides many examples of actions that are not direct, but occur through some intermediary. Endocrinology is particularly rich in such examples, and repeatedly we find the pituitary acting in the role of *Sattva*, the enlightening agent that regulates and controls the action of a gland (*Rajas*) on the passive structure of the body (*Tamas*). Similar examples can be found in the physiology of blood-coagulation, of digestive processes, and of the oxygenation of the blood. It may be argued, of course, that this is mere coincidence, and that there is no

*The idea of the triad appears also in certain Western philosophies, notably in that of Hegel.

correspondence between these physiological triads and those of the Sankhya philosophy. It must be remembered, however, that there are other ideas in the ancient Sankhya philosophy that are now accepted by certain Western thinkers, for example, the idea that time and space exist only in the mind, and are not attributes of reality. It is quite possible, therefore, that in the concept of the three *gunas* there exists the germ of some principle that Western thought has not yet recognized.

Mind, according to the Vedânta, is material, and therefore is itself the result of the action of the three *gunas*. After describing the hindrances to thought in the untrained mind, the Yoga Sutras of Patañjali continue as follows:

Mind stuff has three aspects (*gunas*), as appears from the fact that it has a disposition to vividness, to activity, and to inertia. The *Sattva* of the mind (vividness) when commingled with *Rajas* and *Tamas* acquires a fondness for supremacy and for objects-of-sense; while the very same *Sattva* when pervaded with *Tamas* tends towards demerit and non-perception, and passion, and towards a failure of its own rightful supremacy; and the very same *Sattva* – when the covering of error has dwindled away and it is illuminated and but faintly pervaded with *Rajas* – tends towards merit and knowledge and passionlessness and its own rightful supremacy.

In relation to the mind, *Rajas* acts as a distracting force, and *Tamas* as inertia. Both of these are obstacles to meditation, and it is only when the illuminating quality of *Sattva* is supreme that the mind can become an instrument for the acquisition of higher knowledge. Because the untrained mind is always subject to distractions, not only from without but even more so from within, it must be taught restraint. This is one of the subjects discussed by Arjuna and Krishna in that immortal work, the *Bhagavad Gita*.

The mind [says Arjuna] is fickle, boisterous, strong, and obstinate, and I think that to restrain it is as difficult as to restrain the wind.

Krishna replies that the mind may be restrained by 'practice and indifference to worldly objects'. He goes on to say that devotion cannot be attained without self-restraint, but that the man who has self-restraint and works to achieve devotion may

succeed in acquiring it. He gives no further explanation of what
is meant by 'practice and indifference to worldly objects'. For
this information we have to go to the Yoga Sutras of Patañjali,
where Yoga is defined as 'the restraint of the movements of the
mind', and practice as 'the effort for keeping it steady'. Patañjali also explains what is meant by the second requisite mentioned by Krishna, 'indifference to worldly objects'. This, says
Patañjali, 'is the consciousness of having subdued desires for
objects visible, and those also which are only heard of'. Instructions are then given in the Yoga Sutras for the attainment of this
state of non-attachment.

The religion, the culture, and even the social institutions of
the two hundred and fifty million people who call themselves
Hindus is based on the Vedas. The knowledge on which these
are based has been handed down orally together with the
Upanishads, in which philosophical truths are often presented
in story form. The Upanishads, many of which are of extraordinary beauty, are of the greatest interest, since they present
in a manner that is easy to understand the quintessence of the
wisdom of the Vedas. They are, in fact, philosophical poems.
As an illustration may be given the Maitri Upanishad, translated by J. G. Bennett. The story concerns a certain King Brihadratha, who 'having established his son in the sovereignty, and
reflecting on the transiency of this body, ceased to value the
things of this world and went forth into the forest', in search of
understanding. There, living the life of an ascetic, he meets a
teacher, Shakayanya, of whom he asks divine knowledge.
Shakayanya, after offering him other gifts, finally agrees to give
him that for which he has asked, knowledge of what is the
Self.

Maitri Upanishad: Second Prapathaka.
1. Then the blessed Shakayanya, well pleased, addressed the king
and said, 'Great King, Brihadratha, glory of thy race, soon indeed
shalt thou attain to knowledge of the Self and reach the final goal.
This Self which thou seekest is verily thine own.'
'What Self is that, Lord?'
2. He answered: 'Thou must go aloft out of the darkness of thy
present state into that which breathes without breathing, that

which, though motionless, reaches all worlds. There only wilt thou find the Self.

'For thus saith the blessed Maitri, "That Serene One who is beyond the senses, dwells in the highest consciousness and is united with the truth. That is the Self, that is the Immortal, the Fearless, that is Brahman!"

3. 'Now indeed, O king, this is divine knowledge, the knowledge contained in all the Upanishads, revealed to us by our blessed teacher, Maitri. To thee will I relate it.'

The Valakhilyas verily had put away all evil deeds. With vigorous effort they lived the holy life. They went to Prajapati Kratu and said: 'Lord, this body is like a cart, without intelligence. To what Being, higher than the senses, belongs the power whereby this body has become united with mind? Who is the driver? What thou knowest, O Lord, reveal to us.'

Prajapati answered:

4. 'It is from above and not from below, that this body is endowed with intelligence. There is that Self, above the senses, above the mind, pure, clean, tranquil, unbreathing, selfless, endless, undecaying, eternal, firm, and everlasting. He abides in his own greatness. By him this body is endowed with mind. Thus is it that the driver stands upon the cart.'

Then they said:

'Lord if that Highest Being is beyond our joy and suffering, what is the body and what is mind to Him? How canst thou say that, for His Sake, mind becomes the driver?'

He answered:

5. 'Truly, that subtle, intangible, invisible One pervades the body with but a small part of Himself, and that small part is not conscious of the whole, even as a sleeper, before he awakens, knows not the waking state.

'Now indeed, that which each man calls himself, is merely that small part of man which has the marks of desire, restless striving, and self-conceit: this they call individuality. And yet this mind must take possession of the body, in other words, this mind must be its driver.'

Then they said:

'But Lord, if this mind, which is to be the driver of this body, is truly a part of that passionless Being, how does it not know its Master?'

He replied:

6. 'That Highest Being is differentiated by stages into the mindless

body, the five bodily powers, the human personality, and the psychic functions.

'In the last stage, he pierces the opening of the senses, he goes forth and enjoys the external world. Through the senses, he perceives external objects, his reins are the organs of perception, his horses the organs of action. This body is the cart and the driver is the mind. The whip is the formation of decision. Thus driven, the body performs its duty, like the wheel controlled by the potter. Thus comes this body into the possession of consciousness. Thus, indeed, mind becomes the driver.

7. 'Verily, the Self – so we are told – is not reached by actions bright or dark, is not touched by this return to body after body here on earth. Unmanifest, subtle, unknowable, incomprehensible, free from self. He abides yet acts not. Pure and stainless, He abides in Himself. Hidden by the veil of the *gunas*, He remains firm. Yea, He remains firm!'

Maitri Upanishad: Third Prapathaka.

1. Then they said, 'Lord, if thou declarest thus the greatness of this Self, then what is that other which is also known as self. Who is he that, reaping the bright and dark fruits of action, is born again, better or worse, his course upward or downward, by dualism led astray?'

2. Prajapati replied:

'There is another indeed called the material essence, which suffers the good and evil consequences of actions bright and dark. This is he whose course is upward or downward, by dualism led astray.

'There are five subtle substances which are called by the name of matter. Now the combination of these is said to be the body, the active principle of which is called the material essence.

'This essence, like a drop of water on a lotus leaf, is controlled by the three *gunas*, the forces of nature. Thus controlled, he is confused, and being confused, he knows not the Great Self, the Master who abides within. Carried along by the stream of *gunas*, unsteady, wavering, bewildered, full of desire, distracted, this material essence falls into the state of self-conceit. Then, when he thinks: "This is I", and "That is mine", he binds himself with himself, as a bird is bound with a snare.

'And so it comes about that, suffering the bright or dark fruits of actions, he is born again better or worse, his course upward or downward, by dualism led astray.'

Maitri Upanishad: Fourth Prapathaka.

1. Then indeed those Valakhilyas, with passions subdued, filled with wonder, drew near and said 'Lord, adoration be to thee! Instruct us further. Thou art our way of escape. There is no other.

'What is the means by which this material essence may be freed from its state of separation and attain to union with the Self?'

Then he said to them:

2. 'It has been said in the scriptures, "Like the waves in great rivers, what that material essence has once done cannot be turned back. It is borne on towards death irresistibly, like the tides of the sea. It is bound like a cripple, by the bonds of good and evil deeds. It is bereft of liberty like a prisoner in his cell, filled with fear like one before a judge. Intoxicated is it with delusion, like one drunk with wine, driven hither and thither like one in the power of an enemy. Bitten is it by external objects, like one bitten by a great snake. It is like one in great darkness, the darkness of passion. Deluded is it, like one deceived by enchantment or by visions in a dream. Its reality is unsubstantial, like the pith of a banyan tree. Its dress is ever changing, like that of an actor. Falsely fair is it, like a painted scene."

'Again it is written: "Objects of sound and touch and sight are valueless, yet valuing them, the material essence becomes attached, and through attachment, remembers not the highest state."

3. 'The remedy for the material essence is this: the acquisition of knowledge through the scriptures and devotion to his rightful duty. Devotion to his necessary duties, and the requirements of his state in holy life: this is the rule of right action. All other rules are subsidiary to this. By following this rule, his tendency is upwards, otherwise he can only sink to lower levels still. The way of right action is taught in the scriptures. Neglect of right action cannot lead to progress in the holy life. It is sometimes said that great efforts can relieve a man of duty. That is not right. And yet without great efforts, there is no success in gaining knowledge of the Self, nor any perfection of work. For thus has it been said:

> "Goodness is won by great effort,
> Discrimination is won by goodness,
> From discrimination is the Self attained,
> Attaining Whom, there is no further birth." '

Maitri Upanishad: Sixth Prapathaka.
Shakayanya then revealed to Brihadratha the origin of the world

and the union of the Self with Brahman, the supreme, the immortal Soul of the world.

Having spoken these things, his thoughts collected, Shakayanya did obeisance to him, and said, 'By this Brahma-knowledge, O King, did the sons of Prajapati ascend the path of Brahman.

'This deepest mystery should not be taught save to a son or to a pupil, not to one who has not a tranquil mind. Nevertheless, it may be taught to a devoted pupil who is properly prepared.

'Let him seek conditions which will sustain the fire of his ardour. Let him abide in goodness, intent upon the Truth, speaking the Truth, meditating upon the Truth, worshipping the Truth. Thus shall he continue and he will verily attain the true Brahman, with whom uniting he becomes other. So he gains the reward of freedom from all bonds, he is liberated from expectation, from fear, and from desire. He attains the imperishable, immeasurable bliss and abides therein.'

In this great religious poem is to be found the essence of the Vedânta teaching.

CHAPTER II

YOGA

THE Sankhya philosophy has something in common with the philosophies of Kant and Hegel. Kant, like the Sankhya philosophy, asserts that through our sense organs alone we cannot perceive the nature of things in themselves, but only the properties that we have projected on to them. By means of sensuous perception and inference we shall never stand face to face with reality, and any hope that with a little more knowledge the intervening veil will be torn aside is futile. All that we shall gain from more knowledge is a better acquaintance with the veil and not with that which it conceals.

But where Eastern differs from Western Idealism is that Eastern Idealism maintains that although sensuous perception can take us no further, there are other faculties that can. As these faculties do not work automatically in a man, they must be developed by effort, practice, and devotion.

It is perhaps incorrect to state categorically that all Western philosophies deny that there are any means of going further along the path to truth than sensuous perception permits us. Kant points out that man is an object in the universe; and consequently he himself is a phenomenon behind which stands a noumenon. As well as possessing an empirical self, he also possesses a transcendental self. Man's empirical self is a chaos of wishes, desires, and actions that are as completely predetermined as are the movements of matter in the physical world. His transcendental self belongs, however, to the noumenal world, and it is this Self that is capable of knowing the real. Kant identifies the transcendental self with the moral self and states that when we act in accordance with the laws of our moral being, we can escape from the limitations of the senses. He makes no attempt to lay down precisely what are the moral laws that we must obey if we are to reach the transcendental self, demanding only that we should act in accordance with certain general principles which we intuitively recognize as being morally binding. These general principles are of a kind that all people, irrespective of creed, accept as moral. But although the principles are recognized intuitively they are never opposed to reason. Kant asserts that wrong conduct is self-contradictory and so can never become universal without being stultified. If everyone were to lie, nobody would believe anybody else, so that lying would become useless. This is the meaning of Kant's maxim: 'Act only according to that maxim which you can at the same time will to be a universal law.'

So far Kant and the Vedântist philosopher see eye to eye. In order to apprehend higher truth beyond the range of sensuous perception, man must act in conformity with moral values that he recognizes intuitively. There exists, moreover, a parallel between Kant's form of intuition and his categories of understanding, and the Eastern philosopher's *Savitarka* and *Savichara*. Intuition apprehends *directly* and therefore requires only exposition; our ordinary understanding of the universe comes indirectly and must be followed by inference. The yogi makes use of the method of direct apprehension, or what Guénon calls intellectual intuition.

No Western philosopher can tell us how the transcendental self that apprehends directly can be developed. Here the Vedântist philosopher is far more explicit, and by referring us to the ancient system of mind-control known as *yoga* indicates the path to higher levels of thought and to knowledge that lies beyond the range of sensuous perception.

The word 'yoga' having two recognized Sanskrit roots, can have two possible meanings, one 'to meditate', and the other 'to join'. In the latter sense it is similar to the English word 'yoke', implying a joining of the unenlightened nature of man to the enlightened and divine part of himself, so that the higher guides and transmutes the lower. The word 'yoga' also signifies a disciplining of the mind by mental concentration. Patañjali, in his aphorisms, believed to have been written in the second or third century before Christ, defines yoga as 'the restricting

of the fluctuations of the mind-stuff'. When the mind is so controlled 'the seer abideth in himself'. When this control is lack-
ing the self identifies itself with the interminable flux of the
mind, so that instead of having a spiritual insight into the true
nature of existence, there exist only mental obscuration and
ignorance. The whole aim of yoga is to get rid of this ignorance,
and to make direct contacts with what yogis and buddhists call
right knowledge.

Yoga is of immense age. Its origin in India is generally
belived to be contemporary with the arrival of the Aryan conquerors, but some authorities are of the opinion that it existed
in the pre-Aryan Age. The Tamil-speaking Dravidians, the
Aryans' predecessors, have always asserted that they, the indi-
genous people of India, possessed knowledge of yoga and taught
it to their conquerors. Recent excavations in Sind and the Pun-
jab have unearthed evidence that seems to corroborate this
statement. Amongst other images found have been those of a
human form seated in the *asana* which is characteristic of the
Buddha, and apparently representing Siva, 'Lord of Beasts,
Prince of Yogis'. Across the top of the image runs a script
which, till now, no one has deciphered. The Dravidian-speaking
peoples have always claimed that Siva was their god and that he
taught their fathers yoga practices.

Archaeologists believe that human culture spread from three
great sources – the Egyptian, the Mesopotamian, and the culture
of the Valley of the Indus. The last-named proved to be the
most successful since it survived longest. Sir John Marshall,
commenting on recent Indian excavations, remarked that, although in the lowest levels finds were abundant, no weapons or
city walls were unearthed in the upper levels of later ages with
the exception of a few small spear-points more suited for deco-
ration than for use. Gerald Heard discusses the significance of
these discoveries in his book *The Sources of Civilization*, and
attempts to find an answer to the question how cities without
defensive walls and arms could have survived for such a long
period. He suggests that it was due to the existence of a high
form of culture in which yoga practices played a large part.

To the Indian philosopher truth is not only a fact, but is also

a value, and the purpose of the yogi is, therefore, both to discover truth and to practise it in living. An intellectual assent to
a doctrine is not enough; as the result of the discovery of truth
a new life must be inaugurated. Hence, the personal discipline
to which the Eastern philosopher willingly submits himself.
This discipline comprises what are known as the eight *Angas*
of yoga, self-restraint, observance, posture, regulation of breathing, withdrawal of the senses, steadying of the mind, meditation,
and contemplation. The aim of all these is to assist the disciple
to ascend from the restricted and low level of consciousness of
ordinary existence to the larger vision of the yogi. Yoga is,
therefore, a practical method for developing in a man many
capacities that he does not ordinarily possess.

For many thousands of years the sages of India have known
that by right training and effort a man can gain extraordinary
control over his body and mind. Yoga is eminently 'practical',
but it must be remembered that it is only this when taught by
a master or *guru*. The numerous books on 'Yoga' that have
swept in a fashionable flood through the drawing-rooms of
England and America are, no doubt, interesting, but they are
useless. Even translations of authentic texts, like the Yoga Sutras
of Patañjali, are useless, for no one, unaided by a teacher, can
understand or put into practice what he reads there. The books
themselves are written in a manner that strongly suggests that
they are commentaries, or note-books, which are only meant to
recall to a student's mind what he has already learnt from his
teacher. They supplement, and do not stand in the place of the
teacher.

Yoga acts on the liberal principle that men of different nature
can best achieve their object by concentrating on different
aspects of yoga. Thus men of deep religious feeling will find in
Bhakti-yoga (or the yoga of right religious action) the best
approach to the subject. *Karma-yoga*, or the yoga of right
action, is suited to those who have not retired from the world,
and *Jñana-yoga* (yoga of knowledge) is for men of wide education. And because control of the body is an essential step to
control of the mind, *Hatha-yoga* (the yoga of power over the
body) must be an accessory to the study of other aspects of

yoga. Finally there is *Raja-yoga*, or the yoga of the development of consciousness, which stands in the same position relative to the mind as Hatha-yoga does to the body. All these yogas are not separate studies, but different aspects of the same subject, which permit of a variety of approaches for different types of men.

It is with Hatha-yoga, or the yoga of body control, that the Western world is best acquainted. This is due to the fact that the outward manifestations of Hatha-yoga are obvious, whereas changes in consciousness are not. For this reason popular writers have tended to create the impression that yoga is little else than a method of acquiring bodily tricks. It must be remembered, however, that the attainment of control over the body is only a *means to an end*, and not an end in itself. A healthy and well-regulated body is an aid to the attainment of a controlled mind and of a higher level of consciousness. For this reason the body has to be brought under the discipline of yoga.

Having indicated the general character of yoga we can now consider separately its various branches.

Hatha-yoga. Not only must the body be brought into a state of health, but it must be taught to do its work expeditiously and with the least possible consumption of energy. In every machine there exists a ratio between its expenditure of energy and the work that it performs, and although physiologists have shown that the body, judged on this basis, is an immeasurably more efficient machine than the best petrol engine, it nevertheless wastes a great deal of its energy. One of the purposes of Hatha-yoga is to reduce this wastage to a minimum, so that more energy can be directed to the attainment of higher states of consciousness. By special methods control can be exercised not only over movements which are normally under the dominance of the will, but also over involuntary activities, such as respiration, digestion, and the circulation. Control over the muscles is assisted by the adoption of certain postures (the *asanas*). (Among these *asanas* is the well-known sitting posture assumed by the Buddha, in which each foot is placed on the opposite knee, heels upwards.) Many of the *asanas* are extremely difficult and to be able to assume them for an indefinite time, not only without physical strain, but with every muscle relaxed, is beyond the power of an ordinary man.

Because of the close links that exist between the outward posture and the inner state, different *asanas* may be assumed for the carrying out of different mental exercises. It is well known, for instance, that the attitude usually adopted for prayer induces an inner feeling of reverence and worship. So also are other *asanas* suited to the different yoga mental practices.

Pranayama is the control of the breathing, but *prana*, to the yogi, signifies more than the breath. *Prana* is the vital force that pervades the whole body, and is the mainstay of every form of activity. It is also the common factor behind the function of the five senses and of what are known as the five motor organs. He who gains control over *prana*, at the same time gains control over all organs of automatic action.

Hatha-yoga also concerns itself with the overcoming of pain, and popular literature is full of statements about the ability of yogis to submit to pain that no other person could tolerate. Some of these statements, however, really refer to fakirs, who are using the control they have obtained for other purposes than those of the yogi, and sometimes only as a means of livelihood. Yogis have very little in common with fakirs. Well-authenticated cases are on record of masters of Hatha-yoga who have gained such control over vital processes that they have been able to pass into a state of suspended animation resembling that of a hibernating animal. A famous instance of this was Saruhu Haridas, who is recorded to have been buried for four months under the supervision of the Maharajah of Lahore, early in the last century, and to have been disinterred alive. The yogi was sealed in a chest by the Maharajah, then buried, and barley seeds sown over his grave. The grave was enclosed by a wall, and guarded night and day by sentries. On the day of interment the yogi's face was shaved, and it is reported that when disinterred his face was still smooth, indicating that growth had been suspended. It is interesting to recall that the pituitary gland is believed to exercise control over the phenomenon of hibernation. Feats like this resulting from the mastery of Hatha-yoga are of the greatest interest to physiologists, but when divorced from spiritual ends, may, as Patañjali points out, become impediments rather than aids to progress.

Karma-Yoga, or the Yoga of Right Action. This is a necessary adjunct to every other kind of yoga, but is of special importance to the man who has not become a recluse, but has remained in the world of affairs. In the *Bhagavad Gita*, when Arjuna is in a state of perplexity not knowing what he should do, and forced by circumstances to take part in a battle that seemed to him useless and stupid, he seeks Krishna's help. He describes himself as bewildered and not knowing whether to fight or to withdraw. He realizes that only by renunciation of the world can the highest level of living be attained, and he is deeply concerned because, at that moment, he is on the eve of leading his army into battle. Krishna agrees that the contemplative life is the highest, and describes the attitude of the seer.

With the mind concentrated by yoga, and with an attitude of evenness towards all things, he beholds himself in all beings, and all beings in himself. Alike in pleasure and in pain, established in the Self, regarding a clod of earth, a stone, or gold alike, the same to the loved and to the unloved, steady, the same to censure and praise, to honour and disgrace, and to friend and foe, relinquishing all undertakings, – such a person is said to have transcended the *gunas*.

But as Krishna explains, Arjuna has not relinquished the world; he is the captain of the hosts for whose leadership in battle he is responsible. Arjuna's present duty is to fight.

If through self-conceit you think that you will not fight, vain is this resolve; your very nature will constrain you.

Krishna points out that it is useless for a man to give up external actions until he has been able to give up the desire that is behind them. So Arjuna's proper course is to do his duty.

He who is free from the notion of egotism, whose intellect is not affected by good or evil, kills not, though (outwardly) he may kill these people, nor is he bound (by the action).

Karma-yoga is the form of yoga that, if it were available, would be most applicable to European and American conditions of life. The principles that it inculcates would not only eliminate that state of fear and anxiety in which nine out of ten of us live, but actually increase the efficiency of the active life to which we are inevitably committed.

Bhakti-Yoga. This is the yoga of the religious man, the man with a strong emotional feeling of the existence of a Divine Mind. It is the simplest of the yoga paths. A man either feels the presence of God, or he does not; no intellectual proof is possible, or demanded. If he does feel it, the emotion is linked with a desire to surrender himself to God. Because Bhakti-yoga is akin to Christianity and other religions, it is an aspect of yoga that is more intelligible to the average European. But it is the *experienced* religion of the religious mystic and not institutional religion that is akin to Bhakti-yoga. Bhakti-yoga, like other forms of yoga, includes methods of concentration, meditation, and contemplation, but the object on which the devotee in this case concentrates is 'God', and not the 'Self'.

Patañjali, although he himself did not believe in a personal God, acknowledges the great value of Bhakti-yoga to those who formulate their religious feelings in this way.

Amongst various ways of attaining yoga, one of the quickest is through complete devotion to God. God is spirit, untouched by human modifications, in whom is infinite that omniscience which in man is but a germ.

Jñana-Yoga. As Bhakti-yoga is the approach to yoga that is suited to the devout and emotional man, so is Jñana-yoga that which is suited to the scholar. Finding that by the use of logic and the perception of the five senses, it is impossible to solve the enigmas of life and of the universe, the intellectual man is inevitably brought to the realization that only by the cultivation of *new* faculties can he go further in his quest. Jñana-yoga is the gateway to a new method of apprehension, the direct apprehension that comes through meditation and contemplation. But as riches constituted the chief stumbling-block to a higher way of living to the young man of great possessions in the gospels, so does his learning often prove an obstacle to the scholar who would tread the path of Jñana-yoga. Before he can *know* more, he must *be* more and get rid of much that he has already learnt, and few people are prepared to make the particular form of sacrifice that this implies.

Raja-Yoga. This yoga has the same relationship to the mind that Hatha-yoga has to the body. As Hatha-yoga establishes control over the body, eliminates unnecessary activities, and increases bodily efficiency to its utmost, so does Raja-yoga control the mind, still what Patañjali calls its 'fluctuations', and increase its capacity as an instrument of knowledge. From the point of view of Raja-yoga, the mind is an inner mirror that reflects truth, but because it is darkened by nescience, the truth is inevitably distorted. Only by eradicating wrong ideas, false divisions and classifications, and by stilling the fluctuations that disturb its tranquillity, can a true image be reflected in the mirror of consciousness. First a man must see the distortion in the mirror, and then by the methods prescribed by Raja-yoga, set the mirror in order so that it may be capable of giving a true picture of reality.

Raja-yoga is chiefly concerned with consciousness. In the ordinary state the mind is lost in confused thought and feeling. It is a welter of disconnected thoughts, fantasies, broken recollections, disjointed phrases, even single words and images. The noise of this inner traffic is as unceasing as the noise heard through a window that opens on some busy thoroughfare. And much of the traffic has no purpose or meaning, for the same thoughts, the same broken phrases return again and again, running along well-worn tracks. There are few silences in ordinary life. Part of the work of Raja-yoga is to stop this meaningless and unprofitable traffic of the mind, so that it may become conscious of what, at other times, it has been unaware.

Yoga [says Patañjali] is attained by the control, and ultimately the suppression at will, of all forms of thinking, and is gained by determined and sustained effort, coupled with increasing detachment and dispassion. At first it is achieved spasmodically, but in time, and with steady effort, it becomes an habitual state.

Progress in Raja-yoga is divided into various stages according to the degree of broadening that the consciousness has attained. When the disciple has reached the final stage, he sees himself not as an isolated and separate being, but as a drop in the ocean of the spirit and as a drop that in itself contains all that is in the ocean.

The eye of the sea is one thing, and the foam another; leave the foam and look with the eye of the sea.

Day and night there is the movement of foam-flecks from the sea: thou beholdest the foam, but not the sea.

There are other classifications of yoga, for example that given by Evans-Wentz in *Tibetan Yoga and Secret Doctrine*. It is not proposed to describe these alternative classifications here.

In one sense Yoga may be regarded as an applied psychology of religion, and from this ancient science have been derived many religious invocations, prayers, chants, meditations, as well as the telling of beads. Evans-Wentz states that there are reasons for believing that the training of the candidate for initiation into the ancient mysteries was largely based on yoga. So also, in his opinion, were many of the practices of the early Christian Church.

When the early Christians, both Gnostic and non-Gnostic, dwelt in the desert and mountain solitudes of Egypt and the Near East, as solitary hermits or in communities vowed to the three vows, of poverty, chastity, and obedience, they grafted into the tree of the Christian Faith a form of yoga which appears to have had sources both in the monasticism of the ancient Egyptian priests and in that of the early Zoroastrians and Hindus. Today, more so in the Latin, Greek, Coptic, Armenian, and Abyssinian, than in the Anglican or Protestant Churches, yogic practices which have had, in at least some degree, this pre-Christian origin are of prime importance. (*Tibetan Yoga and Secret Doctrine*, by W. Y. Evans-Wentz, p. 36)

In all yogas certain milestones, or steps on the path are recognized:

The first step consists of intellectual comprehension of the teachings as contained in exoteric scriptures. The second step is dependent upon gaining spiritual comprehension of the teachings; or, in other words, upon attaining yogic insight into their esoteric significance. The third step consists of glimpses of reality; and the fourth of full realization. Otherwise stated, there are the sowing of the seed, its germination, the growth, and the fruition. (ibid., p. 37)

Whether the similarities that exist between certain religious practices and those taught by yogis are explained by religious teachers having utilized the incredible ancient knowledge of yoga for the purposes of religion, or whether religious leaders re-discovered the value of these methods, it is, of course, impossible to say. It is not the explanation of the similarity, but the existence of the similarity that is of importance. Although the exact technique, and the terms that are employed, differ with different religions, the essentials remain the same. The Hindu would describe the goal of yoga as a joining of the part to the whole, the microcosm with the macrocosm, the individualized aspect; the Buddhist would describe it as meaning the merging of the drop with the ocean, and as the transcending of the *sangsara* (or the universe of phenomenal existence); the Christian and Mohammedan, as meaning union with God. The paths of the yogi and of all devout worshippers run side by side.

CHAPTER 12

HIGHER STATES OF CONSCIOUSNESS

A BOOK is the record of a journey of the author's mind through the world of ideas, and as a traveller who has climbed slowly out of a familiar valley pauses for a moment to look back along his tracks in order that he may know where he stands, so must an author, at a certain stage in his journey, orientate his thoughts by taking stock of what has gone before. If this pause is necessary in the case of a traveller who has made similar journeys before, it is still more necessary to one who undertakes it for the first time.

Medical men are inclined to eschew the company of philosophers. When Descartes drew a sharp line between matter and spirit, he at the same time drew a line between scientists and philosophers. Henceforward scientists took charge of matter and philosophers dealt as best they could with spirit. The scientists were thoroughly satisfied with what had been apportioned to them, for they regarded matter as something that was tangible and real. When examined it behaved reasonably and in accordance with laws that were intelligible to the ordinary man. Physicians, so long as they confined their attention to the body, experienced a similar satisfaction. The body was a tractable object for study. So they took it to pieces, found how each organ worked, noted the changes that occurred when it became diseased, and did their best to rectify the resulting disorder with the remedies at their disposal. What was particularly encouraging was the fact that the methods employed by the scientists and the doctors gave excellent practical results. These were of such a high order that they were sufficient to set the seal of justification upon the methods. How different from this appeared the lot of the philosopher, who could apparently produce nothing except nebulous theories, which when scrutinized by other philosophers were liable to disappear into thin air. It was with something of the indulgence shown by grown-ups to fanciful children that medical men looked at their less fortunate colleagues.

Small wonder therefore that a medical man who has wandered so far from that safe and familiar enclosure should pause for a moment in order to take stock of where he stands. The 'Self', the Absolute, the limitations of sensuous perceptions, knowledge obtained by direct perception; what has he to do with such philosophical conceptions? He is in a strange region where all the well-known landmarks are hidden under mist. Yet the journey has to be made, if for no other reason than that the enclosure in which scientists and physicians worked no longer exists. First came the discovery of the physicists that matter did not behave as they had a right to expect it to behave. Within a short lapse of time it had become 'a kink in time-space', 'an electron mush', 'a wave of probability undulating into nothingness', 'a collection of charges of electricity, which are not charging in anything', 'a system of spatio-temporal events whose qualities are exclusively mathematical' (C. E. M. Joad). Then in the medical world came the discovery that man was more than a collection of organs packed up in a skin wrapping, that disorders of the body often turned out to be disorders of the mind, and that the mind seemed to defy the laws of cause and effect.

The effect of all these discoveries was to force the doctor, however unwilling he might be, to pay some attention to the theories of the philosophers. It is no longer possible for scientists and medical men to get on with their jobs and leave speculation to the philosophers. The Cartesian division has disappeared and scientific, medical, and philosophical theories are becoming hopelessly intermixed. It is true that a few psychologists, such as Dr Watson, refuse to take notice of the change and, by donning the white coat of the scientific researcher and retiring into a laboratory, hope to continue their work undisturbed. But the hope is a vain one, for medicine, psychology, philosophy, and religion can no longer be kept in separate compartments.

Let us take stock of the situation so far as this book is concerned. In the opening chapters it was shown that the behaviour of a man is to a great extent determined by his endocrine pattern, and by the structure of his central nervous system. Man was, to all intents and purposes, found to be a machine driven by the driving-belt of the sensory impressions that reach him from the outside world. An examination of the medical-psychological views of this and of the last century endorsed this view. Dr Watson and his colleagues of the Behaviourist school are particularly emphatic on the subject of determinism. A little later on it was discovered that this mechanical view of man and of the universe was itself determined by the method of scientific inquiry. Since the scientist studies only the relation of cause and effect, he must necessarily discover it in all that he examines. This being so it was thought advisable, before accepting as final the scientists' view that the universe was a vast machine, to seek the opinion of other experts. Eastern and Western philosophical writings were consulted. Here we found many differences of opinion, but at the same time a certain similarity of view. The philosophers agree that although the great bulk of thoughts and feelings and actions in a man are automatic, there yet remains a residuum that seems to be otherwise. The factor of consciousness was then discussed, and reference was made to the teachings of the yogis and of the Vendântist philosophers on this subject. In these we found that it was explicitly stated that although ordinary man to all intents and purposes was automatic, and unable to apprehend reality, there existed in him potentialities which, if developed, changed his whole state. It is to this point that we have come in our investigation.

We live in a dark house, but is it a house into which some light may be admitted? This is, perhaps, the most important question that a man can ask, and it is a question to which the yogis, the Vendântists, the great religious geniuses, and the mystics have all given answers. It will now be for us to examine their answers and to note whether we find any discrepancies in them. First we shall consider the answer given by the mystics.

Many criticisms have been brought to bear on states of consciousness that have been included under the ambiguous term 'mystical'. The first is that they are definitely pathological, occurring in ill-balanced and neurotic people. There is a general

tendency to regard any psychological manifestation of an unusual nature as pathological, and Max Nordau, in his book
Degeneration, discovers what he takes to be stigmata of degeneration in the majority of well-known geniuses. According
to this author there are few great works of art that have not
emanated from degenerate sources. If the great artists have
come under this suspicion in a health-conscious age, it is not
surprising that the great religious geniuses should also be suspected. What seems at first sight to justify this suspicion is the
fact that the word mystical is often used loosely and as a
description of states that are undoubtedly pathological. The
late Sir James Crichton-Browne, for example, included under
this term what he refers to as 'dreamy states'. Used, therefore,
indiscriminately the term mystical may easily become synonymous with unhealthy, and it must be frankly admitted that
many of the accounts of mystical experiences found in literature are in reality accounts of hysterical states. Baron von
Hügel, in the second volume of *The Mystical Element in Religion*, takes the symptoms of hysteria alluded to by Professor
Janet in his *État mental des hystériques*, and shows that they
can be paralleled in the life of St Catherine of Genoa. In his
Psychology of Religions, Dr Thouless also draws attention to this
parallel.

There is first [he writes] the very characteristic hysterical phenomenon of anaesthesia in which cutaneous sensibility is lost over
an area of the body. It is recorded that St Catherine would press
thorny rose-twigs in both her hands, and this without any pain.
There is also found among hysterics an exaggerated affective reaction to contact or to certain colours. Of St Catherine it is recorded
that ... for a day and a night her flesh could not be touched because
of the great pain that such touching caused her. Later she was so
sensitive that it was impossible to touch her very clothes or the bed-
stead, or a single hair on her head, because in such case she would
cry out as though she had been grievously wounded. Professor Thouless also refers to St Catherine's inability to stand or to walk, her
difficulty in eating on account of the spasms of the throat or stomach, and the skin eruptions from which she suffered. He sums up
his conclusions as follows: 'There seems no sufficient ground for
supposing that mysticism is merely hysteria misunderstood by a

superstitious and wonder-loving age, but there can be little doubt that certain forms of mysticism and hysteria are on their psycho-physical side closely related. Possibly the extent of their connexion is that both are characterized by a dissociation of personality, and that the symptoms that they have in common are the symptoms of this dissociation. At the same time, it must be noticed that St Catherine of Genoa is a mystic in whom the relationship is particu-larly marked, for she was suffering at the end of her life from a psychogenic disease, a condition which is by no means universal amongst mystics.

It must be admitted that many geniuses, both artistic and religious, do actually display pathological traits. It would seem as though Nature, having given them with one hand a priceless gift, redresses the balance by withdrawing with the other some of the advantages possessed by less highly endowed individuals. What is true of geniuses is also true of many men and women who seem to possess unusual psychic powers, and have had un-common psychic experiences, such as knowledge of events occurring in the future, or at a distance. It may even happen that illness itself temporarily enhances a man's psychic powers. Some of R. L. Stevenson's best writing was done during bouts of fever. The mind of Nietzsche, like an electric bulb carrying too heavy a charge, flashed into white heat and then, broken by the strain, went out in darkness. So also may the disturbances occurring in the brain of an epileptic awaken faculties for the moment, just as the brain of a drowning man may recount the whole panorama of life in a few seconds of time. An excellent account of an exalted state of mind before an epileptic fit is given by Dostoievsky in *The Idiot*. Since the author himself was an epileptic it may be assumed that this description is based on personal experience. Speaking of the epileptic, Prince Mishkin, he says:

He remembered that during his epileptic fits, or rather, immediate-ly preceding them, he had always experienced a moment or two when his whole heart and mind seemed to wake up to vigour and light; when he became filled with joy and hope, and all his anxieties seemed to be swept away for ever; these moments were but presenti-ments, as it were, of the one final second (it was never more than a second) in which the fit came upon him. That second (of course) was inexpressible. When his attack was over, and the prince reflected on his symptoms, he used to say to himself: 'Those moments, short as they are, when I feel such extreme consciousness of myself and consequently more of life than at other times, are due only to the disease – to the sudden rupture of normal conditions. Therefore they are not really a higher kind of life, but a lower.' This reasoning, however, seemed to end in a paradox, and to lead to the further consideration: 'What matter though it be only a disease, an abnormal tension of the brain, if when I recall and analyse the moment, it seems to have been one of harmony and beauty in the highest degree – an instant of deeper sensation, overflowing with unbounded joy and rapture, ecstatic devotion, and completest life?' ... These instants were characterized – to define it in a word – by an intense quickening of the sense of personality. Since in the last conscious moment preceding the attack, he could say to himself, with full understanding of his words: 'I would give my whole life for this one instant', then doubtless, to him, it really was worth a lifetime.

The second objection, namely, that knowledge obtained through mystical states has no objective value, must now be examined. One of the arguments that is commonly used by the school of psychology that denies the validity of all direct knowledge is the statement that the facts of religious consciousness can be explained by scientific laws. If psychology can explain the experiences of the religious man along strictly scientific lines the transcendental nature of religious knowledge is discounted. Many psychologists would go further than this. They would affirm that a scientific explanation of the transcendental means by which the religious man has reached his conclusions not only discounts the means, but also, the conclusions. Such an argument is not logically justified. Even if scientists could explain mystical states it would only imply that they could find no *psychological* support for the truth of the knowledge reached in these states.

The problem of the objective validity of religious knowledge can be resolved into two parts, first, the validity of the means by which it is obtained, and second, the objective value of the knowledge itself. We will first deal with the value of the means. Those that claim that religious knowledge *is* valid assert that it is knowledge belonging to a higher state of consciousness. The human mind has been compared to a spectrum by F. W. H. Myers. Ordinary consciousness is comparable with the visible part of the spectrum, and such organic processes as are unconscious with the infra-red parts of the spectrum. From the part of our consciousness comparable with the ultra-violet rays come the insight of the poet, the intuition of the prophet, and the illumination of the mystic. Myers continues :

It is that prolongation of our spectrum upon which our gaze will need to be most strenuously fixed. It is there that we shall find our inquiry opening upon the cosmic prospect, and inciting us upon an endless way.

Professor Thouless is inclined to deplore the insistence of the religious man on the existence of supra-conscious levels of the mind, on the grounds that it justifies flights of the imagination and longings for that which we do not possess. He states that his chief objection to the term 'supra-conscious' is that 'it is founded on no sort of *scientific* evidence at all'. With this statement we must agree. Science works by measurement, and by establishing the relationship between cause and effect, and consciousness admits of no measurement. It is the one thing that cannot be objectively examined. All that science can attempt to do is to examine the phenomena that may result from the existence of different states of consciousness, and psychology, as a whole, has paid but little attention to this subject. It was long before psychologists even recognized subconsciousness, beyond noting the fact that many impressions coming from the viscera were never registered by the brain. But a much wider kind of subconsciousness is now postulated in order to give a satisfactory account of such phenomena as post-hypnotic suggestion, and of certain observations made in the realm of mental pathology. The idea of subconscious mental processes is now accepted in order to provide necessary links in an otherwise incomplete chain of mental causation.

It is only the Western schools of psychology that will not accept the idea of the Super-conscious mind. Eastern schools have long accepted it, and, as we have seen in the preceding chapter, the science of yoga is based on it. It is a practice amongst Buddhists, and Buddhism is closely allied to yoga, to increase consciousness by observing sensations, emotions, thoughts, and movement as a preliminary to contemplation. In other words, every effort is made to cultivate a greater awareness.

Nevertheless, Western psychologists look upon mystical experiences as being experiences in a lower rather than in a higher state of consciousness. One of the features of mystical illumination is the sense of conviction and of given-ness which is attached to it. The revelation appears to have come from outside and is invested with an intense sense of its truth. Professor Thouless stresses the fact that this character of given-ness belongs not only to perceptions of external reality, but also to any experiences which result from the passage of mental processes from unconscious regions of the mind to conscious.

Dreams and the vague images and intuitions which cross our minds in the waking state, equally with religious feelings, seem to be outside the stream of thought, and like religious feelings they have been rationalized by attributing their origin to something outside the person experiencing them.

Psychologists who deny the existence of higher levels of consciousness would have us believe that what the religious man and the yogi regard as an illumination from above is really an intrusion from below, what they mistake for an experience of higher consciousness is actually the experience of a dream in a waking state. Neither the psychologist nor the mystic can be convinced by any outside argument. The intensity of consciousness that is associated with any experience can be gauged only by the individual who experiences it. It would, however, seem extremely improbable that all mystical experiences are merely dreams.

The person [writes Dr Bucke] who passes through this experience (of cosmic consciousness) will learn in the few minutes, or even moments, of its continuance, more than in months, than in years of study, and he will learn much that no study ever taught or can teach. Especially does he obtain such a conception of the *whole*, or at least, of an immense whole, as dwarfs all conception, such a conception as makes the old attempts mentally to grasp the universe and its meaning, petty, and even ridiculous.

No dream has ever left such a lasting impression on the dreamer as this. But Professor Thouless is strictly judicial and sums up what he believes to be the situation as follows:

> We must be careful, however, to notice exactly how far these considerations have carried us. They have given us no reason for supposing that no valid argument can be drawn from the validity of religious experience from psychological data. They have shown only the weakness of this one simple, and rather crude, argument, from the *given-ness* of such an experience – the argument that because I feel these experiences have not come from my own mind, they are due to divine action.

Dean Inge in his *Studies of English Mystics* makes an excellent comment on the objections raised by specialists to mystical experiences.

> The real question [he says] is whether our higher endowments are best interpreted from above or from below. Is their true nature to be found by inquiring what they grow out of, and with what physical conditions they are associated, or by inquiring what they may grow into, and to what regions of spiritual truth they may conduct us? The former is the method of pessimism ... The more a thing is good, the higher it has risen from its first state, and consequently the more it can be degraded by identifying it with its original forms ... Pessimism maintains that all human endeavour is futile, all progress illusory; that the attractiveness of physical or moral beauty is merely a bait by which nature entices us to subserve her purposes to our own hurt; and that the mystics are persons who by reason of their unstable nervous system are more completely duped than their neighbours.

The second criterion by which the value of religious knowledge may be assessed is the nature of the knowledge revealed, quite apart from the means by which it was obtained. Judged on these grounds it may be said that there is general agreement between religious knowledge and that which has been gained in other ways. The writer was once asked by a traveller, who had come into contact with the mysteries of yoga, how yogis could possibly know, and have long known, much that science was only now beginning to discover. The explanation is surely a very simple one. There exist higher levels of consciousness, and men who have attained them have access to knowledge that is not accessible to those who only function on the ordinary level. To the yogi, therefore, much is known that we, working along a lower level, are only now beginning to discover. There is also available to them knowledge of a nature which is beyond ordinary comprehension.

Michael Faraday in delivering a lecture before the Royal Institution in 1854 referred to the two different methods of arriving at truth, namely the method of the scientist using the intellectual faculties, and the direct apprehension of the religious man. He spoke as follows:

It would be improper here to enter upon this subject farther than to claim an absolute distinction between religious and ordinary belief. I shall be reproached with weakness and of refusing to apply those mental operations which I thought good in respect of high things to the very highest. I am content to bear the reproach ... I have never seen anything incompatible between those things of man which can be known by the spirit of man which is within him, and those higher things concerning his future which he cannot know by that spirit.

To those who have experienced the higher states of consciousness the formulation of the knowledge obtained on these higher levels would appear to be an impossible task. All men and women who have had experience of these states agree on this point, even although the revelation carries with it an intense conviction of its significance. The mystic stands face to face with truth, but is utterly unable to put into words what he has seen. A repetition of the experience, if repetition there be, finds the truth to be the same, but the expression of it becomes no easier.

The gate was opened to me so that in one quarter of an hour I saw and knew more than if I had been many years at a university. (JACOB BOEHME)

The experience of the mystic is always of this nature; he is overwhelmed by the importance and cognitive value of what he is seeing, and this conviction of value remains even after the state of higher consciousness has passed. Yet he can say nothing. It was with some justification that Dr Johnson remarked, 'If

Mr A has experienced the ineffable he ought not to attempt to express it.'

One of the reasons why it is impossible for the mystic to describe his experience in words is that it is mainly an experience of the emotions. When he does attempt to convey its meaning to others, he is forced to make use of pictures and symbols, and because his feelings were so intense he pictures them in the most vivid colours that are obtainable, using the most extravagant words in his vocabulary. Naturally he shows a tendency to fall back on the material with which he happens to be familiar, the Hindu talking of Brahman, the Christian of Christ and the Virgin Mary, and the Buddhist of Buddha. He therefore is attempting to explain one unknown in terms of another unknown, a unique experience by means of an Absolute whose attributes are unknowable except in terms of negation. As a result of these crude and ineffectual attempts to convey what has been experienced, mystical literature often appears ridiculous and sentimental to the reader.

Dean Inge draws a parallel between the methods employed by art and by religion in expressing the truth they want to convey. Art values the things of experience according as they are good or bad, according to whether they fulfil their proper end or not. So also does religion view things *sub specie aeternitatis*, and not according to whether they give pleasure or pain to ourselves.

But the religious representation of reality is subject to more stringent restrictions than the artistic, in that since the main end of art is enjoyment, there is an element of play, of conscious illusion in its productions ... The religious attitude is one of the highest conceivable seriousness ... It reverences its symbols while admitting their inadequacy. We know that they are not creations of our fancy, like artistic symbols, but the spontaneous projections of a deeper faculty which we dare not trifle with. Hence comes that reluctance to subject religious symbols to rationalistic tests, which we observe everywhere in human history.

With so many obstacles in the way of interpretation, it is difficult to extract from mystical descriptions the common factors of knowledge. William James has attempted to do so, in the following words:

It is possible to give the outcome of the majority of them in terms that point in definite philosophical directions. One of these directions is optimism, and the other is monism. We pass into mystical states from out of ordinary consciousness as from a less into a more, as from a smallness into a vastness, and at the same time as from an unrest to a rest. We feel them as reconciling, unifying states. They appeal to the yes-function more than to the no-function in us. In them the unlimited absorbs the limits and peacefully closes the account. Their very denial of every adjective you may propose as applicable to the ultimate truth – He, the Self, the Atman, is to be described by 'No! no!' only, say the Upanishads, – though it seems on the surface to be a no-function is a denial made on behalf of a deeper yes. Whoso calls the Absolute anything in particular, or says that it is *this*, seems implicitly to shut it off from being *that* – it is as if he lessened it.

It may be argued that the capacity of religious doctrine to rationalize experience is itself a criterion, however imperfect, of its inherent truth. This is the criterion that is ordinarily employed to test the truth of a scientific theory. The atomic theory of Dalton, for example, was originated because it gave a coherent and intelligible account of many observations made in laboratories. The method that has been adopted by scientists – a method based on empiricism – is equally valid in the case of knowledge of a religious nature. It is the criterion of truth that we shall employ in this book.

An authoritative work on the subject of higher states of consciousness is Dr R. M. Bucke's *Cosmic Consciousness*. The author was a Canadian psychiatrist, who after an unhappy childhood became a student particularly interested in books dealing with the basic problems of life. At the age of thirty-two, he came across Walt Whitman's *Leaves of Grass*, and at once realized that it contained, in greater measure than any other book, what he had been looking for. But it was at the beginning of his thirty-sixth year that the event occurred that for ever afterwards transformed his thinking and his method of life. He describes how he had spent an evening in the company of two friends reading Wordsworth, Shelley, Keats, Browning, and especially Walt Whitman. They parted at midnight, and he had a long drive in a hansom.

His mind, deeply under the influence of the ideas, images, and emotions called up by the reading and talk of the evening, was calm and peaceful. He was in a state of quiet, almost passive enjoyment. All at once, without warning of any kind, he found himself wrapped around as it were by a flame-coloured cloud. For an instant he thought of fire, some sudden conflagration in the great city; the next he knew that the light was within himself. Directly afterwards there came upon him a sense of exultation, of immense joyousness accompanied or immediately followed by an intellectual illumination quite impossible to describe. Into his brain streamed one momentary lightning-flash of the Brahmic Splendour which has ever since lightened his life; upon his heart fell one drop of Brahmic Bliss, leaving thenceforward for always an after-taste of heaven. Among other things, he did not come to believe, he saw and knew that the Cosmos is not dead matter but a living Presence, that the soul of man is immortal, that the universe is so built and ordered that without any peradventure all things work together for the good of each and all, that the foundation principle of the world is what we call love, and that the happiness of everyone is in the long run absolutely certain. He claims that he learned more within the few seconds during which the illumination lasted than in previous months or even years of study, and that he learned much that no study could ever have taught.

It will be seen from this description that the change in consciousness has many of the features that are usually noted in such experiences. The stage had been set beforehand by the creation of an emotional background through the reading of poetry. Then suddenly and unexpectedly the moment of illumination is ushered in by a sensation as though the whole body was flooded with flame-coloured cloud. The initiate into a new level of existence does not come to believe, but actually 'sees' that the whole of the universe is unified in a living presence, underlying and, at the same time, explaining everything, the God of Christianity, the Brahman of the Hindu. The change of consciousness lasts but a few moments, yet in that time more is learnt than during years of study. The lesson carries with it a conviction that is not attached to knowledge acquired through the sense-organs; it is truth directly apprehended.

This change of time, this crowding into a second of a thousand different impressions and emotions, is noted by most people who have experienced higher consciousness, whether occurring spontaneously or induced artificially. The writer remembers the case of a priest who while coming round from nitrous oxide anaesthesia suddenly exclaimed, 'O, Christ, in that moment I lived a hunderd years, so much has happened.' Unfortunately he remembered nothing of his experiences subsequently.

The change in the rate of perception that is a feature of higher states of consciousness is beautifully described in a remarkable passage in one of the Apocryphal Gospels, the Book of James.

Now I, Joseph, was walking, and I walked not. And I looked up to the air and saw the air in amazement. And I looked up into the pole of the heaven and saw it standing still, and the fowls of the heaven without motion. And I looked upon the earth and saw a dish set, and workmen lying by it, and their hands were in the dish: and they that were chewing chewed not, and they that were lifting the food lifted it not, and they that put it to their mouth put it not thereto, but the faces of all of them were looking upward. And behold here were sheep being driven, and they went not forward but stood still; and the shepherd lifted his hand to smite them with his staff, and his hand remained up. And I looked upon the stream of the river and saw the mouths of the kids upon the water, and they drank not. And of a sudden all things moved onward in their course.

A similar experience is thus expressed by the modern poet, Rupert Brooke :

> From the dark woven flow of change
> Under a vast and starless sky
> I saw the immortal moment lie.
> One instant I, an instant, knew
> As God knows all. And it and you
> I, above Time, oh, blind! could see
> In witless immortality.
> I saw the marble cup; the tea,
> Hung on the air, an amber stream;
> I saw the fire's unglittering gleam,
> The painted flame, the frozen smoke.
> No more the flooding lamplight broke
> On flying eyes and lips and hair;
> But lay, but slept unbroken there,

On stiller flesh, and body breathless,
And lips and laughter stayed and deathless,
And words on which no silence grew.
Light was more alive than you. . . .

Dazed at length
Human eyes grew, mortal strength
Wearied; and Time began to creep.
Change glinted on the eyes I loved.
The cup was filled. The bodies moved.
The drifting petal came to ground.
The laughter chimed its perfect round.
The broken syllable was ended. . . .

Examples of flashes of higher consciousness provoked by anaesthetics might be multiplied indefinitely. Two more are chosen, one occurring in a quite illiterate man, and the other in a great public figure. The first was a patient, who was heard to shout in the public ward of the hospital, while coming round from an anaesthetic:

'You don't understand, you don't understand. No one understands ... The Universe ... the universe. I know – I know! Happiness is within you; I know, I know. You don't have to look outside, it's within you ... The Universe, the universe. . . .'

The nurse in charge went up to his bed to quieten him, saying:

'Here, stop that. You're making more noise than anyone else. You and your old universe!'

The vision was broken.

In the spring of 1932, Sir Winston Churchill had an accident in the streets of New York, which necessitated an anaesthetic and a minor operation. Afterwards, he contributed two articles to the *Daily Mail*, describing his sensations when coming round from the anaesthetic. The following is an extract from his description:

The sanctum is occupied by alien powers. I see the absolute truth and explanation of things, but something is left out which upsets the whole, so by a larger sweep of the mind I have to see a greater truth and a more complete explanation, which comprises the erring element. Nevertheless, there is still something left out. So we have to take a still wider sweep ... The process continues inexorably. Depth beyond depth of unendurable truth opens.

Dr Bucke's experience had such a lasting effect upon him that he devoted his life afterwards to the study of what he called Cosmic Consciousness, collecting and correlating other descriptions of it in literature and from living men. He also evolved a theory on the subject of cosmic consciousness, regarding its sporadic manifestation in a few individuals as a sign that it would eventually be manifested in the whole of mankind. In other words, he tried to fit cosmic consciousness into the framework of the evolutionary theory.

His line of reasoning was as follows. The lowest rung in the ladder of consciousness is the acquisition and registration of sense-impressions, that is to say, of percepts. This is the rung on which the lower animals stand, and it is from this that the psychic life of man has evolved. The continuous registration of sense-impressions – percepts – in time led to a further increase in the number of cells in the central sense ganglia, allowing of a number of percepts being combined into a recept. If, for example, many percepts, say of a tree, are registered, eventually the brain becomes competent to combine them into a sort of compound percept, or recept, called a tree.

Now the work of accumulation begins again on a higher plane ; the sensory organs keep steadily at work, manufacturing percepts ; the receptual centres keep steadily at work, manufacturing more and yet more recepts from the old and new percepts ; the capacity of the central ganglia is constantly taxed to do the necessary registration of percepts, the elaboration of these into recepts and the necessary registration of recepts. Then, as the ganglia, by use and selection, are improved, they constantly manufacture from percepts and from the initial simple recepts, more and more complex, that is to say, higher and higher recepts. Eventually the third rung of the ladder is reached, when the higher recepts are replaced by concepts.

The relation of a concept to a recept is, as Dr Bucke explains, somewhat similar to the relation of algebra to arithmetic. A recept is a composite image of many hundreds of percepts ; a concept is that same composite image ticketed and, as it were, dismissed. It is the algebraic sign that stands henceforth for the thing itself, that is, for the multiple recepts.

This ability to form concepts increases the efficiency of the brain enormously, as much as the introduction of machinery increases the capacity of the race to work, or as much as the use of algebra increases the power of the mind to make mathematical calculations. To replace a cumbersome recept by a simple sign is almost like replacing actual goods, such as wheat, fabrics, and hardware, by entries in a ledger. The ability to form concepts implies the possession of a language. It also implies the existence of some degree of self-consciousness. An animal does not possess self-consciousness because it cannot stand outside itself and see that it perceives ; it is conscious only of the object that it sees. A man not only sees, but may be conscious that he sees. The faculties of language and of potential self-consciousness are the prerogatives of the human race, as is also the capacity to form concepts. It is on this rung of the ladder that we now stand. We are capable of a certain degree of self-consciousness, and of communicating with each other by language, and we are able to form concepts.

There is every reason to suppose that if there are rungs in the ladder of consciousness below us, there are also rungs above us. But in addition to the *a priori* grounds for believing this, we have the additional testimony of people who have actually stood on a higher rung, amongst others, the rung of cosmic consciousness. Dr Bucke explains this step in a similar manner to that in which he explained the previous step. The mind becomes overcrowded, as it were, with concepts, and these are constantly becoming larger, more numerous, and more and more complex. Some day (the conditions being all favourable) the fusion, or what might be called the chemical union of several of them, and of certain moral elements in addition, takes place ; the result is an intuition, and the establishment of the instuitional mind.

There exist certain ambiguities and undoubted errors in Dr Bucke's theory of the evolution of cosmic consciousness. First of all, it is not clear whether he believes, or does not believe, that the blending of many concepts with the appropriate emotions is likely to produce a phenomenon that contains entirely new features, non-existent in either the intellectual concepts or in the emotions. The analogy is a good one if by chemical union he means that as oxygen and hydrogen chemically united produce water, unlike either of the two elements out of which it is formed, so also through a special form of union of emotions and intellect an entirely new faculty is created. At one moment, we have a mixture of two gases in a bottle; an electric spark is passed through the mixture, and in a flash there is the new material, water. So also is it with cosmic consciousness. At one moment he who experiences it is conscious of nothing more unusual than perhaps a strong emotion, and then suddenly, and without warning, his whole state and his attitude to the world change. This new state lasts a short time and then, with equal abruptness, disappears. The transition would appear to be far more abrupt than the change, say, from sleep to wakefulness, or from wakefulness to sleep.

What is undoubtedly an error on Dr Bucke's part is to suppose that the attainment of higher consciousness can possibly form part of an evolutionary process, and that the individuals who have experienced it can be looked upon as 'sports', that in time are to become so numerous that they will be the rule rather than the exception. There is little to suggest that man is undergoing psychic evolution, and nothing to suggest that higher states of consciousness are becoming commoner. If anything, the reverse would appear to be the case. The possession of the moral values that Dr Bucke rightly supposes to be a requisite to the attainment of higher consciousness is not a distinguishing feature of modern civilized man. He prides himself more on his intellectual attainments, and on his conquest of the material world, than on his possession of moral values. The world of values is, indeed, at the present moment at a discount, and it is more difficult for a poet or a philosopher to exist in London or New York than it was for him to exist in ancient Athens. Progress is measured in terms of material and not of spiritual advances.

Moreover, quite apart from this question of moral values, it is apparent from an examination of literature, that higher consciousness seldom comes entirely accidentally. It is true that Dr Bucke's experience appears from the outside to have been accidental. He was driving home in a hansom, and suddenly, without warning, the moment of illumination arrived. But much had gone before to explain why, of all the people driving home in hansoms, it was Dr Bucke who had this unique experience. From childhood onwards he had dwelt on the subject of God and the meaning of life. At times, to quote his own words, 'he was subject to a sort of ecstasy of curiosity and hope'. Later, he describes his life as being for some years, 'one passionate note of interrogation, an unappeasable hunger for enlightenment on the basic problems'. Finally, as a preliminary to the drive home in the hansom, he had spent an evening with friends reading aloud the more emotional of the poets, especially Whitman – Whitman, a poet who had himself experienced flashes of a higher state.

A careful perusal of the descriptions of states of higher consciousness collected in Dr Bucke's volume shows that in almost every case illumination was preceded by a long period of striving after truth. The great majority of the people whose experiences are included there were solitary men and women who had lost all taste for the world, and had suffered much spiritually, and often physically. It is worthy of note that prior to illumination, both Christ and Buddha went through a period of temptation, associated with fasting in the wilderness. We are told that Mohammed also absented himself from society and sought the solitude of a cavern on Mount Hara, where in emulation of the Christian anchorites of the desert, he remained days and nights together engaged in prayer and meditation.

When we awaken from sleep in the morning our 'coming to' is usually the result of some sensory stimulus; the sound of an alarm clock, the noise of other people getting up, an increase of light in the bedroom, etc. So also many experiences of higher states of consciousness have been the sequel to some stimulus of an emotional nature. Music, a spectacle of great beauty, love, intense religious feeling, or aesthetic emotions of any kind may all be causes of a change in the level of consciousness.

The following two examples of a sudden change in the level of consciousness have been taken from Raynor Johnson's book *Watchers on the Hills*. The first is an example of Nature Mysticism, that is to say of a change produced by an intense emotional response to the beauty of Nature. L. A. G. Strong places his description of what was undoubtedly a personal experience in the mouth of a character in *Corporal Tune*.

The ledge was an enchanted place. Here one fine day this summer Ignatius had sat for seven hours, absorbed, watching the play of the light on sea, and seven hours had passed as one. The wind altered every few minutes, the sun wheeled across from Ignatius's left shoulder to his right, the preoccupied sea changed its mind and wandered; then by degrees all accustomed images of thought left him, there were neither words nor metaphors, sea and earth and sky existed on their own terms, and he was gradually absorbed into all he saw, till he lost human consciousness, and became one of many objects, a part of the coast, drained of his identity, persisting mindless like a patch of obstinate sunlight gleaming on the water a mile from shore, a patch of which he was without thought aware, just as without thought he was aware of himself sitting on the ledge; dimly, from time to time aware, but without distinction between his body pressing upon the rock or the rock pressing up against his body; human consciousness passed out from him yet not into sleep; into no blurring of sense; something clear and shining, wind touched, shadow crossed; something at once firm and rooted like the sun-warmed rock, cool and flowing like the water, outspread like the pine branches, high as the clouds, volatile as the air – something with perceptions extended in all these, something infinitesimal yet supreme, fragment and whole, wave, beam of light, path that the gull had not yet taken through the air; something which, when the elated mind tried to realize it, broke up thus into a thousand facets, but which in spells of deepest experience sank to a luminous sense of peace; light and water and stillness in a pool as wide as the sky. It was an experience not to be put into words, for the effort to find words at once split up the central Unity of awareness into a series of particular visions; creating multiplicity; shattering a timeless exaltation into restlessness, breaking eternity into succession and the intervals between one object and another. . . .

When he came to himself, his limbs stiff and numb, his mind was so charged with luminous wisdom and tranquility that for a few moments he knew that there was no human problem he could not solve, and that, by the light that was slowly fading within his mind, he could illumine his own life and the lives of others. But the light faded; the great satisfying chord hummed away over the far horizon and there remained only the faint piping notes of petty detail, the straying unresolved motifs and burdens of the symphony.

The second case to be quoted from Raynor Johnson's book *Watchers on the Hill* is that of a young man, now a doctor, whose emotions had been deeply stirred by my own description of the all-pervading and ever-present Brahman.

I was travelling back to camp in early January 1948 in an empty railway carriage after a short leave over Christmas from the army. I pulled *Diagnosis of Man* (First Edition) from my pack and began to read the chapter on Brahmanism. I was reading the words telling of the ever-present and all-pervading quality of Brahman, when suddenly my whole being was seized by an acute state of awareness, and immediately the words assumed a great significance. I knew somehow that they were true, that Brahman (at that time I suppose I translated it as God) *was* all about me, and through me, and in me. The knowledge did not come from without, unmistakably it came from within. The state was one of extraordinary joy; I realized happiness was within me. (I believe I also felt that I controlled great power, so that I could have stopped the train just by willing it, but in writing this afterwards as I do, I cannot be certain of this.) I can remember looking out at the countryside passing by, and everything, the trees, meadows, and hedges were all part of me, and I of them, and all were in a great unity through which was God. Everything was a whole.

The experience lasted a few minutes, and very gradually it ebbed away. But I *knew* with complete unshakable conviction that I had been in touch with Reality in those few minutes.

There could be no better description of higher states of consciousness with which to end this chapter than that given by Plotinus, the founder of Neo-Platonism. Plotinus lived in a period of human history (A.D. 204) much resembling our own. It was a time of change and of crisis, during which the power of Rome was rapidly declining and Europe was in great danger of being invaded by barbarians, a time, in short, in which *anything* might happen. After giving certain bad news in a letter concerning the decay of the Roman Empire and after complaining that he was tired of this prison-house, the body, he states that he calmly awaits the day when the divine nature within him will be set free from matter. He then writes the following:

You ask me to tell you how we know, and what is our criterion of certainty. To write is always irksome to me. But for the continual solicitations of Porphyry I should not have left a line to survive me. For your own sake and for your father's my reluctance shall be overcome.

External objects present us only with appearances. Concerning them, therefore, we may be said to possess opinion rather than knowledge. The distinctions in the actual world of appearance are of import only to ordinary and practical men. Our question lies with the ideal Reality that exists behind appearance. How does the mind perceive these ideas? Are they without us, and is the reason, like sensation, occupied with objects external to itself? What certainty would we then have – what assurance that our perception was infallible? The object perceived would be something different from the mind perceiving it. We should have then an image instead of a reality. It would be monstrous to believe for a moment that the mind was unable to perceive ideal truth exactly as it is, and that we had not certainty and real knowledge concerning the world of intelligence. It follows, therefore, that this region of truth is not to be investigated as a thing external to us, and so only imperfectly known. It is within us. Here the objects we contemplate and that which contemplates are identical – both are thought. The subject cannot surely know an object different from itself. The world of ideas lies within our intelligence. Truth, therefore, is not the agreement of our apprehension of an external object with the object itself. It is the agreement of the mind with itself. Consciousness, therefore, is the whole basis of certainty. The mind is its own witness. Reason sees in itself that which is above itself as its source; and again, that which is below itself as still itself once more.

Knowledge has three degrees – opinion, science, illumination. The means or instrument of the first is sense; of the second dialectic, of the third, intuition. To the last I subordinate reason. It is absolute knowledge founded on the identity of the mind knowing with the object known. . . .

You ask how we can know the Infinite? I answer, not by reason. It is the office of reason to distinguish and define. The Infinite, therefore, cannot be ranked among its objects. You can only apprehend the Infinite by a faculty superior to reason, by entering into a state in which you are your finite self no longer – in which the divine essence is communicated to you. This is ecstasy (Cosmic Consciousness). It is the liberation of your mind from its finite consciousness. Like can only apprehend like; when you thus cease to be finite, you become one with the Infinite. In the reduction of your soul to its simplest self, its divine essence, you realize this union – this identity.

But this sublime condition is not of permanent duration. It is only now and then that we can enjoy this elevation (mercifully made possible for us) above the limits of the body and the world. I myself have realized it but three times as yet, and Porphyry hitherto not once. All that tends to purify and elevate the mind will assist you in this attainment, and facilitate the approach and the recurrence of these happy intervals. There are, then, different roads by which this end may be reached. The love of beauty which exalts the poet; that devotion to the One and that ascent of science which makes the ambition of the philospher, and that love and those prayers by which some devout and ardent soul tends in its moral purity towards perfection. These are the great highways conducting to that height above the actual and the particular, where we stand in the immediate presence of the Infinite, who shines out as from the depths of the soul.

In these incomparable words, which might equally well have come from the lips of an Eastern sage, Plotinus sums up all that can usefully be said on this subject. Discursive thinking, however extended, can never lead to the apprehension of Reality. It is only during those states of consciousness in which man finds himself stripped of all finite conditions, including those of his intellect, that the veil is lifted.

CHAPTER 13

RELIGION

MOST scientific writers who have studied religion begin by attempting to define what is meant by that word. Many different definitions have been offered. It has been defined as 'what we do with our solitariness' (A. N. Whitehead), as 'the attitude which the individual takes up towards the determiner of his destinies' (Prof. J. Bissett Pratt), as 'the feelings, acts, and experiences of individual men in their solitude, so far as they apprehend themselves to stand in relation to whatever they may consider the divine' (William James), and 'as the experience of human nature in the higher ranges of its activity' (J. Haynes Holmes). It is however doubtful whether such definitions are necessary or of very great value, for every man has his own conception of what he means by religion and what for him is a religious experience.

The majority of writers have asserted that religious sentiment is not only a natural and normal element, but a universal phenomenon of human life. Havelock Ellis, for instance, described it as 'a special function which is almost a physiological function'. And if we stretch the definition of religious sentiment wide enough so that it embraces all that is related to the world of values, this is true. There is nobody who does not possess some criterion of value, some ethical code of behaviour, to which he nominally subscribes, even though in practice he fails to live up to it. But only if the definition is so stretched as to include recognition of the whole world of values can the universality of a religious sentiment be maintained. In its narrower sense religious sentiment contains an element of wonder and veneration, and there are many men and women who would appear to have lost the capacity to wonder: 'What does it all mean?'; 'Why am I here, and what am I?' Like men who have grown accustomed to the beauty and mystery of a sunset, and, looking at it, merely think, 'the refraction of light by the earth's atmosphere', so they accept life as a stale phenomenon, a story that has been told so often that it has ceased to have any meaning.

What nature could give us if only our senses and minds were less dulled is very beautifully told in the 'First Conversation' with Brother Lawrence, written down by M. Beaufort, Grand Vicar to Cardinal de Noailles, Archbishop of Paris, and published in 1692.

The first time I saw Brother Lawrence was upon the third of August 1666. He told me that God had done him a singular favour, in his conversion at the age of eighteen.

That in the winter, seeing a tree stripped of its leaves, and considering that within a little while the leaves would be renewed, and after that the flowers and fruit appear, he received a high view of the Providence and the Power of God, which has never since been effaced from his soul. That this view had set him perfectly loose from the world, and kindled in him such a love for God that he could not tell whether it had increased in the forty years that he had lived since.

Men and women who adapt themselves as best they can to existence, yet with no particular interest, no particular emotional feeling towards the universe, can scarcely be termed religious; for religion must always contain this element of wonder, this striving after the unknown and reaching out towards the infinite.

Religious feeling not only contains this ingredient of wonder, but also an instinctive desire to venerate or worship. The religious man attempts to discriminate between values that he believes to be ultimate and those that are only relative, between the pursuit of the infinite and the pursuit of the finite, between the spiritual and the material. He is searching for the real, the perfect, and the permanent, and it is in the presence of these values that he is conscious of the desire to worship.

Every great religion can be analysed into three elements, a philosophy, a mythology, and a ritual. The philosophy is the central core of the religion, the mythology and rituals its outer sheath. Sri Ramakrishna, the leader of the spiritual renaissance that was inaugurated in India during the second half of the last century, has aptly compared the central core and outer husk of a religion to a grain of rice.

Although in a grain of paddy, the germ is considered the only necessary thing [for germination and growth], while the husk and chaff are considered of no importance; still, if the husked grain is put into the ground, it will not sprout up and grow into a plant and produce rice. To get a crop one must needs sow the grain with the husk on. But if one wants to get at the kernel itself, we must remove the husk of the grain. So, rites and ceremonies are necessary for the growth and perpetuation of a religion. They are the receptacles that contain the kernel of truth, and consequently, every man must perform them before he reaches the central truth.

What makes the development of ritual and mythology in religion necessary is that a religion is a synthesis of intellectual and emotional experiences. Whilst words are sufficient for the expression of the intellectual content of a religion, they are insufficient for the expression of its emotional aspect. Emotions can best be portrayed by the use of rituals, symbols, and stories. Hence the importance of art, ceremonies, and mythology to all religion. The Absolute can only be thought of, or stated, through the relative, and the various symbols and rituals of a religion are so many pegs on which to hang spiritual truths.

There is another feature that all the greater religions of the world possess in common. They are the result of revelation. Each has come down from some great religious genius, who has stood on a higher level than his fellows, and has by direct vision apprehended truth. The great religions are, therefore, the products of higher states of consciousness, and are invested with all the authority that comes from such an origin. They are not merely the products of the religious sentiment of an ordinary man, but are revelations coming from a higher level. We accept them as we accept a work of genius in the realm of art, which contains something of ordinary man and also something of a religious revelation. We believe that with further study their value will be revealed. This is the true meaning of the word translated in the gospels as 'faith'. A better translation would be 'trust', a word that implies, not a blind credulity, but the trustfulness that comes from having apprehended some of the message, but not all of it.

Most works devoted to the comparative study of religions are really studies of religious husks. Only a few deal with the grain. And the reason for this is at once obvious. It is only the husk that differs; the grain, the inner soul, of all great religions is the same. Divested of all special names, the fundamental abstractions of all the great world religions are identical, variations of the great eternal Religion, suited to different minds and different races.

Many devout Christians will be shocked by this suggestion, that in its essentials the religion in which they so firmly believe is identical with Buddhism and Sufism. They will point to the many differences that distinguish the Christian from the Buddhist, and to the even greater differences that separate Christ from Buddha. But the differences to which they point are differences in the less essential attributes of the two religions, not differences in their souls.

Thirty years ago the writer of this book was taken over the shrine of a Sufi saint in India by an old Mohammedan. After he had viewed all that was to be seen in the dimly lit building and was about to say good-bye, his aged guide turned to him and said, 'There is no difference between the great religions; a good Mohammedan is the same as a good Christian, and a good Christian as a good Buddhist. *We* also revere the name of your great prophet, Jesus Christ, and one of His sayings is written up over the doorway of the Taj Mahal.' Twenty years were to pass before the truth of the old Mohammedan's words was fully understood.

If it were not so, if each religion differed in its essentials, all would be suspect. There are not many truths, but one truth, although the language in which it is formulated will differ according to a man's type, his education, and his level of understanding. There is only one religion, although the expression of it differs with the culture, temperament, education, and understanding of its exponent. Differences of creed, differences in ritual, varieties of ceremonial are necessary in a world in which men differ so profoundly, and the greater the number of sects, the better the chance that any individual man will find that which is best suited to his own particular needs.

In case the reader should think that this is merely the expression of an opinion based on a theoretical examination of religions, that is to say, on external rather than on inner evidence, reference will be made to the life of Sri Ramakrishna. This great teacher, after he had gained for himself an India-wide reputation for holiness, and after he had become proficient in all yoga practices, was initiated into the religion of Islam. He lived outside the precincts of a mosque and dressed, fed, prayed, and behaved generally like any other Mussulman. All thoughts, visions, and ecstasies associated with Hindu gods and goddesses left him for the time being, and his tranquil mind became the mirror from which Islamic thoughts and images were reflected. By his earnestness and devotion he soon obtained from his new religion all that he had previously derived from Hinduism and yoga. Eight years later he was seized with a desire to see where the path of Christianity would lead him. He devoted himself with equal single-mindedness to the study of the New Testament, and eventually reached the conviction that Christ was an Incarnation of God, 'the Master Yogi, the Embodiment of Love'. This conviction remained with him to the day of his death.

As a result of his own personal experience of the four great religions – for in studying yoga he had also studied Buddhism – he made the following declaration :

I have practised all religions, Hinduism, Islam, Christianity, and I have also followed the paths of the different Hindu sects ... I have found that it is the same God towards Whom all are directing their steps, though along different paths. ... Wherever I look, I see men quarrelling in the name of religion, the Hindus, Mohammedans, Brahmos, Vaishnavas, and the rest, but they never reflect that He Who is called Krishna is also called Siva, and bears the name of Primitive Energy (*Sakti*), Jesus, and Allah as well, – the same Rama, with a thousand names. The tank has several *ghats*. At one, Hindus draw water in pitchers, and call it *jala*; at another Mussulmen draw water in leathern bottles, and call it *pani*; at a third Christians do the same, and call it water. Can we imagine that the water is not *jala*, but only *pani*, or water? How ridiculous! The substance is one under different names, and everyone is seeking the same substance; nothing but climate, temperament, and names vary. Let each man follow his own path. If he sincerely and ardently wishes to know God, peace be unto him. He will surely realize Him.

At a later date, Ramakrishna's disciple, Vivekananda, the dynamic apostle of the religious revival in India and in America, re-echoed the views of his master.

The aim of religion is to get rid of nature's control over us. That is the goal of all religions. Each soul is potentially divine. The goal is to manifest this divinity within by controlling nature, external and internal. Do this either by work (karma-yoga), worship (bhakti-yoga), or psychic control (raja-yoga), or philosophy (jñana-yoga), by one or other or all of these, and be free. This is the whole of religion. Doctrines or dogmas, or rituals or books, or temples or forms, are but secondary details. I accept all religions that were in the past and worship them all. I worship God with every one of them, in whatever form they worship Him. I shall go to the mosque of a Mohammedan, I shall enter the Christian church and kneel before the crucifix; I shall visit the Buddhist temple, where I shall take refuge in Buddha and His law. I shall go into the forest and sit down in meditation with the Hindu, who is trying to find the light which enlightens the heart of everyone ... The Bible, the Vedas, the Koran, and all the sacred books are so many pages, and an infinite number of pages remain yet to be unfolded. I would leave my heart open to them all.

The same idea, that although there are many labels for religion there is only one religion, is the theme of a story in the *Mathnawi*. Four friends, a Persian, an Arab, a Turk, and a Greek, found a coin, and quarrelled over the fruit that they would purchase with it. The Persian wanted *angur*, the Arab *unab*, the Turk *uzum*, and the Greek *astafeel*. Each went into raptures over the quality of the fruit he wished his friends to taste. A wise man passing by happened to hear them quarrelling, and learnt from them the cause of their disagreement. Asking for the coin he went to the neighbouring village and bought a bunch of grapes, the one fruit for which all had asked, each in his own language.

It was pointed out that a new religion starts with a revelation of truth through the agency of higher consciousness. Just as an ordinary man who has experienced higher states of consciousness uses the material with which he happens to be familiar in order to interpret to others what he has seen, so do the great religious teachers utilize for the purpose of exposition the culture of the country in which they happen to have been born. Christ preaching to the Jews, a patriarchal race, referred to God as 'Our Heavenly Father', for the word 'father' meant much to his hearers. He accepted the laws of His country, but gave to them a new meaning, teaching that what was important was not so much the outward observance of the law but the inner attitude of the heart.

Ye have heard that it was said of old time, Thou shalt not commit adultery; but I say unto you that whosoever looketh on a woman to lust after her hath committed adultery with her already in his heart. (Matthew v, 27)

Ye have heard that it hath been said, An eye for an eye and a tooth for a tooth, but I say unto you that ye resist not evil; but whosoever shall smite thee on the right cheek, turn to him the other also. (Matthew v, 38)

Like all orthodox Jews, Christ went to Jerusalem, in order that he might celebrate the Jewish feast of the Passover, and then made use of the unleavened bread as a symbol for a new message to his disciples.

So also do we find Buddha using Hindu mythology and Hindu culture as a means of illustrating his own teaching, giving to old rules and old practices new meaning and life. Occasionally religious teachers utilize symbols and word-pictures that are not generally connected with religious ideas. The Sufi teachers, for example, employ the symbolism of earthly love in order to illustrate what is meant by the love of God. The mystical poems of Persia, such as those of the *Mathnawi*, are full of allusions to human lovers because, as one of their own poets has said, 'Nobody can write in heavenly language and be understood.' Nor could the Mohammedans see anything incongruous in illustrating religious fervour by comparing it with the passion of the lover for his beloved. Human love may be the stepping-stone to the understanding of a greater love that embraces the whole of humanity, and thence it is but one step more to the understanding of the love of God. As Max Müller has put it:

The idea of Sufism is a loving union of the soul with God. The Sufi holds that there is nothing in human language that can express the love between the soul and God so well as the love between a man and woman, and that if he is to speak of the union between the two at all, he can only do so in the symbolic language of earthly love.

The Sufi, therefore, uses the theme of the Song of Songs in order to illustrate his truths.

Unfortunately, humanity is more disposed to dwell on the differences in the outward trappings and expression of religion than on the identity of the inner truths. With the passage of time the inner meaning of the symbol is lost and only the symbol remains; the ceremony is retained, but its significance forgotten. All religions are liable to this process of decay from within outwards, some suffering it more swiftly than others. It would seem, indeed, as though some religions from the very beginning started without any inner vitality. Confucianism may be taken as an example of such a religion. Confucius, himself, was apparently an honest man. He made no claim to having had any divine revelation, and regarded himself as being a reformer and a reviver of old knowledge, rather than a creator of anything new. He was interested in antiquity and earnest in seeking out knowledge from old books. That was all.

In spite of this, his disciples, and we are told that there were three thousand of them, regarded him with all the veneration that is shown to great religious leaders. Those who had immediate access to him, stood, or sat near him, watching the minutest details of his conduct. From one of these disciples we learn that he never shot at a bird that was perching, or fished with a net. We are also told exactly how he conducted himself in court, and amongst villagers; how he ate his food, lay in bed, and sat in his carriage; how he rose up in the presence of older men and of those in mourning, and how his countenance changed when he was angry, and when he saw a great display of viands on the table. He was a master of all that was correct in manners, a supreme authority on deportment and ceremony.

Existing side by side in China with Confucianism was a religion of an entirely different character, Taoism. Only in China could two religions so divergent in outlook and so different in method have lived together amicably. Whereas Confucianism concerned itself with every item in a man's behaviour, the Taoist paid attention only to the inner attitude of the heart and mind. The two teachings held scarcely anything in common, but seemed to have tolerated each other, however critical they may have been of each other's points of view.

There are people [wrote Han Fei Tzu, to the king of Ch'in] who walk apart from the crowd, priding themselves on being different from other men. They preach the doctrine of quietism but their exposition of it is couched in baffling and mysterious terms. I submit to your majesty that this quietness is of no practical value to anyone, and that the language in which it is couched is not founded on any real principle ... I submit that man's duty in life is to serve his prince and nourish his parents, neither of which things can be done by quietness. I further submit that it is man's duty in all that he teaches to promote loyalty and good faith, and the legal constitution. This cannot be done in terms that are vague and mysterious. The doctrine of the quietists is a false one likely to lead people astray.

Han Fei Tzu, like many since his time, judged the value of the religion by the material benefits that accrued from it, and certainly when assessed by such a method, Taoism would be found woefully deficient. It was a religion of inaction, of humility, and of acceptance, acceptance amongst other things of King Ch'in, and of the legal constitution on which Han Fei Tzu set such store. But the writer was certainly justified in his complaint that the exposition of the Taoists was baffling and mysterious. None of the mystical religions of the East have ever placed any reliance on the written word, and have always handed on their teachings by word of mouth. The Taoists went even further. Not only did they consider books on the Tao useless, but since words themselves express only such things as belong to ordinary states of consciousness, they were deemed to be irrelevant to the transcendental knowledge of the Tao.

Do not seek precision [wrote Chuang Tzu when referring to Tao]. I myself have traversed it this way and that; yet still know only where it begins. I have roamed at will through its stupendous spaces. I know how to get to them, but I do not know where they end.

When the Taoist spoke of his experiences, he spoke only to arouse interest in them, and not with any idea of describing them. It is with good reason, therefore, that the Tao is often called the wordless doctrine.

The Tao that can be trodden is not the enduring and unchanging Tao.
The Name that can be named is not the enduring and unchanging Name.
Conceived of as having no name, it is the Originator of Heaven and Earth;
Conceived of as having a name (Teh), it is the Mother of all things.
Always without desire it must be found,
If its deep mystery we would sound.
But if desire always within us be,
Its outer fringe is all that we shall see.

Under these two aspects, it is really the same; but as development takes place, it receives the different names. Together we call them the Mystery. Where the Mystery is the deepest is the gate of all that is subtle and wonderful. (*Tao Teh King*, MAX MÜLLER)

As in all other mystical religions, he who would understand the Tao must himself partake of its nature and, as a first step, he must free himself of all personal reactions and desires. The same idea is expressed in St John's gospel. 'He that loveth not God, knoweth not God; for God is Love.' The Tao that cannot be named is the infinite, the Tao with the name, Teh, is the infinite in operation, the Mother and Creator of all things. The parallel between this and the Brahman, and the creative power of the Brahman manifested in Mâyâ, should be noted.

The *Tao Teh King* is reputed to have been written by Lao Tze. The story of its authorship is as follows. Lao Tze, disgusted with the decadence of the times, decided to withdraw from the world, and with this in mind proceeded towards the pass leading from China to the West. On his journey, he was recognized by Yin Hsi, himself a well-known Taoist, who insisted that Lao Tze, before going into seclusion, should leave behind some written record. To this Lao Tze eventually agreed, and wrote the *Tao Teh King*. Many sinologists, amongst others Arthur Giles, throw much doubt on this story of the authorship of the *Tao Teh King*.

In order to give some indication of the nature of Taoism, the following extracts from this so-called work of Lao Tze are appended.

The highest excellence is like [that of] water. The excellence of water appears in its benefiting all things, and in its occupying, without striving [to the contrary], the low place which all men dislike. Hence [its way] is near to [that of] the Tao.

It should be noted that water is held up to the Taoist as a model because its nature is always to seek the lowest place. This is a very common image in Taoist sayings.

When gold and jade fill the hall, their possessor cannot keep them safe. When wealth and honours lead to arrogancy, this brings its evil on itself. When the work is done, and one's name is becoming distinguished, to withdraw into obscurity is the way of Heaven.

Who can [make] the muddy water [clear]? Let it be still, and it will gradually become clear. Who can secure the condition of rest? Let movement go on, and the condition of rest will gradually arise.

Therefore the sage holds in his embrace the one thing [of humility], and manifests it to all the world. He is free from self-display, and therefore he shines; from self-assertion, and therefore he is distinguished; from self-boasting, and therefore his merit is acknowledged; from self-complacency, and therefore he acquires superiority It is because he is thus free from striving that therefore no one in the world is able to strive with him.

He who stands on his tiptoes does not stand firm; he who stretches his legs does not walk [easily]. [So], he who displays himself does not shine; he who asserts his own views is not distinguished; he who vaunts himself does not find his merit acknowledged; he who is self-conceited has no superiority allowed to him. Such conditions, viewed from the standpoint of the Tao, are like remnants of food, or a tumour on the body, which all dislike. Hence those who pursue [the course] of the Tao do not adopt and allow them.

Man takes his law from the Earth; the Earth takes its law from Heaven; Heaven takes its law from the Tao. The law of the Tao is its being what it is.

The Tao produced One; One produced Two; Two produced Three; Three produced all things. All things leave behind them the Obscurity [out of which they have come], and go forward to embrace the Brightness [into which they have emerged], while they are harmonized by the Breath of Vacancy.

It should be noted that the Taoist saying 'three produced all things' is in conformity with the view of the Sankhya philosopher that all phenomena are the result of the interaction of the three *gunas*. (See Chapter 10.)

He who knows other men is discerning; he who knows himself is intelligent. He who overcomes others is strong; he who overcomes himself is mighty. He who is satisfied with his lot is rich; he who goes on acting with energy has a [firm] will.

He who does not fail in the requirements of his position continues long; he who dies and yet does not perish has longevity.

The Tao in its regular course does nothing [for the sake of doing it], and so there is nothing which it does not do.

If princes and kings were able to maintain it, all things would of themselves be transformed by them.

If this transformation became to me an object of desire, I would express the desire by the nameless simplicity.

Scholars of the highest class, when they hear about the Tao, earnestly carry it into practice. Scholars of the middle class, when they have heard about it, seem now to keep it and now to lose it. Scholars of the lowest class, when they have heard about it, laugh greatly at it. If it were not [thus] laughed at, it would not be fit to be the Tao.

The softest thing in the world dashes against and overcomes the hardest; that which has no [substantial] existence enters where there is no crevice. I know hereby what advantage belongs to doing nothing [with a purpose].

When the Tao prevails in the world, they send back their swift horses to [draw] the dung-carts. When the Tao is disregarded in the world, the war-horses breed in the border lands.

There is no guilt greater than to sanction ambition; no calamity greater than to be discontented with one's lot; no fault greater than the wish to be getting. Therefore the sufficiency of contentment is an enduring and unchanging sufficiency.

If I were suddenly to become known, and put into a position to conduct a government according to the great Tao, what I should be most afraid of would be a boastful display.

He who has in himself abundantly the attributes of a Tao is like an infant. Poisonous insects will not sting him; fierce beasts will not seize him, birds of prey will not strike him.

He who knows the Tao does not care to speak about it; he who is ever ready to speak about it does not know it.

Sincere words are not fine; fine words are not sincere. Those who are skilled in the Tao do not dispute about it; the disputatious are not skilled in it. Those who know the Tao are not extensively learned; the extensively learned do not know it.

The sage does not accumulate for himself. The more that he expends for others, the more does he possess of his own; the more that he gives to others, the more does he have to himself. (MAX MÜLLER'S translation)

The thesis of the Taoist is similar to that of the Vedântist. To know reality, a higher state of consciousness must be reached, a state that is only attainable if personal desires, preconceptions, and fantasies are laid aside. Hence Lao Tze's attack on that much-vaunted and highly prized entity of modern life, what is known as individuality or personality. Our personal idiosyncrasies only allow us to see that which is purely subjective, limited, and in conformity with its views. Personality must be rendered passive, if that state of consciousness is to be reached in which *subject* and *object* become one. 'Never to have known that whereby we know is to cast away a treasure that is ours.' (Lu Shih Ch'un Ch'in, quoted by Arthur Waley, in *The Way and Its Power*.) But on this higher level of thought, the language which was created to meet the demands of lower levels is unable to express what has been seen. 'The name that can be named is not the enduring and unchanging name.'

Obviously there could be no mutual understanding between the followers of Confucius and of Lao Tze, and for this very reason we are fortunate in possessing a description of a meeting between the two leaders from the brush of that inimitable sage Chuang Tzu. Lao Tze was fifty years older than Confucius, who always referred to him as the Old Philosopher. Chuang Tzu gives the following description of their meeting ;

Confucius had lived to the age of fifty-one without hearing Tao, when he went south to Pe'i, to see Lao Tze.

Lao Tze said, 'So you have come, sir, have you? I hear you are considered a wise man up north. Have you got Tao?'

'Not yet,' answered Confucius.

'In what direction', asked Lao Tze, 'have you sought for it?'

'I sought it for five years', replied Confucius, 'in the science of numbers, but did not succeed.'

'And then? . . .' continued Lao Tze.

'Then', said Confucius, 'I spent twelve years seeking for it in the doctrine of the Yin and Yang, also without success.'

'Just so,' rejoined Lao Tze. 'Were Tao something which could be presented, there is no man but would present it to his sovereign, or to his parents. Could it be imparted or given, there is no man but would impart it to his brother or give it to his child. But this is impossible, for the following reason. Unless there is a suitable endowment within, Tao will not abide. Unless there is outward correctness, Tao will not operate. The external being unfitted for the impression of the internal, the true sage does not seek to imprint. The internal being unfitted for the reception of the external, the true sage does not seek to receive.'

Confucius was a man who set great store on correct behaviour and he had attained a great reputation for integrity and charitableness.

'Reputation is public property; you may not appropriate it in excess. Charity and duty to one's neighbour are as caravanserais established by wise rulers of old; you may stop there one night, but not for long, or you will incur reproach.

'The perfect men of old took their road through charity, stopping a night with duty to their neighbour, on their way to ramble in transcendental space. Feeding on the produce of non-cultivation, and establishing themselves in the domain of no obligations, they enjoyed their transcendental inaction. Their food was ready to hand; and being under no obligations to others, they did not put anyone under obligation to themselves. The ancients called this the outward visible sign of an inward and spiritual grace.

'Those who make wealth their all in all, cannot bear loss of money. Those who make distinction their all in all, cannot bear loss of fame. Those who affect power will not place authority in the hands of others. Anxious while holding, distressed if losing, yet never taking warning from the past and seeing the folly of their pursuit – such men are the accursed of God.

'Resentment, gratitude, taking, giving, censure of self, instruction of others, power of life and death – these eight are the instruments of right; but only he who can adapt himself to the vicissitudes of fortune, without being carried away, is fit to use them. Such a one is an upright man among the upright. And he whose heart is not so constituted – the door of divine intelligence is not yet opened for him.'

Confucius spoke of charity and duty to one's neighbour, and Lao Tze answered as follows:

'The chaff from winnowing will blind a man's eyes so that he cannot tell the points of the compass. Mosquitoes will keep a man awake all night with their biting. And just in the same way this talk of charity and duty to one's neighbour drives me nearly crazy. Sir! Strive to keep the world to its own original simplicity. And as the wind bloweth where it listeth, so let virtue establish itself. Wherefor such undue energy, as though searching for a fugitive with a big drum?

'The snow-goose is white without a daily bath. The raven is black without daily colouring itself. The original simplicity of black and of white is beyond the reach of argument. When the pond dries up and the fishes are left upon dry ground, to moisten them with the breath or to damp them with a little spittle is not to be compared with leaving them in the first instance in their native rivers and lakes.'

On returning from a visit to Lao Tze, Confucius did not speak for three days. A disciple asked him, saying, 'Master, when you saw Lao Tze, in what direction did you admonish him?'

'I saw a dragon,' replied Confucius, 'a dragon which by convergence showed a body, by radiation became colour, and riding upon the clouds of heaven, nourished the two principles of creation. My mouth was agape: I could not shut it. How then do you think I was going to admonish Lao Tze?' (*The Bible of the World*)

There exists in Chinese literature another account of Lao Tze's conversation with Confucius. It is found in the *Shih Chi*, or 'Historical Records' of Ssu-ma Ch'ien, which was written in the second century before Christ.

Confucius journeyed to the land of Chou to make inquiry of Lao Tze concerning ceremonies; Lao Tze made reply: 'The men about whom you talk are dead, and their bones are moldered to dust: only their words are left. Moreover, when the superior man gets his opportunity, he mounts aloft; but when the time is against him, he is carried along by the force of circumstances. I have heard that a good merchant, though he have treasures safely stored, appears as if he were poor; and that the superior man, though his virtue be complete, is yet, to outward seeming, stupid. Put away your proud air and many desires, your insinuating habit and wild will. They are of no advantage to you. This is all I have to tell you.

Confucius's comments to his disciples upon this meeting are given by the same authority as follows:

> I know how birds can fly, fishes swim, and the animals run. But the runner may be snared, the swimmer hooked, and the flyer shot by the arrow. But there is the dragon – I cannot tell how he mounts on the wind through the clouds, and rises to heaven. Today I have seen Lao Tze, and can only compare him to the dragon. [The dragon is the Chinese symbol for greatness.]

Taoism and Confucianism are excellent examples of two different types of religion, the one mainly concerned with the inner state and the other with external behaviour. They cater for two classes of humanity, Confucianism supplying the needs of men who would have found Taoism too mystical and too contemplative, and who sought expression for their religious feelings in leading an active upright life in conformity with certain well-defined and easily understood values. In Lao Tze's words, the followers of Confucius travelled along the road of charity, but instead of 'stopping a night with duty to their neighbours on their way to ramble in transcendental space', they remained in the caravanserai indefinitely. The message of Confucius is summed up in the following text taken from *The Four Books*, translated by James Legge. 'What the Great Learning teaches is – to illustrate illustrious virtue, to renovate the people, and to rest in highest excellence.' Confucius placed great emphasis on the 'renovation of the people' and considered that the highest aim a man could have was to fit himself to. become an administrator. He was essentially a practical man of affairs who, although he recognized the contemplative method of living, was a little suspicious of it. 'Pay reverence', he said, 'to the invisible entities, but keep them at a distance.' His disciples were not encouraged to spend their time trying to find answers to unanswerable questions. On one occasion they asked him to tell them about death. He answered: 'If you cannot understand what life is, how can you understand about death?' He felt that his chief work was to encourage the study of the classical writers and to promote the culture of the 'superior person'. If the people were to be properly looked after a supply of these 'superior persons' must be available to princes for administrative posts. One of his aims was similar to that of Plato, namely, the production of a perfect state governed by administrators who had the welfare of the people at heart and who were especially equipped for their office. 'Confucianism' is the favoured religion of the West, where it takes the form of an unostentatious and charitable Christianity. It is the religion of the decent conscientious Englishman and American with a strict code of honour, a feeling for the oppressed, and a respect for the ancient traditions of their countries. It is the religion taught in innumerable churches, in the universities and public schools, and in Scout Rallies, the religion of service. That it survives in a world that seems to be losing all spiritual values is a fact for which it is impossible to be too thankful. It is not for all to ramble with the Taoist in transcendental space. Krishna in the *Bhagavad Gita* says :

> I have already declared that in this world there is a twofold path
> – that of the Sankhyas by devotion in the shape of true knowledge,
> and that of the Yogins by devotion in the shape of action.

Confucianism and the more evangelical forms of Christianity are related to Karma-Yoga, the Yoga of Right Action. It will be recalled that Krishna discusses with Arjuna inaction, wrong action, and right action, describing the last-named as duty performed without attachment to the fruits of action. 'He who is possessed of devotion, abandoning the fruits of actions attains the highest tranquillity.' Christ and Buddha also taught that it was only when good works were performed free from all personal aims that valuable results were likely to follow.

Confucianism and Taoism catered for two different types of humanity in ancient China, the active and the contemplative, types that generally find great difficulty in understanding each other. Especially difficult was it for the Confucianist to understand the Taoist, for, as the latter confessed, he had no words in which to express what he knew to be true. Higher states of consciousness were not only unattended by tangible phenomena but their results could not be expressed in the language of everyday life.

CHAPTER 14

BUDDHISM

IN the previous chapter emphasis was laid on the unity of all religious truths; it was pointed out that only in its outward trappings and methods of exposition does one religion differ from another. In this and in the following chapter two of the greatest religions in the world's history, Christianity and Buddhism, will be compared and contrasted. Before dealing with the tenets of these religions it will be advisable to indicate certain differences in their respective attitudes to doctrine.

Although Buddhism, like Christianity, has an enormous literature, all the works that it contains are really nothing more than gigantic commentaries on a few comparatively simple directions given by Buddha to his disciples. They are not regarded as infallible writings to be accepted on the grounds that they are authoritative. The initiate into Buddhism approaches the religion in exactly the same way as a scientist approaches a scientific problem to be solved by experimental study. A few preliminary instructions are given by one who is older and more experienced than himself, and it then remains for him to put the matter to the test. No form of faith is demanded of him other than faith in the possibility that by careful experimentation he will succeed in discovering the truth. Only by the results that he obtains from his experiments will he know whether what he has been told beforehand is true or not.

Primitive Christianity in the first century after Christ took up a somewhat similar attitude to the discovery of truth. Knowledge was obtained by direct experience and an intellectual assent was not demanded of the initiate. Church councils had not yet formulated doctrines that priests were pledged to teach, and members of the Church compelled to accept under pain of excommunication. Intellectual assent meant nothing ; experience meant everything. But whereas Christianity after the expulsion of the Gnostic heresy, and even before it, departed from this attitude, Buddhism has maintained it.

Disciples are discouraged from speaking of that which they have not yet experienced.

For a religious devotee to preach the doctrine to the multitude before having realized it to be true, instead of meditating upon it (and testing its truth) in solitude, is a grievous mistake. (*Precepts to Gurus*, translated from the Tibetan by Evans-Wentz)

What is regarded by some people as being the essential difference between Buddhism and Christianity is that, in the former, there is no idea of a personal God. For this reason Buddhism has sometimes been called a philosophy rather than a religion. That the Buddhist does not describe the Universal Spirit that underlies all creation in terms of personality is true, for personality inevitably implies some degree of limitation. Only too often the personal deity is invested with the attributes required by the worshipper. He is the God of the Chosen People, the God of Battles, the Great Physician, or the Almsgiver according to the needs of the moment. The Infinite is unspecifiable and both the Hindu and the Buddhist define the unknowable only in negative terms of 'not that'. Moreover, Buddhism refuses all dualistic conceptions, the Creator and the Created, God and man, the Worshipped and the worshipper. As Guénon has phrased it:

In reality, Buddhism is no more atheistical than it is theistic or pantheistic; all that need be said is that it does not place itself at the point of view where these various terms have any meaning.

In any case, the Buddhist acknowledges a hierarchy of higher beings, the hierarchy of the Buddhas. So long as there exist beings so high above him, the Buddhist feels no need for the existence of a Personal Deity, whose attributes are, in any case, utterly beyond his powers of comprehension.

Other differences between the two religions result from variations in their underlying philosophy. Both religions recognize the existence of cause and effect, and that what a man sows, that also shall he reap, but the Buddhist belief in reincarnation provides a long series of lives in which the reaping and sowing will take place. Whether the Christian doctrine of the forgiveness of sins and the Buddhist doctrine of *karma* are reconcilable or not depends on the meaning we give to the word forgiveness. If it be taken to mean the non-rising of an inevitable effect from a previous cause, or the arbitrary wiping out of that effect after it has been produced, then, of course, the two ideas are irreconcilable. But forgiveness can never mean this, for should I kill a man, that man remains dead whether I be forgiven or not. Forgiveness does not entail the complete elimination of the results of an action. The effect of the sin on my character is all that can be altered by forgiveness, and this entails first that my action should be recognized as a sin, then repented of, and finally made the occasion for a decision that the offence will not be repeated. It is the continuation of the feeling of guilt and the effect that this will have on my character that are remitted, not the external consequences of my act. There exists therefore no unbridgeable gulf between the Christian idea of forgiveness and the Buddhist view of *karma*.

Because the Buddhist believes that errors committed in one life are atoned for by suffering in another, any idea of a hell is inconceivable to him. However long a man may suffer in future incarnations for what he has done in this life, eventually, even if aeons have to pass, the Round of the Wheel will take an upward turn. So also is the idea of a heaven, where the enlightened ones remain in bliss, and forgetfulness of the suffering of their fellow-creatures on earth is inconceivable to them. Compassion is for the Buddhist what Love (sometimes translated as Charity) is for the Christian. It is the first-fruit of knowledge, for no man can witness the useless suffering of his fellow-creatures without being filled with compassion. The Buddhist rejects the idea that any being is unalterably evil, and, more fortunate than Origen, who was punished by his fellow-Christians for maintaining that in the end the Devil would be saved, he can show compassion for all creatures that are alive. And because of this pity the Buddhas, the Enlightened Ones, who have gained liberation from the wheel of existence of their own free will return to earth to help their suffering fellows.

Go on, with hearts overflowing with compassion; in the world that is rent by suffering, be instructors, and wherever the darkness of ignorance may happen to reign, kindle there a torch. (Buddhist writing.)

I seek no reward, not even to be reborn in the celestial worlds, but I seek to bring back those who have gone astray, to enlighten those who live in the darkness of error, to banish from the world all sorrow and all suffering. (Sayings from two Chinese sages)

It was from this very point, namely the universal existence of suffering, that Buddha started in his search for enlightenment. Here was a fact, the acceptance of which called for no act of faith. Suffering was a disease that affected the whole of mankind. When a patient is sick, it is necessary first to discover the cause of the illness, and then to apply a remedy if any remedy be available. These were the two questions for which Buddha sought answers.

The answer that he eventually found to the first question, as to the cause of the sickness, was 'ignorance'. Man suffered because he remained in ignorance of the real nature of things and especially of his own relationship to the Universe. Ignorance is to Buddhism what original sin is to Christianity, and by ignorance is meant not only lack of knowledge, but what is of still greater importance, the existence of wrong ideas. It is nescience rather than ignorance that is the cause of man's suffering, and before knowledge can be given it is necessary first to get rid of that which is false. Wrong ideas must be eliminated before true ideas can find a place.

The means by which spiritual knowledge can be attained was called by Buddha the Eightfold Path to Deliverance. By deliverance is meant not only deliverance from suffering, but also from the wheel of the *Sangsara*, that is to say, from the repetition of birth, death, and rebirth into the phenomenal world. When ignorance has ceased, desires born of that ignorance no longer arise. The absence of desire in turn leads to the cessation of useless activity and this deprives the wheel of existence of its motive power, so that it no longer turns.

Action is no longer needed when once the harmony of knowledge has been achieved. In real knowledge there can be no action, because there is nothing to change or improve. Change and imperfection go hand in hand. Once Enlightenment has been attained the wheel of change stops, and stability begins, in which there is no action and no rebirth or death. Action breeds action for ever. Enlightenment breeds enlightenment for ever. (MARCO PALLIS)

The quintessence of the Buddhist doctrine in embodied in the Four Truths which may be tabulated as follows :

1. Suffering
2. Cause of Suffering } together constituting the diagnosis

3. Cessation of Suffering } together constituting
4. Way leading to a Cessation of Suffering } the cure

The way to the cessation of suffering is known as the Eightfold Path. Buddha states that, for deliverance, eight requirements are necessary. These requirements fall naturally into three groups that may be described under the three terms wisdom, morality, and concentration of mind. The eight requirements for the elimination of suffering and the attainment of knowledge were according to Buddha as follows :

Right views
Right resolve } Wisdom
Right speech

Right action
Right means of livelihood } Morality

Right effort
Right attention or awareness } Concentration of Mind
Right meditation

The possession of right views is the first essential, without which nothing can follow. Naturally, Buddhists believe to be right those views that find expression in the teaching of Buddha. It is not necessary, however, that these should be accepted blindly, but only that they should be examined and pondered over. All that the disciple is urged to do is to examine the foundation of his own beliefs and to reflect where these beliefs lead, and then to examine impartially those enunciated by Buddha.

Although the acquirement of right views comes at the commencements of the Eightfold Path, it is also the final goal. The object of him who follows this path is to reach right and perfect knowledge, so that he may be liberated from the illusory and painful round of the Sangsara. Right views are therefore the Alpha and Omega of the whole of Buddhistic teaching. Whilst the intellect suffices for the earlier steps along the path, alone it is insufficient for the attainment of higher knowledge. Much, therefore, of the disciple's work is directed to the removal of the hindrances that prevent him from reaching that state of consciousness in which truth may be directly apprehended.

The preliminary formulation of right views is naturally followed by a determination to make progress along the path to enlightenment. This is the second requirement, right resolve, and it is Buddha's formulation of Christ's admonition that he who has set his hand to the plough must not look back. The four requirements, right speech, right action, right means of livelihood, and right effort, all constitute the ethics of Buddhism. It is obvious that in a religion that teaches a man to look upon every living creature as his fellow, some means of livelihood must be ruled out. No Buddhist could earn his living as a butcher, trafficker in drugs, or as a soldier. An intellectual assent to a doctrine is insufficient, for a truth must be lived in order to be understood.

The four branches of the path concerned with conduct may, therefore, be regarded as being both a result and a cause of attaining right views. As the disciple learns to define more and more accurately his relationship to his neighbour and the whole world, so is his conduct inevitably drawn more and more into line with those views. His beliefs help his conduct, his conduct his beliefs.

The penultimate requirements are perfect attention and awareness, practice in which is essential for the final requirements, right meditation. These, like right views, are really necessary from start to finish for, if thought and actions are to be of value, they must be made responsible and deliberate. They must cease to be blind reactions, even if they happen to be good reactions, and become thoughts and activities that are deliberately dedicated to the purposes of enlightenment. From the very beginning it must be the disciple's aim to remove as much of his life as possible from the power of accidental influences and to bring it into line with his resolve. A nature which is entirely swayed by the emotions (even when those emotions are good) is like a weathercock, blown this way and that way by the breath of every impulse. It is with the aim of increasing control that some Buddhist teachers prescribe for their disciple certain physical exercises that bring under the will movements that are normally made quite mechanically.

The converse method employed in Europe and America, namely that of making activities even more automatic than they already are by the use of slogans, press propaganda, drilling, and marching in step, would be looked upon with little favour by Buddhists. A man, they would say, is already sufficiently automatic without the use of additional methods to make him more so. The aim of the Buddhist is the reverse, namely to make a man more aware of his activities so that he may ultimately be able to control them. The disciple is therefore told to direct his attention to all his movements, thoughts, sensations, and feelings, so as to become more aware of them. Madame David-Neel, who has made a lifelong study of Buddhism, and from whom I have borrowed freely in this chapter, describes this part of the disciple's training as follows:

Nothing of what goes on in us should escape us. Neither should we miss anything which happens around us, or within the range of our senses. The Buddhist scriptures tell us that one must be conscious that one gets up when one gets up, that one sits down when one sits down, and so on with all movements. We should be conscious of the feelings which arise in us and recognize them. Now there is born in me covetousness or anger; now sensual desires are arising ... When the power of attention is enhanced, and one has reached the point where one misses none of the phenomena·which are occurring in and around oneself, one proceeds to investigate them, and to search for their causes.

Why should anger suddenly blaze up in me? Because this man has offended me, has injured me....

And what effect will my impulse of anger produce in me? Will it in any way profit me? ...

All the feelings – envy, sensuality, etc. – may be the objects of this kind of examination. One must associate with them the more refined feelings of pride, vanity, etc., and also those feelings which are considered praiseworthy: sympathy, benevolence, modesty....

He who pays attention, according to the Buddhist methods, should not give way to his impulses without examining them. Neither should he approve or blame himself, basing his blame or approval on the injunctions of moral codes whose authority and justness he has not investigated.

If he performs a charitable deed, if he accomplishes an act of devotion, he should question himself as to the motives which he obeyed, should scrutinize his feelings and their origins, just as when he has committed an action said to be evil. The result of this kind of interrogation will often result in a shifting of moral values and will show in a much less favourable light the noble action on which one was ready to pride oneself.

According to this writer the Hinayâna Buddhists practise this continuously, distinguishing four directions for the attention: on the body, on sensations, on thoughts, and on the working of the mind. Another Buddhist practice for assisting the cultivation of attention is that the disciple at the end of each day should be made to recall the actions he has performed, the feelings which he has experienced, and the thoughts which he has entertained. Recollection is directed backwards, beginning with the last action, thought, sensation, or feeling, and ending with the first moment of awakening. The most insignificant details are recalled equally with the most important, the idea being to allow nothing to become obliterated. Buddhism assigns to the memory a very important role, and everything that has been seen, heard, or perceived must be remembered. In the ordinary way only a small proportion of the innumerable sensations and thoughts passing through the brain are clearly registered in consciousness. This exercise of recalling in the reverse order all the events, thoughts, and feelings of the day is not peculiar to Buddhism. It is part of the mind-control practised by Hindu schools of mental training. Some Buddhists, notably Tsong Khapa, the reformer of Tibetan Buddhism, maintained that some measure of control has to be exercised over the working of the mind even during sleep. In his principal work, the *Lam-rin*, he writes:

It is essential not to waste time given to sleep, either by remaining when once asleep inert as a stone, or by allowing one's mind to wander incoherently in absurd or harmful dreams.

Practice in attention is a stepping-stone to the final requirement of the Eightfold Path, meditation. For this final requirement the disciple is recommended to seat himself in an isolated spot, and to contemplate the procession of thoughts and images which without his having desired it, arise and hurry through his mind like an endless slide passing through a lantern. By so doing he will come to realize that his life is but a succession of phenomena, arising and disappearing with dizzy rapidity. The origin of this movement of thoughts, images, and emotions is at present unknowable to him; it is what is called 'energy arising by itself'. Also he will in time perceive that surrounding objects, like himself, are nothing but a vortex of movement. A tree ceases to appear as a solid enduring object, but will be seen as a continual succession of sudden manifestations, the apparent continuity of which is due to the rapidity with which these 'flashes' follow each other.

As a result of what he has seen both in himself and in the objects of his contemplation, the disciple will cease to believe in his individuality. He will know that he possesses no permanent and compounded ego, and knowing this, he will have arrived at the fundamental doctrines of Buddhism, namely that all aggregates are impermanent, that all aggregates are doomed to suffer, and that all the constitutive elements of existence are devoid of a 'Self'. This constitutes the creed of all Buddhists to whatever school they may belong, a creed that is put forward not as an article of faith, but as a subject to be examined, and only accepted if it be found to be true.

This idea of non-individuality is a difficult one for Europeans to grasp. Perhaps the best way of understanding it is that suggested by Marco Pallis in *Peaks and Lamas*. He pictures all living things as a river, formed from many tiny trickles in the mountains. It gathers innumerable tributaries as it flows, and increases its volume by increments from a thousand different sources. Men have mapped out the branches of the river and have given names even to the tiny channels from which these are formed. The river exists, but what drop of water that takes part in its formation has the right to say 'I am the river, I am I?' The drop exists but only as part of the river. 'Self-denial', there-fore, means much more to the Buddhist than it does to the Christian. To the latter it implies only the avoidance of selfish-ness, and the struggle with the feeling of one's own importance, a feeling that generally results in the invasion of the rights of others. But the Buddhist would say that this struggle with self-indulgence is merely the treatment of a symptom. The cause of the disease lies deeper, in the belief that a separate self, a perma-nent ego exists in this flux of sensations, thoughts, and emo-tions. Self-denial to the Buddhist is literally self-denial. In a Tibetan work, *The Powerful Good Wish*, quoted by Pallis, it is written:

Immersed in ignorance and obscured by delusion, the Knower (Mind) was afeared and confused. Then came the idea 'I' and 'Other' and hatred. As these gained force a continuous chain of Action (*Karma*) was produced. The Root Ignorance is the abysmal ground of the knower's unconscious Ignorance. The other Ignorance is that which regards self and others to be different and separate. The thought which regards beings as 'two' begets a hesitating doubting state. A subtle feeling of Attachment arises, which if allowed to gain force, gradually resolves itself into strong attach-ment and a craving for food, clothing, dwellings, wealth, and friends ... There is no end to the Action flowing from ideas of dualism.

How then does the Buddhist regard a person? He sees a per-son as composed of five parts, called *Skandhas*: a body, sensa-tions, perceptions, mental formations (ideas, wishes, etc.), and consciousness. The terms 'I' and 'individual person' are to the Buddhist merely convenient terms for describing a changing combination of physical and psychic phenomena. Each of these five skandhas, or parts, of a person are in turn compounded. The body is formed from an initial supply of material derived from the parents, that is supplemented later by the material ob-tained from nourishment. Even the body has no real personal existence, but is the product of the transformation of food. Nor can an 'I' be located in any other of the four aggregates of the person, that is to say in the rolling panorama of sensations, perceptions, and mental forms that constitute the 'psyche'. In vain does one seek in the physical or mental parts of an individual for something that is not in turn dependent on something else, that exists by itself, 'independent and self-produced, unconnected with anything else', a 'veritable I'.

Madame David-Neel quotes a Tibetan parable that makes clear the Buddhist view of a person.

A 'person' resembles an assembly composed of a number of members: In this assembly discussion never ceases. Now and again one of the members rises, makes a speech, and suggests an action; his colleagues approve, and it is decided that what he has proposed shall be executed. Often several members of the assembly rise at the same time and propose different things, and each of them, for private reasons, supports his own proposal. It may happen that these differences of opinion, and the passion which each of the orators brings into the debate, will provoke a quarrel, even a violent quarrel, in the assembly. Fellow-members may even come to blows.

It also happens that some members of the assembly leave it of their own accord; others are gradually pushed out, and others again are expelled by force, by their colleagues. All this time newcomers introduce themselves into the assembly, either by gently sidling in or by forcing the doors.

Again, one notes that certain members of the assembly are slowly perishing; their voices become feeble, and finally they are no longer heard. Others, on the contrary, who were weak and timid, become stronger and bolder; they become violent, shouting their proposals; they terrify their colleagues, and dominate them, and end by making themselves dictators.

The members of this assembly are the physical and mental elements which constitute the 'person'; they are our instincts, our tendencies, our ideas, our beliefs, our desires, etc. Through the causes which engendered it, each of them is the descendant and heir of many lines of causes, of many series of phenomena, going far back into the past, and whose traces are lost in the shadowy depths of eternity.

It is thus that the psychologists of Tibet explain the contradictory tendencies of which we are conscious, and also our gradual or sudden changes of opinion and of conduct. Both one and the other depend on the temporary composition of the assembly which is the 'person', the 'I', and on the character of the members who are for the time being in the majority and elect its president.

The Buddhist argues that the only thing that could be regarded as 'real' in a person would be something that was self-engendered and homogeneous, a 'self' whose existence did not depend on external causes. Such a 'self' would have also to be 'eternal', otherwise if it came into existence at a particular moment of time, this would mean that some cause had produced it. Also, if it disappeared, this would prove that its existence had depended on certain conditions and that these conditions having ceased, its existence had also ceased.

What then is real in a man? This can only be realized when the disciple ceases to identify himself with this impermanent aggregate of physical and psychic attributes. When he has learnt this lesson personal preferences and aversions cease to have a meaning for him. He has reached the goal of non-attachment to self and abandoned his partisan attitude to life. With the departure of desire and aversion, there departs also the capacity to suffer. He is no longer compelled to act as a cog in the wheel of existence. He has reached the goal of Deliverance and Enlightenment – *Nirvana*.

The word *Nirvana* has been much misunderstood by Europeans. Literally, it implies extinction, like the snuffing out of a candle. But that which is extinguished is nescience and its train of consequences, not the soul. Buddha taught that in life we are carried along by the three 'streams' of *raga* (passion), *dosa* (anger), and *moha* (illusion). He defined Nirvana as the state in which freedom is gained from these controlling influences. And Buddha's definition was followed by words pregnant with meaning.

When thou hast understood the dissolution of all the fabrications, thou shalt understand that which is *not* fabricated. (DHAMMAPADA)

To attempt to describe the positive as opposed to the negative side of Nirvana would be useless, as useless as to imagine what it is like to be living in a higher state of consciousness.

To regard 'Nirvana' as synonymous with the annihilation of

the soul is therefore totally incorrect. There is a story that the Buddha himself was asked the question:

'After death, does a Buddha [he who has attained Nirvana] exist, or does he not exist?' The Buddha did not reply, but he explained the reason for his silence on this point. A reply to this question would be profitless for him who received it, said the Buddha. 'Whether the Buddha exists or does not exist after death, one fact remains: there is birth, decrepitude, death, suffering, on which subjects I have given my teachings, showing the origin, the cause, and the ending of suffering, and the Way which leads to this ending ... I have not said whether the Buddha exists or does not exist after death because that has nothing to do with the foundations of the doctrine and does not lead to the absence of passion, to peace, to supernormal faculties, to the supreme wisdom, to Nirvana. (MADAME DAVID-NEEL)

This chapter could not close more fittingly than with the description of Buddhism given in the Dhammapada.

To refrain from all evil, to increase all good, to control one's own mind,
This is the teaching of all the Buddhas.

CHAPTER 15

CHRIST AND BUDDHA

IT was said that Christianity and Buddhism have much in common. This is explained by two facts, the similarity of the central truths expressed by all great religions, and the background against which Christianity grew up. Christianity can indeed only be understood after this background has been studied.

During Christ's lifetime there were several sections of Judaism. Neander divides the Israel of that day into three main sections, the Pharisees, who taught the dead letter of the law, the Sadducees, who did not believe in any spiritual life, and various mystical sects. The best known representatives of this third section of Israel were the Essenes, the Therapeutae, and the Nazarenes. Although all these mystical branches of Israel had their distinguishing features they were closely allied, and therefore equally hateful to the orthodox priests and Pharisees. So fearful was the dominant party of the mystical movement in Judea that according to Jerome all devout Jews were required to utter the following curse thrice daily: 'Send Thy curse, O God, upon the Nazarenes.' The term Nazarene, or Nazirite, is derived from the root word, *nazir*, signifying separation, or retirement from the world. The true Nazirite was a recluse, a prophet who dedicated himself to a spiritual life and made a vow of chastity and to abstain from wine. He lived a life of great austerity and allowed his hair to grow long, like that of an Indian yogi. John the Baptist was a member of this sect. Actually we know less about the beliefs of the Nazarenes than about those of the closely-allied Essenes and the Therapeutae, but by studying one of these three sects we are at the same time learning much about the others. A great deal of interesting information on this subject will be found in *Buddhism in Christendom*, by Arthur Lillie. The Therapeutae, as their name implies, were healers of body and soul. From Philo we learn that they and the Essenes lived an ascetic life, spending 'their time in fasting and contemplation, in prayer or reading. They believe themselves favoured with divine illumination – an inner light. They assemble on the Sabbath for worship, and to listen to mystical discourses on the traditional lore which they say has been handed down in secret amongst themselves.' He gives further details of their beliefs and their way of living. They believed that God had breathed into man some of his own divinity and that contemplation of this divine essence was the noblest exercise of man. Their aim was to enter into communion with the spiritual part of their nature. The similarity between the beliefs and practices of the Essenes and those of the Buddhists is emphasized in this description. Alliance with a higher world is the union desired by all Buddhists and yogis. A great many writers have no hesitation in asserting that the Essenes and the Therapeutae derived their beliefs and their practices directly from Buddhist missionaries living in Alexandria. Whether this be so or not it is impossible after studying the lives of the Essenes and Therapeutae to doubt that these mystical branches of Judaism borrowed much from Indian sources. Even a writer so unsympathetic to Eastern religions as Dean Milman gave it as his opinion that the Therapeutae sprang from 'the contemplative and indolent fraternities of India'.

This helps us to understand the uncompromising hostility of the orthodox Jewish priest to both John the Baptist and Christ. It is generally accepted that the former belonged to the Nazarene sect, but few ecclesiastical scholars would probably be prepared to admit the possibility that Christ was in sympathy with the mystical side of Judaism. Nevertheless, we find the opponents of Christ bringing the same indictment against Him that was brought against John the Baptist. Christ was also accused of being a member of the hated sect, the Nazarenes. This was the accusation written upon the Cross, 'Jesus the Nazarene, the King of the Jews'. It is true that orthodox churchmen prefer to regard the words ὁ Ναξαραῖος (John xix, 19) when applied to Christ as meaning 'of Nazareth', rather than 'the Nazarene'. They justify this translation by the statement in the Gospel of

St Matthew (ii, 23) that after the return from Egypt Jesus remained in the village of Nazareth with his parents. It is difficult, however, to explain thus why Pilate should record such an unimportant event alongside of the indictment that Christ proclaimed himself the King of the Jews. The hatred that orthodox Judaism felt for the Nazarenes was later transferred to Christ's follower, Paul. Tertullus the Orator sums up his accusations against Paul in the words:

> For we have found this man a pestilent fellow, and a mover of sedition amongst all the Jews, throughout the world, and a ringleader of the sect of Nazarenes. (Acts XXIV, 5)

In the eyes of the Pharisees and the orthodox priests John the Baptist, Christ, and Paul alike were members of the hated mystical sect.

Even if we disagree with this view that Christ was actually linked up with these mystical sects, and consequently, indirectly with Buddhism, we must admit that he was more in sympathy with them than with the pharisaical brand of Judaism. Otherwise it is difficult to understand why he elected to be baptized by John, and himself made use of a rite widely practised by the Essenes. In any case, the difference between the teachings of Christ and John the Baptist were so trifling that five of the latter's disciples (Andrew, John, Philip, Peter, and Bartholomew) were able to become Christ's Apostles without violating their Nazarene vows. But that Christ did not insist on their practising the methods of living which were formerly obligatory to them is shown by the complaint of John's disciples: 'Why is it that we and the Pharisees fast frequently, but thy disciples do not fast.' (Matthew ix, 14).

We know nothing about Christ during his youth and early manhood. A few pictures are given of him in the gospels as a child, and then he reappears as a man of thirty-three equipped for his mission, learned in the law, speaking as one with authority, and capable of holding his own against the lawyers and scholars who were only too eager to trip him up. What was Christ doing during those all-important years? There is nothing but legend on which to base any answer; one legend that he was working with John the Baptist, and the other that he was in an Essene monastery. Nobody can say how much or how little truth lies in these legends, but there can, at any rate, be little doubt that Christ had heard of Buddha before he started his mission. In spite of the poorness of communications in the ancient world, culture permeated along the caravan routes, and through the agency of travelling scholars and holy men. Oral teachings took the place of books, and what is more likely than that a serious-minded young man who knew, in his inmost heart, that he was dedicated to a mission to his country would take every opportunity that presented itself of sitting at the feet of a scholarly or devout traveller who arrived in the neighbourhood of his home? Whatever may have been the nature of Christ's divinity, he lived the life of an ordinary man, and as such, would equip himself to the best of his ability for his great mission to mankind. But it must be confessed that we possess only the scantiest knowledge concerning Christ. He left no writing, and even although the gospels may have been initially compiled in the first century, it is unlikely that they were completed until much later. Only in the second generation was the necessity felt for putting down on paper Christ's sayings, and the main incidents in his life. Previously to that, these sayings were spread by word of mouth, a method that seldom guarantees any high degree of accuracy. The evangelists finally collected these orally transmitted sayings, with any scrap of writing that may have been in existence, and compiled the gospels. The similarity of the Synoptic Gospels is explained by the hypothesis that Matthew and Luke used Mark's earlier version, together with an additional source, now lost, and known as Q. Critics have advanced the opinion that, regarded as historical documents, the gospels are probably quite inaccurate, and that in writing them, their authors were more eager to explain the faith of the Church (which by then had been formed), than to report verbatim the sayings of Christ. And even when no deliberate effort was made to justify the views of the developing Church by putting into Christ's mouth appropriate words, it is an undoubted fact that much of Christ's message has been lost later in transcription and translation. Every translator is familiar with the temptation to drag obscure sayings into line with preconceived views of what they are likely to mean. Even a change in punctuation, or the substitution of an indefinite for a definite article, may be sufficient to alter the meaning of a difficult passage, and of these there are many in the gospels. So, in the words of a great scholar of the gospels, we must accept the fact.

that the form of the earthly, no less than of the heavenly, Christ, is for the most part hidden from us. For all the inestimable value of the Gospels, they yield us little more than a whisper of His voice; we trace in them but the outskirts of His ways. (*History and Interpretation of the Gospels*, by R. H. Lightfoot)

The criticism of the historical accuracy of the gospels does not alter the fact that they could only have been written by men living on a higher level than the rest of mankind. However much they may have suffered in translation they bear unmistakable evidence of being the work of a higher type of humanity. Even if it were proved that Christ never existed but that the writers of the gospels created him for their own purposes, as Plato is said to have created Socrates, the value of the gospels as a higher revelation on which a religion can be founded still remains. That is one of the reasons why many of the sayings found in the gospels are difficult of comprehension by ordinary humanity.

Whether Christ was influenced by non-semitic factors or not, the builders of the early Church undoubtedly were. This is particularly noticeable in the description of the circumstances of Christ's birth. These details are not given in the earlier gospel, that of St Mark. I have but little knowledge of the history of the textual criticism to which the New Testament has been subjected by learned and able scholars and I am fully aware of my incompetence to make any pronouncements on this subject. The explanation of the similarities in the stories of the coming of Christ and of Buddha which most readily offers itself is that the description of Christ's birth was a later interpolation which was added after those responsible for the gospels of St Matthew and St Luke had completed their work, and at a time when the

Church was laying special emphasis on the divine origin of its founder. The Jews, as a race, put great weight on written authority, and were never tired of asserting that the events in the gospel were in accordance with the words uttered by some Old Testament prophet. They had the lawyer's attitude to religion, and liked to see everything properly documented and confirmed by a recognized authority. It was likely that they were anxious to see included in the gospels a suitable setting for the coming of Christ and to add to the splendour of the ideas his words conveyed the visible testimony of miraculous portents and signs. When this desire is present there is a similarity in the miraculous setting that is chosen. Since Buddha preceded Christ by five hundred years, it is possible that those who added this account of the coming of Christ to the gospels borrowed from Indian literature. Many years passed before the story of Christ's life was put on paper, and the details of Buddha's miraculous birth were recorded only a hundred and fifty years after his death. Consequently it is probable that legend played a large part in the description of Christ's birth, as it undoubtedly did in that of Buddha.

Buddha, like Christ, was reputed to be of virgin birth. His father was informed by angels of the coming of a miraculous child, and, according to the *Lalita Vistara*, 'the queen was permitted to lead the life of a virgin for thirty-two months'. She was told, as was Mary, in a vision, of the wondrous son that she would bear. On the day of Gautama's birth, an old priest plays the part of Simeon in the gospels, coming down from the mountains to predict the future greatness of Gautama. When he asked the angels why they rejoiced, they replied that 'they were joyful and exceedingly glad because the Buddha had been born, the Buddha on whom the hopes of humanity rested'. Then, having examined the child and confirmed the presence in him of the thirty-two signs of Buddahood, he did reverence before him and returned whence he came.

At the threshold of his career, Buddha, like Christ, was tempted by the Evil One, *Mara*. He was offered world dominion if he would give up his quest. Buddha replied: 'He who has seen pain and the source of pain, how could such a one bow to lusts?' The Evil One then vanished, and Buddha continued in his search for truth. Miracles also are accredited to Buddha, the blind receiving their sight, the deaf their hearing, and the lame the power to walk. He also became transfigured in the presence of his disciples, of which, like Christ, he had twelve. With compassion for all men, he set out to preach the way of salvation, healing the sick and even feeding the multitude from a small cake placed in his begging bowl. After the multitude had been fed many fragments remained over.

Buddha taught the same golden rule as Christ, summed up in the words, 'Do as you would be done by, kill not, nor cause to kill.' Like Christ, Buddha taught by practical demonstration. On one occasion, when the monks of a monastery neglected to look after a sick brother, the Buddha washed and tended him with his own hands, saying afterwards to those who had failed in their duty: 'Whoever shall wait upon me, let him wait upon the sick', thereby proclaiming the oneness of humanity and the view that services to the sick and destitute were services rendered to his cause.

As a mother would guard the life of her one and only son, at the risk of her own, even so let each one practise infinite sympathy towards all beings in all the world. Let goodwill without measure, impartial, unmixed, without enmity, prevail throughout the world, above, beneath, around.

Buddha and Christ drew the same sharp line between the two worlds of the Spirit and of Mammon. They urged their disciples to lay up for themselves treasure in heaven, where neither moth nor rust would corrupt nor thieves break through and steal.

A man [said Buddha] buries a treasure in a deep pit, which lying day after day concealed therein profits him nothing ... But there is a treasure laid up in the heart, a treasure of charity, piety, temperance, soberness, a treasure secure that cannot pass away. When a man leaves the fleeting riches of this world, this he takes with him after death.

The doctrines of non-violence and of rendering good for evil were equally prominent in both teachings. When a disciple proposed to return to his native town to preach to his fellow-townsfolk, Buddha said:

'The people of Sunarparanta are exceedingly violent; if they revile you, what will you do?' 'I will not return the blow.' 'And if they try to kill you?' 'Death', answered the disciple, 'is no evil. Many even desire it in order to escape the vanities of this life; but I shall take no steps either to delay or hasten the time of my departure.'

It may be said that the doctrine of non-attachment that is so important in Buddhism has no place in Christianity. Non-attachment to worldly goods or pleasure is, however, implicit in all Christ's teaching. When Christ turned to the rich young man who had asked what he should do to be saved, and said: 'Sell all thou hast and give it to the poor', he was not thinking of the benefit that the gift would bring to the needy. He saw that the young ruler was so attached to his position and possessions that they constituted the chief obstacle to his salvation. Therefore his first step was to free himself from these encumbrances. 'Take no thought of what ye shall eat, what ye shall drink, and wherewithal ye shall be clothed' is itself a warning against the dangers of attachment, as were also his instructions to his disciples when he sent them out on their mission.

Renan, in his life of Jesus, points out that the parable was essentially a Buddhist and not a Jewish method of teaching. He then remarks that obviously Christ could not have had any knowledge of Buddha. But what right had Renan to make this assumption? Not only did Christ make use of parables in his teaching, but some of these parables were very similar to those narrated by Buddha. Buddha describes himself as a 'Sower of the Word'. There also exists a strange parallel between some of the incidents in the gospels that were used as an object lesson for teaching and the incidents recorded of Buddha's disciples. Peter's attempting to walk on the Lake of Galilee, and sinking because of lack of faith, bears a strong resemblance to a story told of one of Buddha's followers in the *Jataka*. In this we read of a young and eager disciple who, finding no boat, decided to walk upon the water. In mid-stream the waves rise, and losing faith he begins to sink. Max Müller comments on this parallel, stating that although the idea of walking on water is a common one, that of sinking for lack of faith can only be accounted for by some historical contact, or transference.

Our natural inclination [he adds] would be to suppose that the Buddhist stories were borrowed from our Christian sources, and not vice-versa. But here the conscience of the scholar comes in. Some of these stories are found in the Hinayana Buddhist Canon, and date therefore before the Christian era.

Yet if it be true that, in its early formative stage, Christianity derived help from the older established Buddhism, there is nothing that need distress Christians in that idea. Whether historically connected or not, Christianity and Buddhism were twin expressions of one great spiritual movement. The existence of similarities, far from discrediting either religion, reveals the unity of religious feeling, a unity that is so complete that even the words and parables used by the great teachers are often the same. The gospels, and more especially the interpolations in the later gospels, tell us what those who followed Christ had to say about the life and teaching of their divine leader long after he had left them. Sometimes these additions rested on an historical basis, sometimes they were purely legendary. Would it be surprising if in narrating these legends the authors were unconsciously influenced by the stories that were told of Buddha? Later it will be seen that the services of the early Church were strongly influenced by the numerous cults and religions that were brought to Alexandria by the scholars of different races and creeds who flocked to that city of learning. The ancient mysteries of Egypt, the religions of Syria, Persia, India, and of even more distant lands, met in this rallying-point of culture, and all exerted some influence on the impressionable and formative period of the Church.

But although the teachings of Christ and of Buddha had so much in common, there were certain differences between them of a non-essential nature. Christ was a Jew, and made use of the Jewish culture and tradition in his teaching. He announced that he had come not to alter the ancient law, but to fulfil it. Repeatedly he uses the words: 'Ye have heard how it was said of old', and then he gives to the old law a new significance and life. His disciples were ill-educated men, his audiences simple peasants, and he appealed to that which they all had in common, a reverence for their ancient traditions, and for the law and the prophets. The philosophical discussions of Buddha would have been meaningless to them, for even the educated Jew cared far more for an authoritative theology than for philosophy. India, on the other hand, since the dawn of its culture, has been the home of philosophical and metaphysical speculation. There was no need for Buddha to appeal to authority, for his audience were accustomed to philosophical discussions and put little reliance on the written word.

This accounts for many of the differences between Christian and Buddhist doctrine. Buddha looked upon the Absolute as Super-personal Spirit, Christ referred to the Absolute as the Father, with the attributes of a personal God. In Christianity there is no idea of reincarnation, or of the working out of the law of *Karma*; in Buddhism no parallel to the redemption of the world through the death of a divine spirit made flesh. This was essentially a Jewish idea, an idea that lies behind the offering of sacrifices and the story of Abraham and Isaac.

It may be objected that I have arrived at the conclusion that the essential teaching in Christianity and Buddhism is the same by eliminating from Christianity what is its very core, the doctrine of the Incarnation. This doctrine, ever since its foundation at the Council of Nicaea, has placed Christianity on a different level from all other religions and to an orthodox Christian, a Christianity shorn of it can no longer be regarded as being Christianity. For such a person the comparison of the Divinely inspired Buddha with Christ is the comparison of light reflected from a mirror with the sun itself. But I have neither the knowledge nor the disposition to discuss the nature of the Divinity of Christ, a theme which has given difficulty to theological scholars since the foundation of the Church. I am not attempting to assess the authority with which Christ and Buddha spoke, but am comparing their messages and interesting myself in the similarity I find in their teachings.

It has been said that to understand any one religion, it is

necessary to study two, and no two religions throw more light upon one another than Christianity and Buddhism. The Western mind tends to be matter of fact, logical, and intolerant of symbolism, and yet symbolism is the only language in which a religion can express itself. Moreover, as Christianity itself is an Eastern religion it has borrowed many of its symbols from the East, amongst others the symbol of the Trinity. A greater understanding of Christianity can therefore be obtained from a study of Buddhism, and, what is of chief importance, an understanding of that vital essence of the religion which is soonest lost. 'Five hundred years, Ananda,' said Buddha, 'will the doctrine of the Truth abide.' Buddha died in 470 B.C., and five hundred years later the new Teacher, whose advent Buddha had foretold (Maitreya, the Buddha of Brotherly Love), was preaching the same truths on the shores of Lake Galilee.

CHAPTER 16

THE CHURCH

AFTER the loss of their leader, it was natural that the apostles and all those who had accepted Christ's message should band together in the small community that eventually was to become the Church. They formed a brotherhood in a hostile world, for only by living together could they find strength to put into practice the teachings of their Master. An account of their method of living is given in the Acts of the Apostles ii, 42-7.

And they continued steadfastly in the apostles' teaching and fellowship, in the breaking of bread and the prayers....

And all that believed were together, and had all things in common:

And they sold their possessions and goods, and parted them to all, according as any man had need.

And day by day, continuing steadfastly with one accord in the temple, and breaking bread at home, they did take their food with gladness and singleness of heart,

Praising God, and having favour with all the people. And the Lord added to them day by day those that were being saved.

Here was an experiment in a spiritual form of Communism. The only conditions under which Communism is possible are those which exist when men, of their own free will, have given up all their personal possessions for the sake of some great ideal, and these conditions were fulfilled by the founders of the Christian Church. Information about the Christians in the second century is to be found in the Epistle to Diognetus.

Christians are not distinguished from the rest of mankind either in locality or in speech or in customs. For they dwell not somewhere in cities of their own, neither do they use some different language, nor practise an extraordinary kind of life. Nor again do they possess any invention discovered by intelligence or study of ingenious man, nor are they masters of any human dogma, as some are. But while they dwell in cities of Greeks and Barbarians, as the lot of each is cast, and follow the native customs in dress and food and other arrangements of life, yet the constitution of their own citizenship, which they set forth, is marvellous, and confessedly contradicts expectation. They dwell in their own countries, but only as sojourners; they bear their share in all things as citizens, and they endure all hardships as strangers. Every foreign country is a fatherland to them, and every fatherland is foreign. They marry like all other men and they beget children; but they do not cast away their offspring. They have their meals in common, but not their wives. They find themselves in the flesh, and yet they live not after the flesh. Their existence is on earth, but their citizenship is in Heaven. They obey the established laws, and they surpass the laws in their own lives. They love all men, and they are persecuted by all. (*The Apostolic Fathers*, by Bishop Lightfoot. Quoted by the Bishop of Chichester in *Christianity and World Order*)

Christianity started as a Jewish faith, and to St Paul belongs the credit of freeing it from its parochial character so that it became a world religion. The Jewish followers of Christ had reconciled themselves to the fact that their Messiah had come to establish a spiritual and not a temporal kingdom, but they still clung to the idea that Christianity was for the Jews only. Paul boldly contested this view and asserted that Christians were freed from the obligation to observe the Jewish law. This caused a serious conflict amongst his followers, but he carried his point and Christianity spread widely beyond the confines of Judea. Christianity in its universal form soon won great victories, and with the convention of Constantine finally became permanently established in the Roman world.

In spite of this the nationalistic bias of Jewish thought continued to exert a very strong influence on the early Christian Church. St Paul had won his victory, and Christianity was for all mankind, and not only for the Jews, but a nation that prided itself on being the chosen race was not going to abandon any of its exclusiveness. Men can often be recognized in the gods that they create, and the Jews had created for themselves a God who often displayed anger and jealousy, the God of the Old Testament. Some of this Jewish narrowness and jealousy was carried into the Church. The early Church recognized no other path to salvation than that which it prescribed, and this attitude to other religions is retained by many modern churchmen. In claiming uniqueness the churches do not mean only that Christianity offers the best and surest means of attaining spiritual salvation, but that it is the one and only means, all other religions being founded on doubtful doctrines. This narrow view, sometimes regarded as loyalty to the Church, is peculiar to Christianity, for even the more fanatical of the Mohammedans recognize Christ as one of the prophets; and Buddhists show no exclusiveness or desire to proselytize. It may of course be objected that if amongst all the different religions of the world, there is one which is true, then all the other religions cannot be true because they are different. But truth is a goal which may be approached from several directions and the nearer we get to it the less are the differences due to the variations in the angle of approach.

At first the community of Christians was only a fellowship of men and women who awaited the return of their leader. Any arrangements they might make were in the nature of an interim programme, to fill the gap between the first and second coming of Christ. Soon he would appear again to take charge of everything, and to found a new spiritual kingdom on earth. Whatever hardships they were called upon to endure were only temporary hardships, whatever arrangements they made would only be temporary arrangements. But with the passage of time and the disappointment of their hopes, it finally became imperative for the Christians to organize their meetings and to formulate more clearly their beliefs. Up till then complete liberty of action had been allowed to all taking part in the services, as it is allowed at the present day to members of a Quaker community. This had, however, led to confusion and even to discord during meetings. Particular men were therefore nominated to take charge of these, and at the same time, the services became more elaborate and more stereotyped in form. The sacrament of baptism became very important and only properly baptized members were admitted to the community. This, in turn, made it necessary to decide what requirements in the way of belief should be demanded of those who sought membership of the Christian community.

This was no easy matter. Both the Catholic and the Protestant Churches claim that their only criterion in drawing up their formularies of belief, is 'What did Christ teach?' But Christ's words are often difficult to interpret and more than one meaning can be given to them. He had been far less explicit than Buddha in formulating the philosophical basis of his teaching. It was necessary therefore for the Church to define its own beliefs, and to make good any deficiencies by borrowing from other sources the philosophical doctrine that it lacked. Slowly and painfully this was done, but not without provoking much conflict amongst its leaders. The chief cults that vied with Christianity at that time were Mithraism, the Egyptian Mysteries, and Alexandrine theology, the last-named being a blend of Greek, Hindu, and Jewish thought. From all these sources the Church took something. From Greek philosophy, under the guidance of Philo, it derived the doctrine of the Logos, from the Egyptian Mysteries, materials for the Church services, and from the Gnostic sect, a great amount of Greek and Hindu thought.

Gnosticism is of special interest since it exerted a strong influence on the early Church. It had existed long before Christianity, and much of its teaching had been derived from the Upanishads. This is apparent when we consider its most important tenets. The Gnostics believed: (1) that the Divine Being is indefinable and infinite, above all thought and expression; (2) that the Cosmos is a blend of divine and non-divine principles and represents the descent of spirit into matter; (3) that the deliverance of the spirit from its union with matter, or the world of sensuality, is brought about by asceticism and contemplation, and that these practices lead to Gnosis, or Wisdom; (4) that Gnosis is not achieved by the accumulation of intellectual knowledge, or logical thought, but by seeing God; (5) that the perfect Gnostic is the man who is free from the world and master of himself. He is emancipated from the dead letter and the outward symbols of religion, having realized the truth. He lives in God and may truly be said to have passed from death to life. Many Gnostics believed also in the pre-existence of and in the rebirth of the soul. They practised certain rites to which the initiated alone were admitted.

In the first century after Christ, Gnosticism became fused with Christianity and supplied much of the philosophy that the Church lacked. Gnostics accepted the Christian creed and looked upon themselves as Christians, but the partnership between Gnosticism and Christianity proved an uneasy one. and ended in the Gnostics being condemned as heretics and ejected from the Church. Undoubtedly the Church suffered afterwards from the loss of its Gnostic element.

Not only had the Gnostics contributed much of that vital energy that is essential in the life of all religion, but it had supplied the Church with much of its philosophy and symbolism. It is unnecessary to attempt to furnish even a brief sketch of the early struggles of the Church to establish its doctrines and to formulate its creed. Unfortunately it is just as easy to become hypnotized by words in a religious as in a philosophical argument, and rival schools of theology soon appeared in the Christian assemblies. The leaders of these different factions felt deeply the truth of what they proclaimed, and theological quarrels became common and bitter in the early years of the Church's foundation. This was particularly so when attempts were made to formulate clearly the nature of the divinity of Christ and the doctrine of the Trinity. The ecclesiastical scholastics cared more for intellectual discussions than for the principles enunciated in the Sermon on the Mount. Some of the Church's leaders saw the danger that this growth of theology and doctrine brought with it:

Faithful souls [wrote St Hilary of Poictiers] would be contented with the word of God, which bids us 'Go teach all nations, baptizing them in the name of the Father and of the Son and of the Holy Ghost.' But alas, we are driven by the faults of our heretical opponents to do things unlawful, to scale heights inaccessible, to speak of what is unspeakable, to presume where we ought not. And whereas it is by faith alone that we should worship the Father, and reverence the Son, and be filled with the Spirit, we are now obliged to strain our weak language with the utterance of things beyond its scope; forced into this evil procedure by the evil procedure of our foes. Hence, what should be matter of silent meditation, must now needs be imperilled by exposition in words.

But the scholastics of the Church once having started on the task of defining the indefinable were not easily deterred. Council after council was summoned, words piled on words, and confusion multiplied. Again in A.D. 360 we find Hilary writing, 'Since Nicaea we have done nothing but compose creeds. Every year we make new creeds and define invisible mysteries ... Tearing one another to pieces, we have been the cause of one another's ruin.'

At the numerous church assemblies and councils heretical views were denounced and those who held them expelled from the fold. It was agreed that the original dependence on the Holy Spirit for light and guidance was no longer adequate, since heretical as well as orthodox members of the community claimed to have enjoyed the divine illumination. Other safeguards against heterodoxy therefore now appeared to be necessary. These were provided by proclaiming that the apostles had appointed bishops as their successors, and that the latter were in possession of a divine grace that enabled them to transmit and interpret without error the teachings that the apostles had committed to them. In this manner arose the famous theory of 'apostolic succession', a succession upon which the Roman Catholic Church still bases its exclusive authority. Naturally the Church was now in a much stronger position. Not only did it possess an authoritative apostolic doctrine, but also a permanent apostolic office to which alone belonged the right to determine what that doctrine should be. Pragmatically the adoption of the doctrine was entirely justified. But actually it has no meaning. The only true succession in the Church has been through its line of saints. By this is meant not necessarily the succession of saints recorded in the Church's calendar, but of men and women who, in spite of manifold difficulties, have striven to follow the teachings of Christ. It is difficult to see how even the most enthusiastic churchman can read the history of the medieval Church and still retain the idea of an unbroken line of inspired apostles.

Christianity, under the growing dominance of the Church, soon became a very different religion from that which Christ had taught. Christ had an abhorrence of dogma and refused to become involved in the arguments dear to the heart of the lawyers and priests of Judea. Throughout his life his chief opponents had always been the priests and Pharisees who had insisted on salvation by orthodoxy, and on attention to the letter of the law. But now, within a few hundred years of his death, the Church made the acceptance of dogma a *sine qua non* to salvation. In the Athanasian Creed, printed in the Prayer Book, are found these words. 'This is the Catholic Faith : which except a man believes faithfully, he cannot be saved.' And again 'Which Faith except everyone do keep whole and un-defiled without doubt he shall perish everlastingly.' Christianity became a religion based on the authority of the Church, and baptism was made conditional on the acceptance of a super-naturally imparted tradition. Out of a teaching that paid little attention to rites and formalities was built up an elaborate ecclesiastical structure. Loyalty to the Church was demanded of its members rather than loyalty to Christ's teaching, and as the Church soon became a national institution this meant loyalty to the State. As the Church became politically-minded the effect on its teaching became more apparent. The interpre-tation of God's will at the Council of Clermont in A.D. 1095, that it was the duty of all Christians to go forth and slaughter the Saracens, was a foretaste of what was to come. Religion, hence-forth, was to be used to sanctify men's passions.

During the Middle Ages this transformation of a religion into a political organization was completed. A contemplative spiritual religion had become a dogmatic creed promulgated by a despotic Church jealous of its temporal power. Christianity still continued to stir the emotions and sentiments of its adherents, but had lost much of its power to transform man's nature. It was now only with the utmost peril that a Christian dared to utter a word against any church doctrine. Authority was supreme and if need be it could call in the help of the Inquisition, for it was by means of the thumbscrew and stake that the Church preserved the sanctity of its doctrines. Heresy became punishable by death and there is little doubt that if Christ had returned to earth, he would have been in danger of being burnt for heretical views regarding his own divinity. It was not a layman but an officer of the Church (Canon Barry) who wrote: 'The one really formidable argument against the truth of the Christian religion is the record of the Christian Church.'

The Church merely reflected the cruelty of mankind. It had elected to become a political organization, and as such, was neither better nor worse than other political organizations. But in spite of its lamentable failure, Europe owes a great debt to the Church. During the darkest years of its history Christian monasteries kept alight the lamp of culture in a barbarous world. There were countless individuals in monastic orders who in secret deplored the cruelty and political intrigues of their Church, but were unable to take any effective steps to change its methods. Usually they appeared outwardly to be orthodox churchmen, but sometimes, as in the case of the ecclesiastical alchemists, they hid their spiritual beliefs behind the façade of some external activity. And even although the Church had lost its spiritual essence, it still remained the home of scholarship. What intellectual life survived during those Dark Ages survived mainly in the Church. Certain ecclesiastical scholars gathered round them all the cultured and learned men of the day, so that the Church remained the centre of the intellectual life of Europe. It was the Church also that made possible the beginning of scientific inquiry. (Copernicus is said to have conceived the hypothesis of the earth's revolution round the sun as a result of his study of the doctrine of the Trinity.)

It would be unjust to the Church to suggest that because it had become a political institution it ceased to have any spiritual significance. Although its leaders were usually more interested in theological discussions than in the teachings of Christ, there were countless men living in monasteries, or moving about amongst the poor, who strove to live in accordance with the precepts embodied in the Sermon on the Mount. And even when they failed to live up to these ideals, the mere fact that monasteries existed, that services were held in Churches, and that men had given up worldly ambition for the sake of something that they held to be of greater value, was a continual reminder that there existed another, and a spiritual, world. Nor did it matter that many of these humbler followers of Christ were ill-educated men who could only conceive of a Universal Spirit in crude anthropomorphic terms, as a personal God to be worshipped through the medium of holy images and saintly relics. Different forms of worship are as necessary to different types of men as are different conceptions of time and space necessary to varying levels of intelligence. Learned theologians might discuss, till they were exhausted, the exact nature of the Trinity, but the simple ministrations of the priests gave to the common people the nourishment that was needed to keep the spiritual side of their nature alive.

It is no more possible to standardize the means by which men find expression for the religious sentiments within them than it is possible to standardize the art by means of which they express their feelings for beauty. Different methods of worship are as natural as are different schools of music and painting. It is not the breaking up of the Church into different sects that is to be deplored, but the tendency on the part of each of these sects to claim for itself a monopoly of truth, and to regard other schools of Christianity with scorn, or even with open hostility.

It is satisfactory to know that of recent years there has been a determined effort on the part of different denominations of Christians to sink their differences and to work together for the common good. The Churches hope, thereby, to be able to exert their influence on society so that it may be encouraged to live in accordance with spiritual instead of purely material principles. At the Oxford Conference held in 1937 delegates from most of the Christian Churches, with the exception of the Roman Catholic, discussed the difficult problems of war, the relation of the Church to the State, and a number of social problems, such as unemployment and poverty. It was hoped that by a well-organized effort on the part of the Churches sufficient pressure could be brought to bear upon society to induce it to tackle some of the more flagrant social evils. The difficulties attendant on such an effort immediately became apparent, for three contradictory schools of thought were found to exist. The first group of churchmen consisted of those who insisted on a literal obedience to the commandments of the Sermon on the Mount: 'Resist not evil'; 'If any man will sue thee at the law and take away thy coat, let him have thy cloke also'. (Matthew v, 39-40). A second group went to the opposite extreme and declared that whilst these principles must govern the intimate personal life of the individual, they could not be applied in the wider sphere of community life. Those who belonged to this group felt indeed that there was no moral standard that was applicable to humanity at large. Thirdly there existed a school of thought which attempted to steer a middle course. Whilst there existed no possibility of applying the full commandment of the gospels in any wholesale fashion, there was available a moral standard for the common life that had some relation to it. It was felt that in time this could be made to approximate more nearly to the full commandment.

Without wishing to discuss at length these different opinions, it would seem to be obvious to the writer that any attempt to foist the principles enunciated in the Sermon on the Mount on an unwilling society is foredoomed to failure. The Church itself as a body has failed to live according to these principles, however much the individuals that made up the Church have striven to follow the example set by Christ. An attempt to apply them generally to society would have results as unexpected as those that followed the forcible introduction of teetotalism into America, and of communal living into Russia. Who among the ardent prohibitionists would have expected that the result of their efforts would be to increase drunkenness in their country and to initiate the rule of the gangster? Could any idealistic socialist have foreseen that within a few years there would appear in Russia a despotism more ruthless than any that had preceded it and a greater slavery of those whom he had hoped to liberate? So also would the forcible introduction of an ethic that is far above the level of human conduct have entirely unexpected results. There is much also to support the view that Christ set for his disciples a much higher standard than he expected of the multitude. Generally he spoke to the crowds that followed him only in parables, explaining their meaning afterwards to the small inner circle of disciples. Clement of Alexandria, who was separated from Christ by a shorter period

of time, was probably in a better position than we are to understand his method of teaching. He held that Christ's teaching
was twofold, and that the higher knowledge was imparted only
to some of his disciples. 'It was not designed for the multitude,
but communicated to those only who were capable of receiving
it orally, not in writing' (*Clement of Alexandria*, by Dr Kaye).

What is of importance to note is that at the very beginning of
a sincere attempt on the part of the Churches to work together,
there has been found to exist this deep cleavage in opinion. At
the same time and in spite of all these differences in opinion,
each section of the Church regards itself, not merely as a community of Christians, but as a corporate body invested with
supernatural powers and enjoying direct divine guidance.

The life of the Christian [writes the Bishop of Chichester],
wherever he is engaged, is maimed and incomplete unless it finds
its focus in communion with God and in common prayer with God's
people. It is by actively worshipping membership in the church, by
actual partaking in the liturgy and the services, and actual hearing
of the Word and sharing in the Sacramental life, that he learns and
helps others to enjoy the secret of true community and receives the
grace for a new way of living.

These words would seem to imply ability on the part of each
section of the Church to bestow that grace which is necessary
for a new way of living. By his church membership the individual not only benefits from his association with others more
experienced and more developed than himself, but merely by
partaking in the Church liturgy and sharing in the services he
receives a special grace without which a new way of living
would be difficult or impossible to him. And because the bishop
himself recognizes and deplores the differences in opinion in
the various Churches, each of which claims the power to bestow
this special grace, he proposes that a kind of 'Christian Consultative Body' should be formed. In addition he would like to
see elected a 'Standing Theological and Expert Commission',
assisted by an adequately staffed secretariat. It is suggested that
it should be the work of both these bodies to arrive at the implications of the Sermon on the Mount and to map out a common
ground for action.

But is it necessary to await the deliberation of a Standing Theological and Expert Commission in order to discover the implications of the Sermon on the Mount? And if the Commission be summoned, will it necessarily find them? In a letter written to a friend by Gregory of Nazianzus, who presided at an Ecumenical Council in A.D. 381, I find these words:

> My own inclination is to avoid all assemblies of Bishops, for I have never seen any Council come to a good end, nor solve any evils. It usually increases them. You will always find there, love of contention and love of power.

It is satisfactory to know that so many sections of the Christian Church are making an effort to reach agreement, and there is no doubt that the test of absence of contradiction applied by Shankara to philosophical concepts is equally applicable to Church doctrines. Nor need the Churches in their dilemma hesitate to apply such a test, for in their teaching there undoubtedly exists a large measure of agreement. But in this call of the bishop to form a Christian Consultative Body and a Standing Theological and Expert Commission there is heard a note that has been too frequently heard before, a note that once resounded along the miles of corridors of the now abandoned Palace of Peace at Geneva, and would also be heard, were it ever to be built, along the corridors of the Scientific Institute that Alexis Carrel would like to see established as a means of saving man. It is natural that a churchman should entrust the salvation of the world to a Theological Commission, and that a scientist should entrust it to a body of scientists, but unfortunately both classes of reformers would encounter the same difficulty. The theologians might succeed in eliminating some of the differences of opinion that at present split the Churches into parties, and the scientists might succeed in creating a saner society, but both would be equally powerless to effect from without an inner change in the heart of man. Far be it from the writer to suggest that the results obtained from the labour of the theologians and the scientists would be worthless, even if it failed to achieve that which it had set out to do. In some parts of modern Europe (for example in Germany, Russia, and Italy) conditions for the living of a life in accordance with any ideals are so difficult as to make it almost impossible. If the theologians and scientists could create for the individual seeker after truth a milieu that was more favourable to his efforts they would have done all that could legitimately be expected of them.

In this world there is nothing that is entirely new; every event is a recurrence of a similar event in the past. In the days of Shankara there existed a similar controversy between the authority of ritualistic religion and the individual's claim to approach truth directly. Shankara, the philosopher, came to the same conclusion on the subject as did Ramakrishna, the religious devotee, namely that church services and rituals were of the greatest importance as an *aid* to spiritual progress. At the same time Shankara maintained that as *Jñana*, or direct knowledge of the Supreme Spirit, was the chief end of man's endeavour, the exclusive supremacy of Vedic ritualism was to be avoided. He was convinced that the chief danger of a cult of ceremonies lay in the growth of a pharisaical attitude to religion. As Christ denounced the Pharisees, and Paul the lawyers, so likewise did Shankara declare that ceremonial piety by itself was not the end of religion, and might even become a deadly enemy of it. He did not dismiss the Vedic code as useless. He asserted only that whilst the true philosopher

could advance beyond the Vedic rules of life, others were called upon to conform to Vedic regulations, not in the expectation of good things here or hereafter, but out of a sense of duty, and as a help to the development of the moral competency for the study of the Vedânta. Vedic piety helps a man by turning his mind towards the inner soul and then leading him to the realization of the spiritual goal. (RADHAKRISHNAN)

Similarly the Church with its ceremonies and ritual is of assistance in directing attention to the world of spiritual values; it is a beacon that acts as a continual reminder that as well as the life of the body there is also the life of the spirit.

The hope for mankind does not lie in the action of any corporate body be it ever so powerful, but in the influence of individual men and women who for the sake of a greater have sacrificed a lesser aim. There is no possibility of any mass movement in Christianity or in any other religion. As has been pointed out it would seem that Christ himself expected little of the crowds who gathered to hear him and witnessed his miracles. He talked to them only in parables the meaning of which he expounded to his disciples after the crowds had dispersed.

> Therefore I speak to them in parables: because they seeing, see not; and hearing, they hear not, neither do they understand. And in them is fulfilled the prophecy of Esaias which saith, By hearing ye shall hear and shall not understand; and seeing ye shall see and shall not perceive; For this people's heart is waxed gross, and their ears are dull of hearing, and their eyes they have closed; lest at any time they should see with their eyes, and hear with their ears, and should understand with their hearts, and should be converted, and I should heal them. But blessed are your eyes, for' they see; and your ears, for they hear.

The words 'Who hath ears to hear, let him hear' resound through the gospels. In one form or another they are repeated nine times in the Synoptic gospels and eight times in Revelation.

It has been said that in the darkest days of the Church's history there were many who, in order to protect themselves from persecution, sought the truth under the guise of some external calling. As an example of such a body of men may be mentioned the ecclesiastical alchemists. Alchemy was an extremely ancient science which for upwards of seventeen hundred years exerted its influence upon thought, not only in Europe, but in Egypt, Arabia, Persia, and China. Although it is said to have formed part of the traditional knowledge of the Egyptian priesthood, it was probably an importation into Egypt from abroad. Alchemy certainly existed in China prior to this era. It also flourished amongst the Arabs and in Greece, where it was always referred to either as 'the work', or as 'The Divine and Sacred Art'. Although externally it appeared to be a branch of metallurgy, and was popularly regarded as a search for gold, the more important part of the true alchemist's research was spiritual and hidden. This is evident from the clear distinction that is drawn in all alchemical writings between the exoteric alchemy that was visible to the world and the esoteric alchemy that was revealed only to chosen adepts. Although to the world, the alchemist appeared to be engaged only in the transmutation of baser metals into gold, he was in reality striving for an inner transmutation of the spirit. He was therefore essentially a religious man.

The central doctrine of the alchemists was the unity of all things, a doctrine that was engraved on the emerald tablets of the great alchemical leader, Hermes Trismegistus, in the saying 'As above so below'. The laws that ruled the material world also ruled the world of the spirit. The alchemists believed that throughout the whole universe there existed a general movement of the baser towards the finer, and it was man's work to find how best this movement could be assisted. Arnold of Villanova explained the meaning of the search for the philosopher's stone in the following words:

There abides in Nature a certain pure matter, which being discovered and brought to perfection converts to itself proportionately all imperfect bodies that it touches.

That the vital part of the alchemists' work was the inner transformation of the spirit rather than the conversion of lead into gold, is shown by the following quotations:

Out of other things, thou wilt never make one unless first the one arises out of thyself. (ABBOT TRITHEMIUS, C. A.D. 1500)

In order to acquire the golden understanding (*Aurea apprehensis*), a man must open wide the eyes of the spirit, and of the soul, and contemplate and recognize things with the help of the inner light that God has kindled from the beginning in nature and in our hearts.

Know that thou canst not possess 'the science' if thou dost not cleanse thy mind through God, by which is meant that thou purgest thine heart from all corruption. (ALFIDIUS)

To a modern reader whose mind draws a clear distinction between matter and spirit, alchemical writings are apt to appear confused and meaningless. It must be remembered, however, that no such distinction as 'matter and spirit' existed for the alchemist. For him there was instead an intermediate realm that lay between matter and spirit, a realm of subtle bodies, to which a psychic as well as a physical manifestation was attached. Whereas to us there seems to be an incongruity between the alchemist's preoccupation with retorts and crucibles and his search for spiritual change, for the alchemist there was no such incongruity. His external work was a symbol of his inner work, but at the same time it was more than a symbol. Unity existed in everything, and the same laws ruled everywhere.

Alchemy, therefore, provided a cloak for those Christians who could no longer believe in the validity of the Church's teaching and sought to find truth in intimate spiritual experience. There also existed other societies and sects who continued their search in secret lest their heresies should be discovered and punished. However corrupt the Church might be there were always men who, in secret, and as best they could, followed the teachings of Christ. The level of Christianity within the Church is as variable as is the level of Christianity outside of the Church. And it is on this note that I would wish to close a chapter which to many may appear to be an unwarrantable attack upon the Church. Fortunately heresy is no longer punishable by death, and it is permissible to the individual to interpret to the best of his ability, and without risk to his person, the sublime and difficult message of Christ. Of this privilege I have availed myself freely and if to some readers I may seem to have dwelt too much on the shortcomings of the Christian Churches it may well be, as one of my critics has pointed out, that I am more familiar with the failures of Christians than with those of the Buddhists, Sufis, and Taoists.

CHAPTER 17

MYSTICAL CHRISTIANITY

THE birthplace of religious feeling is in the solitude of the soul. It was on the desolate peak of Sinai that Moses saw God. It was under the Bodhi tree on a hilltop that Buddha found enlightenment. It was in the wilderness of Judea, in the stillness of prayer and meditation, that Christ prepared himself for his mission to mankind. Walt Whitman has expressed this idea with striking emphasis :

I should say indeed that only in the perfect uncontamination and solitariness of individuality may the spirituality of religion positively come forth at all. Only here, and on such terms, the meditation, the devout ecstasy, the soaring flight. Only here communion with the mysteries, the eternal problems, Whence, Whither? Alone, and identity, and the mood – and the soul emerges, and all statements, churches, sermons, melt away like vapours. Alone, and silent thoughts, and awe, and aspiration – and there the interior consciousness like a hitherto unseen inscription, in magic ink, beams out its wondrous line to the sense. Bibles may convey and priests expound, but it is exclusively for the noiseless operations of one's isolated self to enter the pure ether of veneration, reach the divine levels, and commune with the unutterable.

From the earliest times there have been men both within and outside the Christian Church who have shut their eyes to the babble of warring creeds, and in the solitude of meditation and in the unfathomable depths of the soul have found the truth they sought. Men who seek what Whitman terms the 'interior consciousness' are called mystics, a term that is generally used with a certain flavour of indulgence by the more charitable rationalists, and with scorn by the uncharitable.

Why is mysticism such an ill-favoured word ? Mainly because the rationalist regards mysticism as a method of seeing things through a golden and sentimental haze, things that can be seen much more clearly and with a greater sense of proportion by the intellect. Although Kant's view that our reasoning can never tear aside the veil that hides the noumenal from the phenomenal world is still widely accepted, it is accepted only theoretically. Men still continue to reason and dispute about the mysteries of existence; theologians still seek to confine God within their human formulae, and to reduce him to the span of their narrow understanding. Words are strung to words, theories piled on theories, and from such activity has grown up a vast intellectual structure of theology, which bears as much, or as little, relation to truth as do the speculations of a savage concerning the nature of the universe coincide with reality. In the savage's view of the universe there is undoubtedly an element of truth, but we accept the picture that he has painted as we accept the crude unskilled drawings of a child. There is no need to quarrel with what he has drawn, and there is also no need to take it seriously.

But is there no better method of seeing spiritual truths than that of peering through the peephole of the intellect? Kant, Spinoza, Schopenhauer, Bergson, and many other philosophers believe that there is such a method.

The teaching of mysticism [says Schopenhauer] tends towards the giving of a direct sense of what perceptions, concepts, and all knowledge in general are incapable of attaining.

And what these philosophers have postulated, the mystics have confirmed. Things of the spirit are seen by the eyes of the spirit. The noumenal world is revealed only to the noumenal man. A study of the classic type of mystical experience reveals an astonishing uniformity of view, a uniformity that embraces all differences of race and of clime, and reaches across the centuries. Here is a Church in which there is no cleavage into sects, each of which claims a monopoly of truth, but a Church universal in which Christians, Buddhists, Sufis, and all other religious men can worship without fear of disagreement. Pierre Nicolle realized this fact very clearly when he reproached the Christian mystics of his time with having discarded the forms of thought that were intrinsically Catholic. The word 'catholic' might

mean universal, but there was a limit to the universality permitted to members of the Roman Catholic Church.

They do not know God as Christians and Catholics [he wrote] but
in a way equally suitable for Mohammedans, Deists, and the majority of heretics. For what does this knowledge of God come to
ultimately? A confused and indistinct idea of an omnipresent God.
But to know this it is not necessary either to be a Catholic, or a
Christian.

Small wonder that staunch members of the Holy Roman Church
were disquieted !

There are critics who would deny the truth of the statement
that mysticism is a universal religion. They would say that
Western mystics differ from Eastern in being more positive and
creative, the Christian mystic affirming the reality of the world
and the meaningfulness of life, and the Eastern mystic denying
them. But, as Radhakrishnan points out, it is difficult to maintain this thesis in the face of Buddha's intense pity and sympathy for every form of sentient life. Pity, and desire to suc-
cour one's fellows, cannot be reconciled with a complete negation of the reality of life. Moreover, the whole of Christ's
Sermon on the Mount can be looked upon as a negation of
ordinary life.

It is a proclamation of unworldliness in its extremest form. It is
the poor, or those who have no care at all for wealth, those whose
concessiveness or submissiveness to injustice knows no limit, and
who take up this burden of misery most readily, who are to enjoy
the blessings of the kingdom. These negative characteristics – expressing an extreme renunciation of the world and all its normal
desires – are constantly emphasized. (BISHOP GORE)

The contrast is not between Eastern and Western mysticism,
but between a religious and a self-sufficient humanist outlook.
It is humanism that affirms the importance of life, and religion
that discounts it. And humanism has become a religion-substi-
tute for many who are unable to accept the idea of truth based
on revelation. But by cutting themselves off from the supra-
human element in religion the humanists – and many so-called
Liberal Protestants must be numbered amongst these – are
reducing religion to a code of ethics. All religions are essentially

otherworldly. All of them regard the world merely as a training ground and as a means of attaining spiritual development.

In spite of the uniformity that is found in the mystical experiences of men and women of all creeds and nations, grave doubt is generally expressed concerning the validity of knowledge so obtained.

The real belief of the Brahmins [says Schweitzer, with what seems to be a note of surprise in his voice] is that man does not attain to union with Brahman by means of any achievement of his natural power of gaining knowledge, but solely by quitting the world of the sense, in a state of ecstasy, and thus learning the reality of pure being.

Precisely so, but this is not merely the real belief of the Brahmin, but of every mystic, brahminical or otherwise. St Ignatius, St John of the Cross, St Teresa, Jacob Boehme, and a long line of Christian mystics are at one with the Brahmin in this.

Ecstasy, like mysticism, is a word which has been used to cover a multitude of states, ranging from hysteria to the raptures of Plotinus and Boehme. All experiences of the divine are ecstatic, but all ecstasies cannot be regarded as being experiences of the divine. The excited outbursts of a neurasthenic have no more in common with the bliss of religious ecstasy than the babbling of a drunkard has with the teaching of Buddha. Ecstasy like mysticism is an ill-used word, but if we refuse to believe that a flash of genius in a great artist is a sign of mental instability, we must also refuse to believe that the revelations vouchsafed to Plotinus were symptoms of mental decay. Indeed, if we truly regarded ecstatic visions as being necessarily pathological, it were best to convert all churches into museums, and, like the Nazis, burn all the books that we fail to understand. It cannot be stressed too often that all religions are based on revelation and that revelation is imparted on a higher level of consciousness.

At the same time a critical attitude must be maintained to mystical writings. In Chapter 2 the pathological theory of mystical experience was discussed and it was agreed that some mystical writings were definitely of a pathological nature. There is also a theory that the knowledge given in ecstasy is simply some concept, which, having long formed a subject for reflection, suddenly assumes the power of hallucination, taking complete possession of the subject, so that his state is changed from one of activity to passivity. The object towards which the former meditation was directed is freed from the check imposed on it by sensations and concepts, so that it becomes endowed with irresistible force, forming a sort of *idée fixe*. This theory of the nature of revelation is supported by Ribot and Murisier. Whilst it may explain the experiences of some of the lesser mystics, it cannot explain those of all. The great mystics always adopted a critical attitude towards their experiences, and were often alarmed in case they should prove to be the temptations of the devil. Strict warnings were issued to all aspiring religious by their spiritual directors in regard to visions and supernatural experiences. They were advised to regard these generally as being designs of the tempter to lead them astray into confusion and spiritual pride. The special danger to which the mystics were exposed was the temptation to clutch at the fruition of their spiritual aim before they had gone through the toilsome preparatory disciplining of the will and the intellect. As a result of this impatience the intellect might be sacrificed and be excluded from the religious life. In such cases there would be no check upon superstitious beliefs, upon fantasy, and upon such excesses of emotionalism as are sometimes witnessed in religious revivals. Walter Hilton, Canon of Thurgarton, who died in 1396, expressed the opinion that violent emotional fervours did not belong to a high state, but were characteristic, rather, of beginners, 'who for the littleness and weakness of their souls cannot bear the smallest touch of God'. He also warned others to be wary of the strange physical and psychical phenomena which sometimes accompany higher states, such as sights and sounds and odours, a sensation of burning heat in the breast, voices, and apparitions of various kinds. He added that although he did not doubt that such things really take place, it was by no means easy to determine whether they were sent by God or were a snare laid by the devil. The best test according to Hilton was to ask whether they tended to distract the mind from devotions and from good actions or to encourage these. If they did act as a distraction it must be concluded that they were sent by the Evil One. The validity of the vision was only to be known by its fruits.

That the great mystics carefully scrutinized their emotional experiences is shown by the detailed analysis they made of them. St Teresa, for example, subdivides the mystical states into which she passed into various 'mansions'. She also made a distinction between what she called a 'spiritual espousal' and a 'spiritual marriage'. In Hilton's *Scale of Perfection* he describes the various steps in the ladder of contemplation by means of which the divine vision is reached. The first step is knowledge of the facts of religion, and the second, feeling without light in the understanding. When in this middle state the aspirant 'cannot tell what it is, but he feeleth it is well, for it is a gift of God'. The third and final step was a combination of knowledge with perfect love. In this state was fulfilled what St Paul says to the Corinthians: 'He that is joined unto the Lord is one spirit.' The true mystic, therefore, is not merely content with a blind emotional fervour, but observes the steps by which he reaches this as carefully as a psychologist notes his inner reactions.

What is above all essential to the mystic is that he should attain the childlike attitude to truth that Christ counselled his disciples to assume if they wished to enter the Kingdom of Heaven. It was the exact opposite of that adopted by the priests and the Pharisees, who approached everything with preconceived views and with complete confidence in the infallibility of their subjective opinions. Mysticism entails the giving up of all egoism, of all personal desires and hopes, and of all personal views and imaginings, so that that which is not personal may be seen with the eyes of the spirit.

Now we have received not the spirit of the world, but the spirit which is of God; that we might know the things that are freely given us of God. Which things also we speak, not in the words which man's wisdom teaches, but which the Holy Spirit teacheth; comparing spiritual things with spiritual. But the natural man receiveth not the things of the spirit of God; For they are foolishness unto him; neither can he know them, because they are spiritually discerned. (1 Corinthians ii, 12-14.)

The best way of understanding the method of the mystic is to study the life of one of them, and to note what he has to say about his experiences. No better subject for such a study could be found than Jacob Boehme, if for no other reason than that he was a plain unpretentious man, who describes his experiences in the simplest possible language. Boehme had no thesis that he wished to prove, laid no claim to any superiority, and took no credit for what he had seen.

I am not come to this meaning, [he writes] to this work and knowledge, through my own reason, or through my own will and purpose, neither have I sought this knowledge, nor so much as know anything concerning it. I sought only for the heart of God, therein to hide myself from the temptations of the devil.

He was born in the village of Alt Seidenberg, close to the Bohemian border, in 1575. His parents being poor, he was put to mind the cattle, and it was in the solitude of the fields that he had his first spiritual experience. Because he was not robust enough to be a labourer he was afterwards apprenticed to a bootmaker, eventually becoming a master of his craft. At the age of twenty-five he married a butcher's daughter and set up a household of his own. A year later he experienced another ecstasy that altered the course of his life. This was followed soon afterwards by a third and still more memorable illumination that clarified for him much that he had not previously understood.

What Boehme had seen he could not keep to himself, and ill-equipped as he was in other respects for such a task, he published a book, entitled *Aurora*. This work was read by a pastor of the local Lutheran church, one Gregorius Richter, and the reading of it so infuriated him that he went straight off to the city council to demand that Boehme should be banished from the neighbourhood. This the council agreed to do, but later, realizing that Boehme had an excellent reputation and had attended church regularly, it allowed him to return on condition that he wrote no more books.

But Boehme's business had suffered badly from the local scandal, and, unable to carry it on, he took a job as travelling salesman in woollen gloves. No longer able to remain silent, he published another book. Gregorius Richter denounced him from the pulpit, and a scurrilous campaign was launched against him. 'His writings smell overmuch of cobbler's pitch.' 'Will you have the words of Jesus Christ, or the words of a shoemaker?' yelled his opponents, the followers of One who had once been a carpenter. Boehme's only reply was 'Not I, the I that I am, know these things, but God knows them in me'. It is gratifying that not all were blind to the quiet dignity in Boehme, and certain influential people, including eminent dignitaries of the Church, treated him with consideration and respect. He died in 1624, at the age of forty-nine.

Whatever one's views of mystical states or of higher levels of consciousness may be, no one can read Boehme's books without feeling that here lies a great mystery. How could a tender of cattle, a cobbler, and a pedlar of woollen gloves, contrive to write them? Boehme had doubtless had some elementary education and had listened to the preaching of the Reverend Gregorius Richter, but this could not have enabled him to attain the profound and tranquil wisdom of the world's greatest religious leaders. Gregorius Richter knew nothing about the unity of all, the Brahman that pervades everything, the identification of man with his lower being, and the necessity for losing all in order that one might attain all. Everyone must explain the enigma of Jacob Boehme's books as best he can, but however varied the explanation may be, all will agree that some explanation is necessary.

The solution that Boehme himself offers is that which he gave to his opponents. 'Not I, the I that I am, know these things, but God knows them in me', or which he offers in the preface to his best-known book, *The Signature of All Things*:

This is the wisdom that dwells in nothing, and yet possesses all things, and the humble resigned soul is its playfellow; this is the divine alloquy, the inspiration of the Almighty, the breath of God, the holy unction, which sanctifies the soul to be the temple of the Holy Spirit, which instructs aright in all things.

In order to explain how a man may come into direct contact with truth, Boehme imagines a dialogue between a disciple and

his master. As no description of the general drift of this dialogue
can possess the value of Boehme's own words, the beginning of
it is appended :

The disciple said to his master: Sir, how may I come to the
supersensual life, so that I may see God, and may hear God speak?
The master answered and said: Son, when thou canst throw thyself into That, where no creature dwelleth, though it be for a
moment, then thou hearest what God speaketh.
Disciple: Is that where no creature dwelleth near at hand; or is
it afar off?
Master: It is in thee. And if thou canst, my son, for a while but
cease from all thy thinking and willing, then thou shalt hear the
unspeakable words of God.
Disciple: How can I hear him speak, when I stand still from
thinking and willing?
Master: When thou standeth still from the thinking of self, and
the willing of self; 'When both thy intellect and will are quiet, and
passive to the impressions of the Eternal Word and Spirit; and when
thy soul is winged up, and above that which is temporal, the outward senses, and the imagination being locked up by holy abstraction', then the ternal hearing, seeing, and speaking will be revealed
in thee; and so God heareth 'and seeth through thee', being now
the organ of his Spirit; and so God speaketh in thee and whispereth
to thy spirit, and thy spirit heareth his voice. Blessed art thou therefore if that thou canst stand still from self-thinking and self-willing,
and canst stop the wheel of thy imagination and senses; forasmuch
as hereby thou mayest arrive at length to see the great salvation of
God, being made capable of all manner of divine sensations and
heavenly communications. Since it is nought indeed but thine own
hearing and willing that do hinder thee, so that thou dost not see
and hear God.
Disciple: But wherewith shall I hear and see God, forasmuch as
he is above nature and creature?
Master: Son, when thou art quiet and silent, then art thou as
God was before nature and creature; thou art that which God then
was; thou art that whereof he made thy nature and creature; Then
thou hearest and seest even with that wherewith God himself saw
and heard in thee, before ever thine own willing or thine own seeing
began.
Disciple: What now hinders or keeps me back, so that I cannot
come to that, wherewith God is to be seen and heard?

Master: Nothing truly but thine own willing, hearing, and seeing do keep thee back from it, and do hinder thee from coming to this supersensual state. And it is because thou strivest so against that, out of which thou thyself are descended and derived, that thou thus breakest thyself off, with thine own willing, from God's willing, and with thy own seeing from God's seeing. In as much as in thine own understanding thou dost understand but in and according to this thine own willing, as the same stands divided from the divine will. This thy willing moreover stops thy hearing, and maketh thee deaf towards God, through thy own thinking upon terrestrial things, and thy attending to that which is without thee; and so it brings thee into a ground, where thou art laid hold on and captivated in nature. And having brought thee hither, it overshadows thee with that which thou willest; it binds thee with thine own chains and it keeps thee in thine own dark prison which thou makest for thyself; so that thou canst not go out thence, or come to that state which is supernatural and supersensual.

The Christian mystic who is probably the best known to English readers is John Yepes, more familiar under the name of St John of the Cross, the author of *The Dark Night of the Soul*. Born in 1542, he was educated by the Jesuits and became a Carmelite friar at Medina. His illumination followed a period of intense suffering, not only spiritual but also physical, for he was imprisoned for the infringement of some ecclesiastical ordinance. Butler, in *The Lives of the Saints*, records that Yepes passed through a period of

interior trouble of mind, scruples, and a dislike of spiritual exercises ... The devils assaulted him with violent temptation ... The most terrible of all these pains was that of scrupulosity, and interior desolation in which he seemed to see Hell open ready to swallow him up ... After some time certain rays of light, comfort, and divine sweetness scattered these mists, and translated the soul of the servant of God into a paradise of interior delights and heavenly sweetness.

There then followed another period of depression, brought to an end by a still greater illumination and happiness.

After his experience of higher states St John of the Cross wrote several books with the object of conveying to others a knowledge of the new life that had come to him. The following passages have been selected from his two chief works, *Ascent of Mount Carmel* and *The Dark Night of the Soul*.

The more the soul strives to become blind and annihilated as to all interior and exterior things, the more it will be filled with faith and love and hope. But this love at times is neither comprehended nor felt, because it does not establish itself in the senses with tenderness, but in the soul with fortitude, with greater courage and resolution than before; though it sometimes overflows into the senses, and shows itself tender and gentle. In order, then, to attain to this love, joy, and delight which visions effect, it is necessary that the soul should have fortitude and be fortified, so as to abide willingly in emptiness and darkness, and to lay the foundation of its love and delight on what it neither sees nor feels, on what it cannot see nor feel – namely, on God incomprehensible and supreme. Our way to Him is therefore, of necessity, in self-denial ... That soul, therefore, has greater communion with God which is most advanced in love – that is, whose will is most conformable to the will of God ... For which cause, therefore, as I have already explained, the more the soul cleaves to created things, relying on its own strength, by habit and inclination, the less is it disposed for this union, because it does not completely resign itself into the hands of God, that He may transform it supernaturally.

Knowledge of pure truth requires for its proper explanation that God should hold the hand and wield the pen of the writer ... This kind of vision is not the same with the intellectual visions of bodily things ... It is most like to the spirit of prophecy ... In so far as this becomes pure contemplation the soul sees clearly that it cannot describe it otherwise than in general terms, which the abundance of delight and happiness forces from it. And though at times when this knowledge is vouchsafed to the soul, words are uttered, yet the soul knows full well that it has in no wise expressed what it felt, because it is conscious that there are no words of adequate significance. This divine knowledge concerning God never relates to particular things ... It is only a soul in union with God, that is capable of this profound loving knowledge, for it is itself that union ... Such is the sweetness of deep delight of these touches of God, that one of them is more than a recompense for all the sufferings of this life, however great their number.

Amongst the spiritual maxims of St John of the Cross there appears the following poem:

I entered, but I knew not where, and there I stood not knowing, all science transcending.

I knew not where I entered, for when I stood within, not knowing where I was, I heard great things. What I heard I will not tell; I was there as one who know not, all science transcending.

Of peace and devotion, the knowledge was perfect, in solitude profound; the right was clear, but so secret was it, that I stood babbling, all science transcending.

I stood enraptured in ecstasy, beside myself, and in my every sense, no sense remained. My spirit was endowed with understanding, understanding nought, all science transcending.

The higher I ascended, the less I understood. It is the dark cloud illumining the night. Therefore, he who understands knows nothing, ever all science transcending.

He who really ascends so high, annihilates himself, and all his previous knowledge seems ever less and less; his knowledge so increases, that he knoweth nothing, all science transcending.

This knowing that knows nothing is so potent in its might that the prudent in their reasoning never can defeat it; for their wisdom never reaches to the understanding that understandeth nothing, all science transcending.

This sovereign wisdom is of an excellence so high that no faculty nor science can ever unto it attain. He who shall overcome himself by the knowledge which knows nothing, will always rise, all science transcending.

And if you would listen, this sovereign wisdom doth consist in a sense profound of the essence of God; it is an act of His compassion to leave us naught understanding, all science transcending.

A multiplication of extracts from the writings of Christian mystics is unnecessary, for all convey the same message. There is a monotony in mystical literature, a monotony from which there can be no escape when all writers express the same ideas, and the only novelty lies in certain superficial differences of language. It would indeed be possible to shorten the messages of all the mystics to those three words of the Vedântist, *Tat Twam Asi*, Thou are the That. The description of the 'That' alone is variable. To the Platonist, it is the eternal Idea ; to the Hindu, it is Brahman ; to the Buddhist, it is Purusha ; and to the Sufi and the Christian, it is God.

The discovery that in man there is a part of the Divine Being brings with it certain implications. The first question that naturally arises is : if there be in man a part of the Divine, why has he become so estranged from it that he has even forgotten its presence ? To this question, the Buddhist replies in terms of nescience, and the Christian in terms of sin. Both of them add, as a corollary, that salvation can only come when man recognizes the divine principle in himself and, for the sake of that which is indestructible and eternal, sacrifices that which is destructible and temporary. This is the whole of religion, and it is this truth that is experienced in a mystical state of consciousness, a state that is associated with a sense of conviction and with an intensity of feeling that are unknown under ordinary conditions. Walt Whitman expresses the emotional tone of mystical knowledge in the following lines :

Swiftly arose and spread around me the peace and joy and knowledge that pass all the art and argument of the earth ;
And I know that the hand of God is the elder hand of my own.
And I know that the Spirit of God is the eldest brother of my own.
And that all the men ever born are also my brothers, and the women my sisters and lovers.
And that a kelson of creation is love.

The question that will immediately be asked is : What guarantee have we that knowledge so obtained is of any objective value ? This subject has already been discussed and we will here content ourselves with referring to the views expressed by William James in *Varieties of Religious Experience*. After having laid stress on the unanimity found amongst the mystics, he makes the suggestion that an impartial science of religion should be asked 'to sift out from amidst the discrepancies a common body of doctrine, which she might formulate in terms to which physical science need not object'. To the writer the interposition of an impartial science of religion would appear to be as unnecessary as formulation in terms to which physical sicence need not object. The agreement amongst religious mystics is apparant to all, and there is nothing in their views to which science need object. It is only psychology and philosophy that are concerned with the formulations of the mystic. Pyschologists have, as a whole, paid little attention to the all-important subject of consciousness, but on *a priori* grounds, psychologists would agree that since there are levels of consciousness below that at which we normally live, so also is it reasonable to suppose that there exist levels above it. No one will dispute that the objective value of an experience in wakefulness is greater than that of an experience in sleep. Consequently it must be supposed that the objective value of experiences on a still higher level is increased. And when we come to refer the matter to the philosophers we find that many of them have already experienced the value of higher states of consciousness, so that the philosophers need have no objection to the formulations of the mystics. Who can read the works of writers such as Spinoza, Swedenborg, and Schopenhauer without being convinced that they have derived their philosophy in part from that knowledge 'that passes all the art and argument of the earth'?

A second question that is likely to be asked is: If higher states of consciousness exist from which knowledge of great objective value can be obtained, why is it that so few of us have experienced them? This question also admits of an answer. Even a cursory perusal of mystical literature of the religious kind reveals the fact that mystical experience is of an intensely emotional character. In most cases we find that the religious mystic has passed through a period of acute spiritual suffering. The language in which he portrays this period of the dark night of the soul is as extravagant as that which he uses to describe the subsequent illumination. Usually the struggle between the higher and lower parts of his nature appear to him in the guise of a fight between angels and devils. It is not for him merely an incident, but a grim battle for survival, a battle that becomes so fierce that he is often brought to a state of physical exhaustion. Then, suddenly, and unexpectedly, when keyed up to an intensity of feeling that few people have ever reached, comes the release and the illumination. Who amongst us have any experience of being keyed up to such a high emotional pitch as this? We have plodded along our accustomed road, taking pleasure in our trivial achievements, disgruntled by our disappointments, and seeking the comfortable middle way of compromise. We have continued to live in a monotonous greyness, knowing nothing of the darkness of the soul's night, or of the brightness of its day. In all probability we have never even bothered to acquire the art of meditation and, this being so, we are unlikely to have had glimpses of higher states of consciousness.

For the business of living we are equipped well enough as we are. Only if we seek new knowledge beyond the range of the senses is it necessary to attempt arduous flights into the empyrean. To most of us, it seems better that we should remain on the ground, fulfilling our domestic tasks and listening to the messages brought to us by bolder spirits, but not sharing their experience. An inglorious lot, perhaps, but associated with certain compensations. Things have been made easier for us. The stern figure of Christ has become less stern, his doctrines have been watered down, and the majority of Christians have come to an understanding with the world. Christianity has for most of us become a comfortable religion, and suited to our needs. There is no *necessity* for us to become religious mystics.

But those who persevere with the discipline of the contemplative life and struggle to silence the chattering of the discursive mind may eventually succeed in penetrating to an inner zone of silence. And having reached it, they will know what Boehme meant when he wrote: 'When thou standest still from the thinking of "self" and the willing of "self", when both thy intellect and will are quiet and passive to the impressions of the Eternal Word and Spirit, and when thy soul is winged up, and above that which is temporal, the outward senses and the imagination being locked up by holy abstraction, then the eternal hearing, seeing, and speaking will be revealed to thee.'

CHAPTER 18

'IF THERE HAD BEEN A CANDLE'

THIS survey of man from the points of view of biology, psychology, Western and Eastern philosophy, and religion, incomplete though it be, enables us to arrive at certain conclusions. From the point of view of science we see man as an elaborate piece of mechanism, his actions determined by man's endocrine glands, his central nervous system, his hereditary endowments, and his environment. From philosophy we learn that his capacity for knowledge is strictly limited, so that by means of the sense organs alone he can never know reality. This is confirmed by Eastern philosophy, but a new idea is added. Man, as he is, can see no more and do no more, but by right effort and right method, he can gain new powers, understand more, and achieve more. Finally we have the confirmation of this idea by religion. Whatever may be the differences in their creed, whatever may be the variations in their philosophy, all religions, without exception, contain this idea of the possibility of change, so that a man may become other than he is. From the point of view of all religions man is a being in whom are lying latent higher powers.

This division of man into lower and higher components is differently expressed in the various psychological, philosophical, and religious systems that we have studied. Kant's division is between *homo sensibilis* and *homo noumenalis*, between the man whose knowledge is limited by his sense perceptions and the transcendental man who can, by direct apprehension, know reality. For Bergson the dividing line is drawn between the intellect and what he calls 'intuition'. Intellect is the faculty that allows us to make artificial cuts across the living flow of reality, and to view separate states of consciousness, which persist only until they are succeeded by other states. Only by intuition, which for Bergson is part of the *élan vital*, can the flow of becoming which constitutes life be grasped. In holding this view of the limitations of the intellect, Bergson is in agreement with Shankara who looked upon man's ordinary mind (*manas*) as being an instrument of restricted utility, a faculty whose value lay chiefly in the practical field of action. It resembles a bulls-eye lantern which allows us to concentrate light on one particular place in our environment, so that we can react appropriately. In the opinion of the Hindu, the intellect belongs to the smaller and lower 'self' of man which is part of his material being. It is to *purusha* (spiritual intuition) that a man has to turn in order to *be* and to *see more*. According to Shankara this 'Higher Self' of man is pure and undifferentiated consciousness. It is a consciousness which is neither personal nor individual – it is cosmic or universal consciousness. Only when a man has ceased to identify himself with the limited life of the intellect and the senses, only then may he establish contact with this higher part of himself. And if he manages to do this he experiences that state known to the Hindu as *sat-chit-ananda*, ('being' – 'consciousness' – 'bliss'). It is the state which is described in Christian literature as a 'peace which passes all understanding'.

In no Western philosophy is the difference between man as he now is and man as he might become more strongly proclaimed than in that of Nietzsche. This is the theme that underlies the whole of that much misunderstood work *Thus Spake Zarathustra*, the idea of the Superman.

I teach you the Superman. Man is a thing to be surmounted. What have you done to surmount him?

All beings hitherto have created something above themselves: will ye be the ebb of this great tide and rather revert to the beast than surmount man?

What is the ape to man? A jest or a thing of shame. So shall man be to Superman – a jest or a thing of shame.

Ye have trod the way from worm to man, and much in you is yet worm. Once were ye apes, and even yet man is more ape than any ape.

But he that is wisest amongst you is but a discord, a hybrid of plant and ghost. But do I bid you become either ghosts or plants?

Behold I teach you the Superman!

The Superman is the meaning of the earth. Let your will say: the Superman *shall be* the meaning of the earth.

What Nietzsche did not understand was that his philosophy of the Superman was strictly in line with the religious teaching of Christ and Buddha, that in each of us there is something of the divine to which we must return if we are to become other than we are.

The idea that man may become other than he is finds expression in many religious ceremonies and symbols. In *A New Model of the Universe*, P. D. Ouspensky states that a grain of corn was a very important symbol in the ancient Mysteries of Egypt and of Greece.

In the Eleusinian Mysteries every candidate for initiation carried in a particular procession a grain of wheat in a tiny earthenware bowl. The secret that was revealed to a man at the initiation was contained in the idea that man could die simply as a grain, or could rise again into some other life. This was the principal idea of the Mysteries, which was expressed by many different symbols.

Christ and Buddha made use of the same symbol, saying that a grain must be cast into the ground, and a grain must die, in order that a shoot should live. Christ's words were misunderstood by many who followed him and for the idea of regeneration in *this* life was substituted that of regeneration in some future life beyond the grave. But this was not the meaning originally attached to the idea of regeneration, or transmutation; it was an emendation that came from the desire to find compensations for disappointment in this life in a glorious resurrection after death. In spite of Christ's insistence that the Kingdom of Heaven was within, the Early Christians preferred the idea that their Lord would soon reappear to found the Kingdom of Heaven on earth. Later, when they were disappointed in this, they put their hopes in a heaven beyond the grave, where they would enjoy the fruits of their work upon earth. Yet Christ's talk with Nicodemus shows clearly that when he spoke of the necessity of a man being born again before he could enter the Kingdom of Heaven, he was not referring to some future existence, but to this life.

Verily, verily, I say unto thee, Except a man be born again he cannot enter into the Kingdom of God.

Except a man be born of water and the spirit, he cannot enter into the Kingdom of God.

That which is born of the flesh is flesh; and that which is born of the spirit is spirit. (St John, iii, 3, 5, 6)

So much emphasis is placed on the idea of death on one plane and rebirth on another in the teaching of Gautama that the term 'twice born' is attached to all higher levels of humanity. Those who have attained enlightenment have deliberately sacrificed their personalities for the sake of higher capacities; they have died that they might live. The words used by Christ to his disciples might easily have been used by Buddha.

If any man will come after me, let him deny himself and take up his cross and follow me. For whosoever shall save his life shall lose it, and whosoever shall lose his life for my sake shall find it. (Matthew xvi, 24–5)

To be a follower of Christ, or a follower of the Eightfold Path, the same requirement was necessary, that a man should sacrifice his personality in order that the higher part of him may live. By personality should be implied all that a man commonly thinks of as himself, his ambitions, his personal theories and opinions, his prejudices, his desires and his aversions, his ideas about himself, his feeling of importance, his fantasies, his day-dreams, as well as much in himself to which he is oblivious. According to all religious systems these characteristics, which are purely subjective, must stand in the way of the man who is struggling to obtain something more objective.

It should be noted that the Buddhist stresses the importance of sacrificing personal feelings, aspirations, and dreams in order that higher states and higher knowledge may be attained. A similar teaching exists in the other Eastern religions and philosophies. Yet there are many European writers who express the opinion that all mystical experiences are only dream experiences. In their view a mystic is a man who has rendered himself highly suggestible by means of some form of self-hypnosis. In this state of self-induced sleep the creations of his own imagination are liberated from lower levels of consciousness and, rising to the surface, speak to him with all the authority of objective phenomena. Instead of being more awake the mystic is more asleep; instead of seeing more objectively he is seeing more subjectively. Face to face with his own dreams, and listening to his own thoughts invested with a spurious authority, he is easily hoodwinked. Arthur Waley appears to take this view of mystics. In the appendix to his translation of the *Tao Te King* he writes: 'That the Chinese Quietist practised some form of self-hypnosis no one familiar both with the Yoga literature of India (whether Hindu or Buddhist) and with Taoism would, I think, be likely to dispute.' To this writer and those who share his opinion all Eastern religions would appear to be based on nothing more substantial than fantasy. To them Christ, Buddha, Lao Tze, and Zoroaster are but great dreamers, men who practised 'some form of self-hypnosis'. They have no message for humanity, for their teaching, being founded on these dreams, makes no contact with reality.

The difficulties which some people have in accepting the idea expressed in this book, namely that there exist higher levels of thought, seem to be insurmountable. If self-hypnosis is the aim of the yogi, why has he taken the trouble to divide his study into five branches, each of which complements and fortifies the others? And why has he insisted on the need for instruction by a teacher? If deeper sleep is the goal of the Buddhist, what need is there for the cultivation of greater awareness and for the arduous training of the attention and the memory? Would not these exercises be more likely to banish sleep than to induce it? If self-hypnosis is all that he seeks why does he embark on all this unnecessary preliminary training? Would it not be better for a disciple merely to seat himself in a comfortable chair and gaze at a fixed point of light, thus inducing a sleepy state? No *guru* is needed for this simple procedure. Or if help be required, would it not be more profitable to enlist the help of a skilled hypnotist? Hypnosis is hypnosis, whether it be induced from without or attained from within. A scholar's knowledge of the Chinese language is not all the equipment that is necessary for the understanding of the *Tao Te King* and works of a similar nature.

This, then, is the great difference between the new and the old psychological systems. Modern psychology regards man as a finished product, something that can never become anything more than it is. The only difference between one man and another is a difference in degree, one being cleverer than another, one more emotional than another, and one better adjusted to life and less handicapped by illusions and inhibitions. By education a man may become cleverer, and by suitable treatment he may be freed from many of his illusions and inhibitions, but essentially he remains the same man. That is all that it is possible to do in the way of changing humanity. The older psychological systems that were closely allied to religious teachings looked upon a man quite differently. To these systems he was an unfinished product, a seed that could either grow into a plant, or else remain with his higher potentialities completely undeveloped. Not that this growth, or change, could be effected easily or brought about by any outside agency. On the contrary, the purpose of the teaching and methods of these systems was to bring about this change.

The differences in the new and the old psychology are reflected in the outlook of Western and Eastern thought. Humanism is the religion of the majority of modern intellectuals in Europe and in America, whilst Eastern thought still remains essentially religious. In England most of us accept Christianity as we accept the Bank of England, the Constitution, and the Queen. It is no longer a religion in the true sense of the word, but a national institution to which we can belong without any great demands being made on us for our membership. Occasionally a religious revival sweeps through the country igniting the more combustible members of the community, and then after smouldering for a while, dies away like a fire that has spent its force. But it is purely a temporary disturbance that leaves behind it no permanent effects.

Man has achieved great material progress during the last thousand years, but he has changed very little in himself. If there has been any spiritual advance in man during that time, it has been a very small advance. On looking back at the golden age of history, the century in which Buddha, Zoroaster, and Lao Tze lived, and which was followed by the Greek Golden

Age, it is difficult to believe that humanity has progressed. Whatever we may have gained we owe to a few outstanding men whose words and whose lives still exert upon us their influence. I am referring to the great religious leaders, and to the gifted artists, poets, and philosophers, many of whom are nameless, whose works are the priceless possession not of one nation, but of the whole of mankind. Such men have appeared in all nations and in all centuries, but because Western man has been so preoccupied with the outside world, it is to the East that we must turn to find the highest level that human thought has reached. In the opinion of the author of this book, Dr Bucke, the author of *Cosmic Consciousness*, made a great error when he suggested that those who have reached a higher level of consciousness are, as it were, biological sports that, becoming more and more common, will in time represent the normal state of mankind. This idea, begotten by Charles Darwin, of a progress *ensured* by Nature, an idea that owing to our victories over the external world has now become an article of faith, must be abandoned. Development in the sense in which the word has been used in this book can never be, as Bucke suggests, automatic. It can only result from ceaseless effort, and from effort of a special nature.

We live in a dark house, fumbling with our hands and knowing only that which is within the reach of our own hands. If we understand Jalalu'ddin Rumi aright, it is a house in which there might be light, the light of higher levels of consciousness. Illuminated by this, all contradictions would disappear and the many would become One. For the Vedântist the One is the Brahman; for the Christian it is God. What for us is separate and with its own form is for the seer and the more fully evolved man an expression of the One Supreme Being.

There exist certain signs that Western science is beginning to change the direction in which it moves. Having completed a semi-circle it now begins to travel in the direction of philosophy and religion.

When Western science [writes Sir John Woodroffe] attributes unity, conservation, and continuity to matter, energy, and motion in a universe of obvious plurality and discontinuity, what it is in

fact doing is to show that none of its conceptions have any meaning except in the assumption of unity and unmoving continuity of
consciousness in the sense of the Vedântic *chit* (consciousness).

All matter, declares modern science, is built up from the same
elements, all energy is evolved from one energy; energy passes
into matter, and matter into energy. To attain unity amid apparent multiplicity is the goal towards which modern science is
surely travelling. It is science that now comes into line with the
Vedânta and religious teaching, 'Truth is One; the sages only
call It by different names' (*Rig Veda*).

Yet whilst the true leaders of thought – the great philosophers, religious geniuses, and scientists – move in one direction,
we who constitute the vast bulk of humanity continue to turn
our eyes in another. Controlled by the mechanisms of our
bodies and of our personalities, we live out the tiny span of our
lives amid a turmoil of multiplicities and contradictions. But
Jalalu'ddin Rumi suggests that this is a fate that can be changed.
Beginning with his words, we shall end with his words:

If there had been a candle in each one's hand, the difference
would have gone out of their words.

The eye of sense-perception is only like the palm of the hand, the
palm hath not the power to reach the whole of the elephant.

The eye of the Sea is one thing, and the foam another; leave the
foam and look with the eye of the Sea.

Day and night there is the movement of foam-flecks from the
Sea; thou beholdest the foam, but not the Sea. Marvellous!

BIBLIOGRAPHY

ALCHEMY

CAMPBELL, DONALD, *Arabian Medicine*, London, 1926
HOLMYARD, E. J., *Alchemy*, Harmondsworth, 1957
JUNG, CARL, *The Integration of the Personality*, tr. Stanley M. Dell etc., London, 1940
READ, JOHN, *Prelude to Chemistry*, London, 1936

CHRISTIANITY

BASTIDE, ROGER, *The Mystical Life*, London, 1934
BOEHME, JACOB, *The Signature of All Things*, London, 1912
CHICHESTER, THE BISHOP OF, *Christianity and World Order*, Harmondsworth, 1940
HERSCHEL, W., *The Gospels in Parallel*, London, 1924
INGE, W. R., *The Fall of the Idols*, London, 1940
  Studies of English Mystics, London, 1906
LILLIE, A., *The Influence of Buddhism on Primitive Christianity*, London, 1893

EASTERN RELIGIONS

BALLANTYNE, J. R. (tr.), *The Sankya Aphorisms of Kapila*, Bibliotheca Indica, 1865
BALLON, ROBERT O. (ed.), *The Bible of the World*, London, 1940
DAVID-NEEL, A., *Buddhism*, London, 1939
EVANS WENTZ, W. Y., *Tibetan Yoga and Secret Doctrine*, 1935
GANGANATHA, J. H. A., *The Tattva Kaumudi* (English translation with sanskrit text), 1896
GUÉNON, RENÉ, *The Crisis of the Modern World*, tr. Arthur Osborne, London, 1942
MÜLLER, MAX, *Sacred Books of the East*, Vols. 19, 20, 39, and 40, Oxford, 1879–1910
PALLIS, MARCO, *Peaks and Lamas*, London, 1939
RADHAKRISHNAN, S., *Eastern Religions and Western Thought*, Oxford, 1939
  The Vedânta, according to Shankara and Ramanuja, London, 1929
SRI RAMAKRISHNA MEMORIAL, *The Cultural Heritage of India*, 3 vols., 1937
WALEY, ARTHUR, *The Way and Its Power*, London, 1934
  Three Ways of Thought in Ancient China, London, 1939

ENDOCRINOLOGY

BERMAN, LOUIS, *The Glands Regulating Personality*, New York, 1921
CANNON, WALTER B., *Bodily Changes in Pain, Hunger, Fear, and Rage*, London, 1915
GEIKIE COBB, I., *The Glands of Destiny*, London, 1927

GENERAL

BUBER, MARTIN, *Between Man and Man*, 1947
  Eclipse of God, London, 1953
CARREL, ALEXIS, *Man the Unknown*, London, 1935
FROMM, ERICH, *Man for Himself*, New York, 1947
HEARD, GERALD, *The Source of Civilization*, London, 1935
LANGDON BROWN, WALTER, *Thus We are Men*, London, 1938
MACNEILE DIXON, W., *The Human Situation*, Harmondsworth, 1958

PHILOSOPHY

BERGSON, HENRI, *Creative Evolution*, London, 1911
FECHNER, *Zend-avesta*, Leipzig, 1851
FOULQUIE, PAUL, *Existentialism*, London, 1948
JOAD, C. E. M., *Guide to Philosophy*, London, 1936
  Guide to the Philosophy of Morals and Politics, London, 1938
  Philosophy of Our Times, London, 1940
NIETZSCHE, F. W., *Thus Spoke Zarathustra*, tr. R. J. Hollingdale, Harmondsworth, 1961
OUSPENSKY, P. D., *A New Model of the Universe*, London, 1931
  Tertium Organum, New York, 1920
ROSE, J. W. (ed.), *Outline of Knowledge*, London, 1931
RUSSELL, BERTRAND, *An Outline of Philosophy*, London, 1927
WHITEHEAD, A. N., *Science and the Modern World*, Cambridge, 1926

PSYCHOLOGY

BROWN, W., *Psychology and Psycho-Therapy*, London, 1921
BUCKE, R. M., *Cosmic Consciousness*, Philadelphia, 1905
COSTER, G., *Yoga and Western Psychology*, London, 1934
HARPER, ROBERT A., *Psycho-analysis and Psychotherapy*, New Jersey, 1959
HORNEY, KAREN, *Neurosis and Human Growth*, New York, 1953
JAMES, WILLIAM, *The Varieties of Religious Experience*, 1902
JANET, PROFESSOR, *États mentales des hystériques*, Paris, 1893

MCDOUGALL, W., *The Energies of Man*, London, 1932

STEPHEN, KARIN, *Psycho-Analysis and Medicine*, Cambridge, 1933

THOULESS, R. H., *Introduction to the Psychology of Religion*, Cambridge, 1923

VON HÜGEL, BARON, *The Mystical Element of Religion*, Cambridge, 1908

WATSON, J. B., *Psychology from the Standpoint of a Behaviourist*, London, 1919

SCIENCE

PLANCK, MAX, *Where is Science Going?*, London, 1933

SHERRINGTON, SIR CHARLES, *Man on His Nature*, Harmondsworth, 1955

TILNEY, F., and RILEY, H. A., *The Form and Functions of the Central Nervous System*, London, 1921

PATIENTS AND DOCTORS

A387

Kenneth Walker regards the relationship between the patient and his doctor as being essential to successful treatment and he has written this book specially for the Pelican series in the hope of enlightening readers on this important subject. There is, he declares, a great deal of misunderstanding on the part of patients concerning the functions and the methods of the medical profession, and this book can be regarded as being a popular guide to doctors and their ways. But if misunderstandings occur they are not necessarily always on the side of the patient, for medical men often fail to appreciate the difficulties and the confusions of their patients in their dealings with the medical profession, and particularly with medical institutions such as hospitals and health services. The author of this book is deeply concerned with the marked deterioration in the patient – doctor relationship which has occurred since the passing of the Health Act. He is equally disturbed by the decline in the prestige of the very person upon whom the successful working of that Act entirely depends – the family doctor. Kenneth Walker has a gift for making difficult matters clear and he writes lightly and amusingly both of patients and of his own colleagues.

Also available:

HUMAN PHYSIOLOGY · A102

THE PHYSIOLOGY OF SEX · A71

SEX AND SOCIETY (*with Peter Fletcher*) · A332

*For a complete list of books available
please write to Penguin Books
whose address can be found on the
back of the title page*